SOCIAL SCIENCE IN ACTUAL PRACTICE

"They said, 'You have a blue guitar.
You do not play things as they are.'
The man replied, 'Things as they are
are changed upon the blue guitar.'"

Wallace Stevens,
'The Man with the Blue Guitar', in
Rag and Bone Shop of the Heart,
edited by Robert Bly, James Hillman
and Michael Meade, Harper Collins,
New York, 1992.

"It was my part at this feast to play
upon my instrument, and I have done
all I could."

Rabindranath Tagore,
Gitanjali, XVI, p. 10, Macmillan,
New Delhi, 1987.

SOCIAL SCIENCE IN ACTUAL PRACTICE

Themes on My Blue Guitar

ROLF P. LYNTON

Sage Publications
New Delhi/Thousand Oaks/London

Copyright © Rolf P. Lynton, 1998

First published in 1998 by
Sage Publications India Pvt Ltd
M–32 Market, Greater Kailash Part–I
New Delhi–110 048

Sage Publications, Inc.   *Sage Publications Ltd*
2455 Teller Road   6 Bonhill Street
Thousand Oaks, California 91320   London EC2A 4PU

Published by Tejeshwar Singh for Sage Publications India Pvt Ltd, phototypeset by Line Arts, Pondicherry and printed at Chaman Enterprises, Delhi.

Library of Congress Cataloging-in-Publication Data
Lynton, Rolf P.
    Social science in actual practice: themes on my blue guitar/Rolf P. Lynton.
      p. cm.   (cloth: alk. paper)   (pbk.: alk. paper)
    Includes bibliographical references.
    1. Lynton, Rolf P. 2. Social scientists—United States—Biography. 3. Social sciences. I. Title.
    H59.L93A3   300'.92—dc21   1998   97–30581
    [B]

ISBN: 0–7619–9207–3 (US-hb)   81–7036–659–3 (India-hb)
       0–7619–9208–1 (US-pb)   81–7036–660–7 (India-pb)

Sage Production Team: Sumitra Srinivasan, Richard Brown and Santosh Rawat

Dedicated to my closest colleagues over these years—twins sent from heaven:

Jerry Scott	1948–53
Ronnie	1953–
Udai Pareek	1962–
John Thomas	1965–
Racine Brown	1967–

CONTENTS

LIST OF FIGURES AND TABLES

Figures

Tables

FOREWORD

Being Known

I fear that I took on too much, a task far more complicated and daunting than I had thought it to be, when I told Rolf months ago that I would write the Foreword to his autobiographical *tour de force*. Words usually come easy to me. I've written at least a dozen or so forewords before, but this time I was stumped. First of all, I'd never, until now, read a book by a social scientist that brought tears to my eyes—tears of nostalgia and laughter, buckets of tears. In the midst of reading this volume I ducked into the bathroom to dry my eyes and saw in the mirror my drooping cheeks (among the curses of aging), and realized that in some rather eerie way Rolf and I were twins. The fact that Rolf and I are exactly the same age—a robust 72 (Rolf still plays squash for goodness sakes!)—isn't the sole basis for our twinship, but it's a reminder. No, there's something deeper than that which perhaps I can plumb and explore as I write. We'll see.

First of all I should say that Rolf isn't your every day social scientist. Yes, that's his day job, but on the side, when he moonlights, when he's at his best, he's a social philosopher, a hungry spirit, who strives to bring meaning into the lives of others. But thank God, he followed W. H. Auden's advice: THOU SHALL NOT COMMIT A SOCIAL SCIENCE. For his writing is plummy and rich, deep and thoughtful, and on top of that he writes with such enviable, almost absurd, lucidity. I promise you, dear reader, that you are going to get more out of this book on social and institutional development and change, more on change agentry, more on the moral and ethical nuances of what's referred to as OD, than you will from any other single volume. I'm not kidding.

Getting back to my being stumped. I began to realize what an enigma he is, this Rolf Lynton. I first got to "know" Rolf in India where I was involved in developing a school of management in Calcutta. Rolf and his wife, Ronnie, were living in Hyderabad, as I recall, and Rolf's reputation, as they say, preceded him. Actually, we had met before while I was at MIT. He was visiting Cambridge and I had read his work—marvellous, difficult, on-the-ground work (literally *under* the ground in the coalmines of England) and then later his seminal work on community development in Ceylon (Aloka). I was so impressed because he was actually *doing* social change and documenting it as he went along, learning all the time, always with his eyebrows raised in wonder and curiosity.

But I really got to know Rolf more intimately when we worked together in India. When I first arrived there, Rolf was already an "old Indian hand", as they say. Some people were a little intimidated by him, from what I could learn, somewhat wary, and one oafish official thought him to be "maybe a Communist". Naturally, I was fascinated.

Well, we got acquainted in India, and I was so impressed with his muscular mind, his resonant voice, his appearance, and most of all his commitment to human betterment and social justice. I also realized that he was puzzling, remote in some way, as if listening to other voices, other, perhaps celestial, sounds, different from the mundane voices and sounds that filled my head. Which is probably why people could project on him—a human Rorschach—anything they wanted. Actually, I enjoyed the mystery of the man.

A coda, a short break from the above. So I called Clurie Bennis who got to know Rolf and Ronnie in India and asked her point blank, "What comes to your mind when you think of Rolf?" She hesitated a long time, a *very* long time for Clurie, and finally said, "Well, it's hard to get beyond the word 'handsome'...there is a tranquillity about him, a serenity that gives the gloss of an enigma. Measured, somewhat detached, all those notes he took during the meetings, an obsessive record keeper. There was a kindness about him". Thank you, Clurie. That helped.

Yes, all that obsessive note-taking and the kindness and tranquillity and spirituality masking a certain mystery—yes, a secret life that you knew existed.

It was interesting to me that the first thought that came to Clurie's mind was the physicality of Rolf. Me too. I recall his Mediterranean blue eyes, slightly graying (even in his forties) wavy hair and his inimitable voice: a gentle and soft German mixed with a heavier British accent. Gorgeous. He shimmered.

Now coming back to this book and twinship. The paradox in Rolf's life is not unknown to many of us: building communities and yet not altogether living in them; a certain separateness and yet a need to belong. So Rolf has two quite separate and inter-related homes—one in India and one in North Carolina. What a contrast! He has that combination of rootlessness, detachment, and remoteness co-mingled with an urgent need to create vivid utopias. That ambivalence is what is most fascinating about Rolf's work and about Rolf himself. I don't think he's alone in this re-spect, and this is where his "twinning" comes in. He talks about five "twins" in his life—the most significant one being his wife Ronnie, herself a creative, generous spirit. Rolf does have two siblings, but he's created many more of them along the way.

Being *known* is the first step in love—*really* being known. I don't think Rolf has really been known by a wider public. I would argue that he has never received the acknowledgment— the broad admiration and esteem—that he deserves. This book is a labor of love. In writing it Rolf has made himself more known and will be loved by more than those who have been touched by Rolf in person and those who have learned from him and been nurtured by him. I want to thank him for this book, for re-moving some, but not all, of the mystery of his personhood and for letting us know him more deeply.

Writing an autobiographical book is hard. I'm going to end this Foreword with a quote from the book. Dietrich Boenhoffer, a Christian clergyman in Nazi Germany who stood up against the Nazis and was imprisoned, characterized to his best friend and fellow pastor the people who influenced him most. "They had", he said, "a kind of *hilaritas*...confidence in their own work...a steadfast certainty that in their work they are showing the world something GOOD (even if the world doesn't like it) and a high-spirited self confidence.... It is a necessary attribute of greatness". That's a fairly accurate description of Rolf Lynton.

Santa Monica   **Warren Bennis**
Spring of 1997   University Professor and
                                      Distinguished Professor of
                                       Business Administration
                              University of Southern California
                                                  Los Angeles

PROLOGUE

/AILBOAT/ ON PUGET
/OUND—/ETTING /AIL

By itself, reality isn't worth a damn. It's perception that pro-
motes reality to meaning.

Brodsky 1986, p. 152

Unless one is a pharaoh one doesn't aspire to become a
mummy.

Brodsky 1986, p. 493

Bobbing on top of currents that have borne my work lifelong, two quite distinct memories tug at me to get on with writing this book. One rings in my head as, "This is the time for telling what you know." The voice is Alexandra's—dear friend and wise colleague. Inserted, in her quiet voice, into our ordinary working discussion that morning in Indonesia, made it quite startling. And clear as a bell it still rings. A three-country group of us were helping provincial governments build capacities for more independent functioning in the public health system (and the central government its inclinations and capacities to delegate more decisions).[1] That was in the mid-1980s and my hair was already white.

The other memory is anchored two years later in Delhi, India. Deepankar, another close colleague but much younger, had come by to tell of his work with coalmining officials in eastern Bihar. It sounded familiar to me, from my work in the mines of

---

1. Chapter 8 on "Going to Size" will be largely about that work.

Scotland 35 years earlier and published then. He borrowed a copy and called the next morning, all excited: It is just like Bihar today, and would it be all right if he made copies for the officials there. Of course. Soon after, and quite independently, another close colleague in India, Vijay, declared a 1963 monograph to be "quite as relevant even now—the situation is essentially the same". In that paper, two of us had declared the ongoing strategies for creating employment in small towns to be quite inadequate and had laid out a radically different approach. We had gone public with it against all advice, some from exalted quarters.[2]

So, I conclude through a forest of continuing misgivings that *some* of my work at least may bear retelling, to myself in the first place for "a clarification of life" (as Robert Frost puts it leading into the *Complete Poems*). Writing of this sort, he muses,

> begins in delight, it inclines to the impulse, it assumes direction with the first line laid down, it runs a course of lucky events, and ends in a clarification of life…not necessarily a great clarification, such as sects and cults are founded on, but in a momentary stay against confusion. (Frost 1964, p. ii)

As I run my course by again, perhaps I can then also raise some of my pet peeves—about much that currently passes for professional work and literature in management for instance—and also indulge my barely-banked passions for improving the world.

By way of material to draw on for this accounting of over five decades, in addition to published writings, I have my own diaries, uncommonly—some whisper obsessively—complete, and also unpublished papers, some of monograph length or more.[3] But how to put all this together, to "tell" (back to Frost) "how it can"? How *is* that, and how will I know when I think I discern it?

One of the things I have learned over the years is not to worry a question of this kind, but to leave it alone. Or to start typing *some* thoughts into the computer as and when they come, usually first thing some morning. Start *somehow*. That way one can

---

2. The work in the coal industry is in Chapter 2 and on area development in Chapter 5.
3. The genesis of my diary, its successive elaborations, and its benefits and costs are the subject of Chapter 3 "Expanding the Moment".

hope—even expect—to hit the right level of discourse, that current in the swirling waters which looks fair to bear one in the direction one wants to go. Confirmation comes from going with it. The "anyhow start" that helps this has then done its job, and one may later discard it, gladly. I know that this sequence will run and produce results—if I (still) do not fuss.

What happens next (and I know it now with the confidence that comes with experiencing the same wondrous unfolding again and again) is that what peeks as mere notion clarifies in the capturing. Several rounds of writing and letting it rest mould it to its proper shape. Clarifications come often with leisure-time reading, not purposefully focused but freely ranging. A phrase, an onward thought, a stray reflection—and the notion comes to life. Usually not full-blown, but a bit here and a bit there.

That fallow period (fallow on the surface but actually gestating, generating, marinating) lasted years in this case. No matter. I was busy with other things. Then came Susan Ketchin's (1994) book, *The Christ-haunted Landscape*, and it crystallized the approach for me. She focuses each chapter on one (American) writer. In a three-fold sequence for each, she tells briefly about the writer's history, then presents a five- to ten-page extract from her or his published writing, and ends with an interview in which the two explore the religious dimension. Susan is delightfully active in the interviews and quite opinionated here and there. She is certainly not merely leading on and transcribing. She lets the reader in on her perceptions and so "promotes" what she sees, hears, and describes in the book "to meaning". I need not settle for her meaning as if that were the one and only, yet I can let it stand and be important. But by knowing "where she is coming from" (in that vivid if rather graceless current idiom), I can also tune into my own perceptions of those same authors and scenes, and follow them through to my own meanings.

A three-fold sequence promises well here too. The first part in each chapter tells how a particular writing came about, that is, the work on which it was based—usually in the field and for practical purpose—and its course right through to publication (or, in several cases, to worldly powers holding it back and hiding it away). The second part extracts from the then writing what may today matter still; it is otherwise unchanged. Keeping it clean that way allows the third part to focus clearly on what learnings can be derived from that original experience and what, in the light of developments in practice and profession and in my own understanding since then, I would now do differently in a like situation. It is the septuagenarian counseling, talking with his 25- or 40- or even 60-year self.[4]

This retracing of roots and developments will usually range widely. Only with patience and minds long-open can each stage and setting be recreated as it really was—as best I can and with the help of others also there at that time.[5] This tack, less clear though it is at the outset, is so much more promising than spur-of-the-moment labeling and attempts to force-fit a life unfolding into some stencil of the mind. It is precisely some of these stencils I want to raise doubts about with my experience in practice,

4. An early reader asked for a simple orderly overview of where all I have cast anchor during my professional journey and in what capacities I worked in each place. Mid-decades serve best:

1935–45	Emigrated from Germany to England boarding school	
	War and war factory	Machinist
1945–55	British Institute of Management—Studies of docks and coal (in Chapters 1 and 2)	Field Researcher
	European Youth Campaign (education)	Watchdog
	Harvard Business School, Human Relations	Training Fellow
1955–65	Sri Lanka and India:	
	Aloka International Training Center for community leaders (in Chapter 4)	Founder-director
	Small Industries Extension Training Institute (in Chapters 5 and 6)	Consultant, Team Leader
1965–75	USA but with international work too:	
	Carolina Population Center and School of Public Health	Faculty, Project Director
	Duke University and SUNY at Buffalo (in Chapter 7)	Doctoral Studies
1975–85	University of South Carolina School of Public Health	Founder-dean, Professor
	Indonesia:	Consultant,
	Ministry of Health (in Chapter 8)	Team Leader
1985–	India, Southern Africa, USA:	
	Ministries of health and of local government, management institutes and faculty development (in Chapter 10)	Consultant, Semi-retired

5. These colleagues are listed on pp 22–23.

much of it rerun in slow motion, in order to see better. Even with patient openness, my accounts will still do only scant justice to the complex realities which were at play at that time and led to what can only now (and with hindsight) be made to look like decision trees of goodly shape. I look, in vain, for reality—in constant creation, germinating, budding, and yielding—in the impersonal, simplified, abstract lines of many published writings in management and the social sciences in general, even at the applied end of the range; they leave me not merely cold and distant but deeply disquieted, worried, and resentful.

In fact, not one but two realities set the stage for any worthwhile account, for each brings its separate history and tends in its own onward direction. One is the outer reality, what Fritz Roethlisberger, of Hawthorne Studies fame, called the stubborn facts of life. For him, engineer as he was by first training, that stubbornness epitomized the human condition most of all and he was both awed and delighted by it, eyes laughing, jaw twisted aside almost to a grimace; he knew good, solid stuff when he hit on it or even saw it from a distance. This outer reality Eric Trist, a trained psychoanalyst, operationalized two decades later as "socio-technical system analysis" and it has become a mainstay of my practice.[6]

Both would have gone along with my insistence of attending to the other reality as well—the *inner* one. Each of the people on a particular task, on a particular day, in a particular place, bring along to it, by virtue of who they are, personal elements which also weigh into the performance of that task in that situation. So each moment becomes singular indeed, in person and context. For Eric Trist, this personal, inner reality would in fact have come first. He *knew* that inner reality comes with a stubbornness hardly less persistent than the outer—according to our stage in life and position in society, to the trajectory of our learning, and to our (hopefully healthy) assertion of self at all times; and he was glad that it was not easily changed. At the moment at which any one of us perceives the moment and "promotes it to meaning" for decision and onward action, at that moment both realities are stubbornly present and so also make up the absolutely essential context for a sound accounting for it. This is true for that moment, the next, and the next—and the moments spin

6. Chapter 1 traces my learning to appreciate the stubborn facts of life.

into threads that weave a life. This is true for each person, as also for a department consisting of many, and for the organization of which it is part, of a project and program, and for communities small and large.

If either of these realities is left out when accounting, it does not matter much what a book or paper is ostensibly about. Neat tables and equations may point toward abstract theory or, in the opposite direction, to the concrete; but no matter. Other publications offer a "situational" something (as in "situational leadership") or join the flood of "how-to" manuals full of detailed instructions for taking this or that managerial step, or for even thinking about it "practically" ahead of introducing a personnel appraisal system, or for re-engineering the whole company, or for running a meeting for taking any decision whatsoever. Contrary to what each proclaims in its different ways, they all look alike to me: impractical, unenlightening, and rather like attempting Hamlet without the Prince and in sunny Italy instead of in the morning mist of Denmark.

Maybe that last image points to the function they all serve most in their shortcomings: to lull readers into sunny climes, away from the truly difficult assessments and taxing realities which actually have to go into improving management, planning, and social and political action.

Is my quite different experience really so singular or even rare? My experience declares much of the current literature as perpetrating fraud and deception on the beginner or unreflective practitioner. Unwittingly maybe, but even so. More kindly, it is pretentious, and certainly sets and signals quite the wrong direction. The realities *are* complex. And, they include the perceptions of the people involved, including most certainly those of the researcher/consultant/writer. The voyage must start, even the mapping of it, with the broadly conceived inner and outer realities identified, chronicled, and accounted for. Both realities. No, it is not neat, nor always sure or complete, well short of perfection certainly. Yes, it is a lot of work. So purpose and means should warrant that extent of work (and the associated anxieties and elations). Useful theory can be derived from it, to guide and simplify the next round of work. And over time, these working guides can be constructed into quite elaborate frameworks of theories. Along with testing and other confirmations when possible, there may be no other way. Otherwise, "reality by itself" may really not be "worth a damn", as Brodsky puts it (1986, p. 152).

The scene changes to India in the mid-1960s, specifically to Hyderabad, right in the center of the country. Manuraj, short, bald, wiry, and very dark, from Kerala in the far south, leads the little singing group he has organized and trained into a new venture: "The Minstrels" will stage Gilbert and Sullivan operettas, starting with *The Mikado*. We rode this music and foolery from the hub of the Empire into this ancient city, the capital of the Jewel's foremost Princely State. Manuraj, as Koko on stage, finds that all his tortuous subterfuges have only led to his having to marry Katisha, and Katisha has "a caricature of a face".

The scene I have drawn of the literature for practitioners is of course a "caricature of a face" too, but in the more common sense of truths overdrawn and emphasized beyond real life. Such challenging clarity comes with leaving out lesser truths and all gradations.

Back to theory and its development. Even abstract and far-out theory is fine when it addresses salient issues in actual lives, in families, in organizations, communities, and large public affairs, and when theorists also show, however indirectly, how their formulations can help responsible practitioners improve their work. If they themselves are not good at making or showing these connections, then they can collaborate with others who are. Cycling theory development through practice at least twice over—at the beginning and at the end of each sally—grounds it well.

This would guarantee attention to the particulars of actual situations arising from practical and theoretical perspectives. To ensure it, researchers of particular "cases" and theorists need to set off together and not rush off in opposite directions, as if detailing contexts were opposed to developing useful theory (when in fact it grounds and anchors it) or as if *good* theory were not the most useful thing for the person on the spot to have in her or his head (Lewin's action-researcher). The two will part company at various places along the way, for each to work out its special concerns, then join up again later. Differentiation is fine as long as it is limited to our capacity to integrate the parts. I learned this, *really* learned this, when charged with working out system innovations and when I tried to develop useful theory for it.[7] I found that enthusiasm for novel things and ways runs way ahead of our patience with visualizing and marshaling the ingredients required for also integrating them. Cheering each new thing is much more fun. It also masks that nothing much will come of it by itself. Matching differentiation with integration makes sober good sense, an elegant principle. Practically, it translates into less aimless milling about and fewer cheers, but these cheers are more measured and truly heartfelt.

"How-to" books get most in the way of that, and there is such an avalanche of them. They convey the notion that *what* needs to be done is quite clear already, and it only needs to be done well and more and more efficiently. Yet, the very opposite is true: clarity about what precisely needs to be done and which can also *get* done is the issue most of the time and the most difficult one at that. The premature "how-tos" then serve mostly as a cheap escape from facing that difficulty, and that is no service at all.

By its relentless flow and pretended universality alone the literature distracts and reassures. Add the high gloss and hyped marketing, and the sessions of a half-day or two days in five-star hotels around the world with authors in person, and realities get easily lost in the melee and the cheers. For practitioners strapped for answers, the companiable melee and the loud cheers become welcome distractions. Meanwhile, issues left unattended or only fussed with get worse and ever more difficult. True exploration, and what is properly "in the field" and what better left out are matters of solid substance and must indeed stand out over the fine shading and detailing that caricaturing quite properly omits.

If, then, I strike a different direction in this book, I mean it not to be just one more direction to take, nor am I frozen in disagreement with any other. I offer it neither for its novelty nor for some long-forgotten tradition that in this age of floundering tempts recapturing. I set out, rather, with the thought that the "direction" I can tell about, distilled as it is from a half-century of living and working on three continents (and for brief periods on another two), is of a different order. Maybe the telling can help gain, maybe *re*gain, useful perspectives on how events actually occur and opportunities for action come about, and how they work

7. See Chapter 7.

out; and, further, how they set up chains of events and opportunities to follow—the flow. Intent is something else again. Here I only insist that, intended or not, the events that follow are not random. They come from somewhere and they go somewhere, and much of that can be seen and foreseen with a little effort. More, sometimes much more, can be—or could have been—seen if I had been wiser at that time. Now, with hindsight, those intricate chains of events and opportunities can be understood and told a little better. In this way, learning can take place, and should—mine and others.

I start with keeping the personal in plain view, right at center stage, imperative and alongside the other inescapably essential components of any real-life situation. I fall short of Poobah who eagerly held every last office that promised tangible rewards at Mikado's Court: I have a role, sometimes more than one, and I take it into account. I do take personal perspective (mine as also of other parties to any situation) to be central to understanding a role, and for decision and action. Without this, "reality isn't worth a damn". In pursuit of the personal then, I persist in ranging into the inner contexts too, along with whatever else mattered in a situation which that perspective of mine allowed me to see, both at that time and also now in retrospect.

In places where a particular description of my part in a situation distracts the reading, skip on. Gilbert and Sullivan's operas are not everyone's cup of tea, nor is war-time Britain or scenes in rural India. I know my disdain for Gilbert and Sullivan, raised as I had been on Bach and Beethoven and the Berlin Philharmonic, almost ended my courtship of Ronnie nearly a half-century ago, i.e., before I even get into Chapter 4 of this book! Skip on, I say. There will be other stages and images, and also straightforward data to make me "come alive" so that readers can "see" a situation I write about through their own eyes. *That* promotion to meaning is what I am after. Right through.

Rejoining the personal dimension with the other essential elements of responsible practice is one of the three broad-gauge learnings from my experience that seem worth sharing. In doing this, in my practice and my writing, I line myself firmly and gladly with colleagues working with social system perspectives at the Tavistock Institute, the Gestalt Institute and other mostly small groups; with Erik Erikson, Robert Coles and Sudhir Kakar; and with

Donald Schon and Chris Argyris as they persevere with distilling theory of action out of the messy mass of daily living and working.

My second overall learning is against sticking too exclusively to any one role and becoming a specialist in that and being known for that. The narrowing, of perspective and familiar competence, gets worse and worse. I favor occasional changes of roles, e.g., researcher to doer, internal consultant to external, working individually to working in a team. If there should be exceptions to this rotating and to experiencing the work first-hand in several roles in turn, I cannot think of even one. I get especially anxious about consultants (many highly reputed and visible, and charging high fees) who have no first-hand experience of the roles of people they profess to help, either none at all or not recent experience, and consult on team-building and -working when they themselves have stayed for so long in individual practice. Not absolutely all roles need be experienced by every last practitioner, of course, nor all equally. But for practising responsibly, creatively and also safely, I find it essential to experience a fair set of them from time-to-time first-hand, fully responsible and held accountable for the results. Each time, practice in the role must be long enough, often enough and intensively engaging enough, to keep alive and current the true appreciation of the nature of situations as they come up to someone *there*.

These motley dimensions come together as stories. All stories in this book are true, in the sense of "from real life", and all are my stories, in the sense of *my* reality promoted to *my* meanings. And in each I will not merely be present and active (we cannot help but be that; it is the human condition, whatever we do to try to avoid, hide or disclaim it), but also as open as I can be about my part, "where I was (or am) coming from". My cards will be on the table, to play the game open, as far as I can. My hope, of course, is that clarity about my part will make readers more inclined to consider what *their* own proper position(s) would be in a like situation, in a story like that. More inclined and also more surefooted.

The writings on which the stories center are in rough chronological order; so, together they also make up much of my story as a whole. They may even show that I learned some things along the way.

My third overall learning underlines companionship: I don't trust myself alone for very long, and need others to confirm that

I am still "seeing straight" or, more often, seeing enough that matters in that situation. This is not a social preference in the first place. I prize time alone and, experience shows, also do well enough working on my own for weeks, even months. But this is also not true, for I have wonderful colleagues on call, even at great distances, and I stay in touch. I find second opinions, also third, part of responsible practice.

Hence, I have also checked these chapters with colleagues who were together with me in those situations at the time, to backstop my truths and set limits to my fancies, and altogether round out the accounts. And I have asked current colleagues too to read and react to selected chapters. Here they all are, chapter by chapter:

1. "One Strike Too Many": Work on the London Docks. Elizabeth Sidney, close colleague and friend in London, then and since.
2. "Facts from Way Down (to Way Up)": Coalmine management and organization. Harold Bridger, then (and still) with the Tavistock Institute in London; George McRobie, then economist with the National Coal Board; Deepankar Roy, consultant; Nandani Lynton, consultant; Glenn Wilson, formerly with the National Union of Mineworkers, USA.
3. "Expanding the Moment": The story of recording my practice. Colleagues who saw me do it: Udai Pareek at SIET Institute; Racine Brown, Walter Isaacs, David Kiel, Lill Mood, and Bob Sigmon at the School of Public Health; Lynne Kohn, counsellor/therapist; Suzanne Stier, consultant.
4. "'Lynton's Crocodile' and Other Companions": Building supports. My very closest and enduring colleagueships over the years. Four of the five "twins" to whom this book is dedicated. Also Lynne Kohn, counsellor/therapist.
5. "Seizing the Moment": Serendipity and risk-taking, wise and unwise. George McRobie, then at SIET Institute; John Lewis, then head of what is now titled the US Agency for International Development in India; Vijay Mahajan, pioneer of an all-India organization for channeling young professional managers into NGOs and, newly, for financing non-farm rural employment.

6. "Seeing Systems—At Last": Changing positions from which to see and work in the world. Modeling. Don Klein, consultant; Lynne Kohn, counsellor/therapist; Udai Pareek at SIET Institute; Bob Tannenbaum, consultant.
7. "Innovative Institutions in Particular": Strategies, structures, linkages and working styles of effective innovative subsystems.
8. "Going to Size": Enlarge a successful program or spin off many new programs. Networking for learning strategies. Bill Cousins, formerly director for urban development, UNICEF; Loren Mead, founder and first head of the Alban Institute in Washington, DC; Tony D'Souza, then program officer for leprosy, Danida, in India.
9. "The Personal Dimension: More Inner Work": Personal presence, what it is, means and does. Nancy Brown-Jamison, Racine Brown, Nandani Lynton, Barbara Sloan, Bob Tannenbaum, consultants; Don Klein, program head, Union Institute; Maya Engh, Pamela Kirkpatrick, Lynne Kohn, therapists; Kay Jamison, producer; John Martin, producer and director; Mallika Sarabhai, close family friend since the 1950s, dancer, choreographer, and co-director of Darpana Academy of the Performing Arts and of Mapin Books; Susan Ketchin, writer.
10. "Transcendent Challenges: The Sound of Sense": Directions worth taking. Abad Ahmad, then vice-chancellor, University of Delhi, North Campus; Vijay Mahajan, then head of PRADAN, India.

As with earlier books, Ronnie, my wife and colleague for life, continues to be in my way the whole time, from sharing ideas, hers as well as mine, to editing and, I know already, wishing we/I had added/left out/put something differently after the text has already gone to press. There are no ways I know to thank her enough.

Thanks, of a different order of course, are due to architect friends Ashoka Katakam and his associates in Hyderabad and Tony D'Souza in Delhi for converting my sketches of crocodiles, jesters' caps and other favorite images into printable figures. Tony's own work on converting leprosy services from outcast status in isolated communities to incorporation in public health services provided in ordinary towns and villages I would dearly have liked to include in Chapter 8, but I was not formally or continuously enough connected with it to do so. Yet, it is the work I know best that has gone furthest in completing the cycle that starts with responding to a "transcendent challenge" (see Chapter 10) by creating an innovative sub-system for change of a strategic order and achieving large system acceptance and transformation (in this case throughout three Indian states with a combined population of over a 100 million as I write).

Warren Bennis responded enthusiastically to my idea he write the Foreword, and I am grateful—once again. In the mid-1960s we both led consultant teams helping to build institutions in India, and together we led a six-institution faculty development program one April in the cold Himalayas. At those heady heights, he shared his idea of a new kind of policy studies program for practitioners. He went on to institute that (at SUNY Buffalo, New York), chaired my doctoral work in it (their first as well as mine), invited me to teach in it (which I did, part-time), and offered me a deanship (which I declined as premature—and in too cold a place). He also, in this our first longer stay in the USA after 12 years in South Asia, brought me fully into what is now the NTL Institute, which continues to be my main network of colleagues. In Buffalo, and later in Cincinnati when Warren was president of the university there, I often stayed at his and Clurie's house, then alive too with children. Warren and I share much personally, important parts rooted in cultural, historical depths and only vaguely apprehended and still unexplored. Classic Warren was his coming into my doctoral "defence" carrying a bottle of champagne. That I deserved to pass, he began the session, was not really in question by now. But would I start off the discussion by telling, briefly, what my dissertation (on institution-building and consulting in India) could tell him about running this State University at Buffalo (where rioting students had just occupied the administration building and the police was deciding whether and when to storm it). Classic Warren too was that the defence was in public, like a Medieval university would have had it, in say Paris or Bologna.

How things come about. In the middle of writing this book, on the way back from some work in China, I stopped off in Seattle.

Ronnie, with frequent flyer points about to lapse, joined me there so we could visit friends whom we had met on our anniversary cruise last year up the breathtakingly lovely fjords of Norway. We had gone there after a week in Berlin, my place of birth and timely emigration, with feelings now aplenty from way back, and also, now, for the city which had invited us to come visit at its cost and had shown in many ways it was trying to make up—to me and the rest of us who had survived, and to itself and Germany no less. So I "was back" in my origins, and the wedding anniversary spanned to the present.

At our friends', I picked off the shelf in the guest room a book of essays by Joseph Brodsky. I am not much of a reader of poetry, but Brodsky had died recently and the many highly appreciative obituaries had heightened my awareness of him and his life. The quotes at the beginning of this Prologue come from that reading and my warm appreciation of his accounts of friendships with Nadeszda Mandelbaum and, above all, with Auden (whose *September 39* I had just reread in China). So back to that war as well.

Sailors Ronnie and I are not, but our friends are, with their own boat, and Puget Sound is aswim with boats. So here the scene was of peace. And expanse of space. One evening, a perfect double-rainbow spanned it. So the imagery of anchoring and of gaily fluttering pennants and of making a voyage came of itself. And with it the quiet "space" to get on with writing the book.

A final word of appreciation—for Tejeshwar Singh, Managing Director, Sage, the Production Team and the Readers. Amazingly, across all the vicissitudes and deadlines of publishing (and 12,000 miles most of the time), they kept my space—quietly, absolutely reliably, with firm good order and flexible good sense, and engaging personal courtesies all along. A heart-warming experience indeed.

References

Brodsky, Joseph, *Less than One: Collected Essays*, Farrar, Strauss, Giroux, New York, 1986.

Frost, Robert, *Complete Poems*, Holt, Rinehart and Winston, New York, 1964.

Ketchin, Susan, *The Christ-haunted Landscape: Faith and Doubt in Southern Fiction*. University Press of Mississippi, Jackson, 1994.

1

ONE STRIKE TOO MANY

Memory Traces to Community
Work by its Very Nature and Setting: "The Givens"
Ill Work on the Docks: The Report
A Flash—Then All is Dark Again
Mapping the "Areas of Freedom" to Act

It is only by concentrating on physical details...that I can prevent my initial impression from being overwhelmed by the...legend.
Laurens van der Post 1982, p. 178

1940, early in the first summer of the Nazi Blitz on London. I stood on Parliament Hill and watched the giant conflagration as the docks burned. Those docks kept Britain going. Even as they burned, I was sure—as most people in Britain were—that they would be made to function again with the speed of dedication. And so they were, for the years of the war. The enduring consequences became clear only later.

The late 1940s were difficult years in Britain; so soon after six years of total war, that was no wonder. People were tired, plain exhausted, each, of others, whole agencies, country-wide. Tired of things dragging on, seemingly not getting any better; of rationing and shortages of everyday items that continued with neither let up nor promise (or so it seemed); of standing in long lines for every little thing, and certainly for big ones, like just getting on the lists for housing and moving that little still quite indefinite bit closer to getting married, starting a family and having one's own place; tired of rules and regulations as if the war were still on; tired of everything in sight being drab and run down, and of gaping holes every few steps down streets full of rubble.

Still years ahead, then, was the Festival of Britain which would recall the Great Exhibition of 1851 and Britain's very own century of undisputed pre-eminence in the world. With its bright colored posters and flags everywhere; the South Bank first cleared then lined with new-age halls for concerts, exhibitions, theater, and generous walkways and places to sit, all sparkling new just across the Thames from dear old parliament; and fresh, open, often clever designs of everyday things to use—yes, the Festival would buoy people's spirits, perhaps the first thing that did since the euphoria of VE-Day that May day long back in 1945. All that was in the future that dreary summer of 1948. At least, not even a hint of it was public knowledge.

Tempers were short. No longer were people inclined at all to make do, to take the extra step or two and then even put on a cheerful face whatever the latest trouble was, which had carried them through the war with such remarkable equanimity. All was now insult: too much had gone on too long. And just then erupted yet another strike in the docks, the one that provoked the study that involved me (Lynton and King, 1949, duplicated and marked confidential).

Tempers in government, even of Cabinet ministers, had limits too, and this latest strike in the apparently unending series crossed those limits. Feisty, down-to-earth Home Minister Herbert Morrison challenged the recently formed committee of leading management and applied social science institutions in the country to advise the government what to do to stop these strikes, all interventions so far having obviously failed. This committee met regularly to work out policies and priorities for applied research towards raising productivity in industry and services, and to see that the most promising were funded. At this meeting, Morrison, in the chair, brushed the set agenda aside and citing the pressures of the moment and the particular responsibilities of those here assembled, his own and of the institutions, simply started with his request.

The gravity of *any* strike at this time was clear, and dock strikes were especially grave. All present knew this. Food rationing was still on, and these strikes interfered most directly with the unloading of tightly calculated supplies from overseas, essential even just to continue the present meager rations. Britain's "export drive" was only barely and uncertainly under way. It had to succeed so Britain could pay for that essential food and for the supplies, raw materials, and equipment required for restocking and reconstruction after six years of all-out war, not to mention making even a token start toward repaying the mountainous war debts (then still talked about as an honest intention). Every major dock strike threatened this ability to pay. Directly, it interrupted the still meager flow of exports, added heavy costs due to delaying of ships in port, and upset shipping and port schedules for months to come. More scary still, each deepened the doubts many around the world already entertained about Britain ever being a dependable trading partner again.

That the strikes in the docks were all *unofficial* made people generally even more uneasy. Were things getting out of control? Were there no limits? Were we mere pawns—the docks, Britain herself—in a *much* larger fiendish campaign of disruption by enemies of the state itself? What was to become the Cold War was heating up then, and card-carrying Communists were prominent among the strike leaders. What else but sinister plotting could account for the speed with which "any little dispute" on some dock led to a walk out on the spot, then immediately spread like wildfire throughout the entire port, and overnight brought ports to a standstill up and down all coasts? And that too not just in and from the London docks—Liverpool, Glasgow, Hull, Cardiff were also very frequent starters of strikes.

Even if international ramifications could be held at bay, the strikes certainly undercut the Labor government and all its grand plans for full employment, the National Health Service, public ownership of coalmining and other major industries, and much else—all for the workers' benefit. Here were the workers themselves undercutting it. The leaders of the Transport and General Workers Union (to which the dock workers belonged, every last one of them if they expected to work there legally), with altogether more than a million members and easily the largest union in the country, had already condemned this strike and "ordered" the men back to work. *They* were of course committed to backing this Labor government and these policies. Former officials were ministers in it, and many more were in parliament. But, going by what had happened in all the earlier strikes, the men would not listen to the union leaders; they scorned them. The leaders could hardly get a hearing at the thinly attended meetings they called. So the strikes, especially major ones like this and in so key an industry which was part of Britain's "lifeline", threatened the country's whole new political direction. Nothing indicated that any of this would be different this time, only worse. What did the professionals have to suggest, Morrison wanted to know. And if not things to do right away, then at least ways to explore and find out, as was their business.

The room went silent; excuses came next: the few senior personnel were already fully committed to important projects approved by this very committee and/or even minimal conditions for a proper study of the docks did not exist. In the end, the director of the quite new British Institute of Management (BIM) volunteered its Field Research Unit to study the strike. The Institute, in the long tradition of autonomous research institutions in Britain, was half-owned and half-funded by the government. The study would start right away.

A call from Tony Mayo, my strikingly tall, beautiful chief, the daughter of Elton Mayo, was the first I heard about it. He, a doyen in the human relations field, had recently retired from Harvard Business School and now lived in England. I was on holiday just then, across the Channel attending a week-long international seminar at Breda Castle, Holland. Incredulous! An overseas call was a very uncommon event then, probably my first ever—I had to be called out of a session to take it on the one phone in the large hall. Would I please come back right away to do this study while the strike was going on? No, I replied quite off the cuff, that would not be useful, could even endanger onward possibilities. (It would have risked my neck too, people told me later. If I had ventured into strike territory just then, I might have been seen next floating down the Thames with a steel hook in my neck, the kind dockers used to redirect the huge nets of full sacks dangling from a winch or crane. Mine was the youngest neck in the BIM to risk!) On the phone I agreed to start the study next week when I would be back, or as soon after that as the strike stopped.

Memory Traces to Community

When, 45 years later, I looked for the report on this study to include in this book, I was quite certain that it was about dock communities: the essential role the dock communities (strung along the Thames on both sides along the entire length of London's East End and right by the work) had played in the lives of dock workers generation after generation as they had made and kept the London Docks great over the decades; the utter devastation of these communities by bombs and fire during the war, starting with the giant conflagration I myself had witnessed that first summer of the Blitz; the consequent dispersals of the workers and their families, to live among strangers in the suburbs; and now, as inevitable as night follows day, the dire consequences of failing to fill that void of community. So sure was I that the report was all about community and the lack of it (prize example: docks), that I did not even scan the table of contents when I found a copy in our chock-a-block filing cabinets on the landing above our rooms in Hyderabad, India. I simply bundled it up with others to take along, to reread, review and think about, and to extract parts that might still have some practical use and deserve comment and updating.

It was only when I read the report right through months later and half-way round the world that I realized there was really very little in it about dockland and community. Though they were mentioned here and there, and "community participation" had a line on the full page of contents, the study had really focused on something else. Central instead was the nature of dock work itself, what it was and how it was organized, and how this pattern had become unworkable as a whole, intrinsically: dock work had become over the years a Humpty Dumpty of many ill-fitting parts; this Humpty Dumpty had managed to maintain his balance over "the duration" (of the war) only with much outside balancing and artificial propping; he had now finally tumbled off the wall and broken up; and no bandaid could put dock work together again as before. This was doubly disappointing when the

Labor government and the Union had only just instituted the National Dock Labour Scheme to reduce the casualness of employment on the docks everywhere, thereby putting a floor under the workers' incomes. Elaborate, good-looking in a logical sort of way, costly, and a direct attack on a perennial grievance—even with all that the new scheme would not do the trick either. The whole business was beyond tricks. And so the study pointed toward more basic directions to pursue.

Dock development since that time has proved this assessment to have been essentially true. Within only a few years, equipment and operations of ports and ships all around the world changed so drastically that these London docks totally disappeared; expensive riverside highrises have taken their place. So the thrust of the analysis then and the story of the report itself seems well worth telling still.

But first, I wonder, what accounts for my so faulty memory of the study and what it was really about, for it was of course the memory of it, its meaning to me, that I had carried forward into my life and work. It was not that what I found, made of, and remembered about dockland communities was mistaken in itself, but that I held it and prized it quite out of balance, on center stage when, in fact, it belonged in the wings. That displacement is worth attention, for "playing games" with memory must be quite common.

I can make out four threads in my memory to account for the distortion, and possibly a fifth one, thinner and fuzzier, running underneath those four.

One goes back to actually seeing these very docks go up in flames those days—and nights—that first August of the war. The German armies were just across the Channel. I was 16, home from school for the holidays via a three months' internment after Dunkirk. The skies were blue day after day. The public pool on Hampstead Heath was a great place to be, just up Parliament Hill where my parents then lived. (They were to move 12 times during the war, all in the same borough.) Only the blimps above, the sky filled with those funny small grey zeppelins swinging silently from their long tethers on the ground, reminded us of war, they and the trenches dug freshly into the Hill, which were ugly and of no obvious purpose. Training for trench warfare, and shades of 1914–18? Then the air raid alarm wailed and we learned what the trenches were for.

The guards ordered the pool cleared, all swimmers into the trenches. A strange spectacle it was; I can see us now: half-naked, still dripping boys and girls, and some adults, strung along the trench, heads barely at ground level or not even that. Waiting. Scanning. Spasmodic chatter; some wise-guy, irreverent joking, pretty inane; response thin and flat. Really like whistling in the dark, to keep spirits up. So to the "All Clear", the even pitch, like a factory siren that signals the end of the shift. Nothing had "happened". Perhaps it had been just another practice. At any rate this siren meant an end to the nuisance interruption of water fun and to the impatient waiting.

Only minutes later the alarm went again, that horrid wailing that threatened never to stop. We grew to hate it. This half-century later my insides still contract when I hear it—factory siren, police car, ambulance, whatever. So out of the pool and into the trenches again, then "all clear and back". We must have been in and out eight or more times that first day of actual raids. For that is what they were. And that night too, all night. Then more and more regularly each night and most days: that was the start of the London Blitz. Any residual sense of "phony war", from the languid first fall and winter of the war, disappeared fast in the screeches and crashes of bombs actually falling, the rattle of anti-aircraft batteries, searchlights criss-crossing and sometimes converging on an enemy plane in the night sky; and in seeing walls collapsed, holes where houses had been, broken glass and rubble in the streets each morning after.

From that green Parliament Hill's gentle slopes, I see London's East End burn, now, in my mind's eye. Miles away, across the sea of roofs of the vast city. I believe, still, I could make out the silhouette of St. Paul's fading in and out of black billowing smoke all around. I could see huge flames too, or so I thought, leaping up into the black sky, but I now doubt that. Certainly, though, there was great redness there as darkness fell, a steady glow below the vast fuzzy thick blanket of black that hung suspended between rooftops and sky. And that made light enough for the bombers which came again that night, and the next. Dockland—along with large swaths of the City—would be hit many times more as London was bombed nightly through that fall and winter and spasmodically after that, and finally with unmanned flying bombs; but the bombing those first nights decimated the dock communities most. Each time, I now know, the docks themselves were got going again in quick order; they were that essential. But the dockland communities, clustered along the Thames on both sides, stayed shattered and scattered, and never recovered.

The disastrous implications of *that* I had good reason to see eight years later, with the recollection of fires still vivid in my mind, and of people running, fleeing, falling, searching, helping, and then being taken to shelter and safety, but in strange places. Force and horror, and surviving: it all dredged up images and imaginings of our own fleeing as a family from Nazi Berlin, the threats and shots there, our resettling in England, and all that was new then—the thread of knowing what that feels like, even with deaths happily only as hearsay and distant reporting.

The second thread I can follow to my remembering community above all else takes me to the actual activities to get the dock study started that fall. They were all in community settings and in off-hours. And I continued to meet and talk with people from those communities right through the study. Community was always the context, so also for my memories.

My anticipation from the very first of what the study would involve determined this location of it. That is, *I* determined the community setting for it. In a situation as fraught with conflict as this, I decided, anchoring the study right was the strategic first step. That meant finding the right auspices and the right place. Nothing mattered more. Right meant that people be drawn together who could speak credibly for the different interests involved and feel encouraged to engage each other afresh, few holds barred. The main "stakeholders" in improving the docks I might now term them.

That meant finding a setting where employers and union officials were free of their formal roles and need not take their fixed positions against the strikers and their leaders. Otherwise, no strikers and strike leaders would come. Other considerations—of trying to set up meetings at work itself, which the bustle, noise and possibly personal danger made improbable anyway—I simply brushed aside with the overriding requirement that workers, union leaders, and employers resume talking again. So "off-site" it had to be. Also off-the-record, at least in the beginning. The groups would start small and informal, and probably be quite local. How from that small and informal start the study could make significant headway and affect the issue nation-wide was not clear. Looking back now, it may have been unclarities and semi-secrecies of such kinds that had led other committee members at the meeting with Herbert Morrison to declare that the basic conditions for a study did not exist in the docks. I too would now review those conditions and set about meeting them differently, using appreciative inquiry and future search methodologies worked out solidly in the 1980s and 1990s; of this reviewing, more later.

What I remember from that fall is the tentativeness of the approach; its slowness and laboriousness, with all the cross-checking and testing that composing even the exploratory meetings involved; and the long gaps between appointments and actual contacts, and between contacts and firm decisions. I need to add here that I tend to work slowly anyway, even in less conflict-ridden situations than this, and do so still even with much more experience. I hesitate to make starts in many places, preferring to see where any promising start may lead before I make another start elsewhere. I do not put beginnings at risk by hurrying and multiplying participants, persons or organizations, and in any case want to minimize risks of harm, to people above all. One implication of this slow-poking is on my overall pattern of work at any time: I need second and third projects to work on alongside the first, to take up the slack and drain off my impatience. So all through that fall I busied myself also with negotiating a much larger study of the newly nationalized coal industry and preparing my part in it (see Chapter 2). By the time the regular meetings started in dockland, the coalmine study was also under way. At the end of a meeting, I went straight for the night train to Scotland and arrived in time for another day-shift down a mine; and, as scheduled in advance, I would interrupt the work there to return to London in time for the next meeting about the docks.

So most of that fall went in making contacts to discern what would be the best anchoring institution, and to identifying workers, employers, and community leaders in different parts of the dockland for understanding the epidemic of strikes and what might be done about it. David King joined me in this in September. It was wonderful to share the work and have him to talk with. Close colleagueship like this I have striven for and have happily also had everywhere in my far-flung career, a basic connectedness—community again. He or I called ahead, walked many streets, found addresses, knocked on doors, sat and drank tea in many rooms and many offices in many houses, at many different hours. The sights, sounds, smells of dockland became utterly familiar that fall; also characteristic habits, phrases, silences of the people there; also our own feelings about them and our understandings.

By December, we had in place a network of contacts who wanted to join and a place in which to meet. One network of young workers' groups—the Young Christian Workers—brought many participants and onward contacts; their regular activity was a weekly meeting to examine a situation at work or in the family in the light of the gospels and decide on appropriate action. To me, they also brought two lifelong friendships and, unbeknown then, set my career off on its international trajectory only three years later.

For our dock study, a "Royal Foundation" no less became the anchoring institution. St. Catherine was in Stepney on the north side of the Thames, just past the Tower when coming from the City. Fr. St. John Groser was its head then. His legendary leadership of the protest marches for jobs and rent strikes during the Depression gave him impeccable credentials with all labor, and his even-handedness and utter integrity in all manner of developments and disputes in the borough gave him an equally unquestioned standing even with conservatively inclined employers, landlords, and shopkeepers. A commanding presence at any time, wiry, tall, strong voiced, often in laughter, with piercing blue eyes, he looked dramatic at this time with his white hair long uncut and blowing free for playing Thomas A. Becket in the film version of *Murder in the Cathedral*. He saw at once that the Foundation would be the right meeting ground and that doing something about the docks an absolutely right venture for it. We became personal friends and consulted and collaborated on various other things afterwards too, and then stayed in touch and visited whenever I touched England later coming from Asia.

The point here is that the communities and this footslogging up and down the streets in those communities, and then later joining with people from those communities regularly to consider the

work which was their very living and discerning how to improve
and guarantee it into the future, imprinted the most vivid, colour-
ful, moving (in short the most personal) images in my memory.
And this accretion and personal deepening, all the thinking and
rethinking around the activities, by myself and with David,
scored deeper still. I/we went over that ground again and again
in the business of working it all out, putting the picture together,
trying this way and that to make the best sense of it all, assessing,
hoping, dreaming. In so many ways the people from those communities, particular individuals and also people in all manner of
groupings, streets, kinds, whole communities, became parts of
me and stayed so vividly in my memory these many years.

It is difficult to sort out what was etched in then and what came
later. I now think that this weighting of community, the over-
weighting by far, that rereading the report surprised me with
these decades later, comes even more from my *later* work, which
was heavily into community-building and community development. So this third thread becomes more visible—and the
skewness of my memory of the docks more understandable—
backwards. In the long string of community work in my subsequent career, these memories of dockland and its people came
live again. The work with coalmining communities, even as the
dock work was still going on; again later, when I was founder-
director of an international training center in South Asia for community leaders in then newly independent countries; when, following that, I helped develop therapeutic communities in a
mental hospital in Oregon, USA; and then again back in India,
when I championed "area development" for creating jobs. The
string is long and continuous, in the States as well as in Asia and
elsewhere: helping a national network of consultants get off the
ground for work with local religious congregations; more and
more work since the mid-1960s in public health (in neighborhood health centers, then starting a new, "community-based"
school of public health, followed with helping Indonesia, then
India, "decentralize" their national health services); and alongside these major assignments, helping to organize and staff "community labs" with the National Training Laboratory (now the NTL
Institute in Washington, DC). For each, the community part of the
dock study is what I must have called up to *use*, and each time
I did in those very diverse settings I also etched them more

deeply still into my own memory. So, with habitual use they crowded out all else in that study, till even its main thrust just dropped away.

That exclusion, this progressive blindness to things of no immediate or ready "use", is a personal version of what Karl Deutsch (1963) terms "self-closure". It is a good term for putting the responsibility where it indeed belongs—namely, with me. I have learned to value the searchlight effect of the term for revealing so very clearly the temptation intrinsic in each major task and commitment: to domesticate it, fit it to *my* span and capacities. And I have learned to counter this lurking blindness by mixing the kinds of work I do and the settings for it, and by working primarily toward innovating, many times drastically. This balancing theme, of diversity while also aiming at deeper discernment, runs through the whole book, and most from Chapter 4 on.

Here, this abiding deep interest in community, the sheer descriptive fact of it, makes visible the thread that runs under the others. It stands out by its oddity: for this career-long interest in community and the daily neighborliness and familiarities with people, ideas, and habits that membership in a particular community means and conveys, is surely the very feature which my own life has been most glaringly without ever since that first emigration from Berlin as a child. That breaking of all ties was forced, and my parents never did strike roots again, in England or, even when time came to retire and they chose to live again in their "own language area", in Switzerland. But I have kept on moving by choice, many times and to very different places, as if to avoid that very rootedness in a community that I also so highly value. Even now, in semi-retirement, my wife and I divide our year between two homes, one in the States and one in India. We "belong"—in the splendid Indian way of putting it—to each place and are wonderfully part of whole families (by now over several generations), are also mindful of them when we are away and stay in touch across two very distant and different places, are in community (but only for part of the year); it is surely a limited commitment, well short of staying in one place through thick and thin. By choice I take hold and engage readily and with enthusiasm, but I am also ready to let go, ready for loss, for deep regret, even for tragedy—always with some reserve. Connectedness is the most important thing for me, building it and husbanding it. I have sensitive antennae out for people cutting themselves off from company—community—and heading into isolation by themselves, test for whether they really wish this or want it, to avoid the risk of exclusion or to play safe. I hold friends dear and close, lifelong, and though very dispersed, connect them up with one another into networks to build a community. That means support, and a supportive network is community—steady, reliable, lasting. So support-building and community-building are major themes I pursue in this book (Chapter 4 is specifically about this).

Work by its Very Nature and Setting: "The Givens"

We are now close to what the dock study and paper *were* most about: the nature of dock work (at that time) and the tendencies the prevailing patterns of it set up (which had become unmanageable). Just one more oddity on the way there: my not remembering *that* as the primary focus of the dock study is doubly curious since attention to "the givens" in any situation, the basic "factuality" (as Erik Erikson calls it) is also deeply engrained in my practice and quite as much second nature for me as concern with community and support. This too I attend to and build on all the time. What is given, fixed, more or less unshakeably fixed, stubborn reality is the first thing I set about understanding in any situation as I enter it. Repetition alone then, even if frequent and even with diligent and successful use, cannot account for my remembering one thing rather than the other, and my making the memory of one so rich and strong that it overwhelmed and at times excluded the other.

Another personal trait, accentuated like the first by emigration and being a stranger, may provide one clue: my acute sensitivity to what all may be required and expected so I can slip in and fit in like everyone else. Immediate context helps unravel this conundrum I think: real people going about the business of actually working things out with one another in their life circumstances and settings—that means something to me, engages me personally. So that is what I carry forward with me as conscious memory and endeavor. Compared with that, analyzing "factuality" is emotionally pale; it has become mere routine over the years, virtually mechanical, like brushing my teeth, using a fork or, much of the time, driving a car. My memories are of what stands out: figure to ground.

None of this belittles factuality. I don't "remember" to breathe, either. The fixed and all-but-fixed contours of a situation are basically important to attend to. We ignore factuality at our peril, personally as well as communally. When factuality is ignored or belittled, that is when castles get built on sand.

"Stubborn", Fritz Roethlisberger of Hawthorne Studies fame used to call those facts. His face would contort in part mock agony, eyes laughing, as he slammed his fist into his other palm, "the stubborn nature of things"; I can see him as I write. This stubborn factuality Eric Trist, Fred Emery and their colleagues at the Tavistock Institute were refining into "socio-techinical system analysis" at about the same time as we were working on docks and on coal. The four "Ts" of it—Task, Territory, Technology, Time—became the basic units for analyzing the nature of work, *any* work, and "primary task" the unit for mapping and monitoring effective organizations. And I acquired a growing repertoire of useful rules of thumb to use, such as, interdependence of tasks spelled trouble unless the performers worked that interdependence out together and then also maintained it over time. Even this one realization (out of several) led managers, for instance, to overlap shifts down coalmines or in hospital nursing, and to major (on occasion massive) reorganization of workplaces (as when Pearl King helped large hosiery mills to shift workers [back] to sitting around a large table so they could make up whole garments without special handling: it was surer, quicker, and led to less anger, no damage in transit, less inspection, and so also lowered cost). The workers around the table worked things out among themselves. In community, in fact.

This became the third study in Jerry Scott's and my book (1951), *Three Studies in Management.* Marvin Weisbord (1987) *Productive Workplaces* has traced the encouraging move towards autonomous work groups and updated it. For working with larger organizations and inter-organizational systems, the two streams of socio-technical necessities in a situation, its factuality, and the creativity, zest, and morale engendered by autonomous working, come together in Future Search methodologies. *All* stakeholder groups vitally involved in a particular matter come together in one room to discern what they hold in common and then get on with working out feasible action(s) in community.

That Trist and his colleagues first crafted such analyses into precision in the rockfastnesses of coal seams seems only right. There, hundreds of yards below ground, whole sets of stubbornly inescapable requirements of nature and technologies had to be followed meticulously, for physical safety's sake at the very least—one's own and one's mates. Those seams tunneled like rabbit warrens under mining "villages", where life in turn, of miners and officials alike and of their families, revolved around the same stubborn facts of that singular work; and that enforced fit was quite enough to make them singular and cut them off from the country at large. Yes, taking a good hard look at factuality there was utterly right, as indeed it was too in the docks and docklands. The stubborn facts about these two industries and their communities were very similar, including their isolation from others in the mainstream, the long periods of inattention and neglect by the world outside, and the similar consequence that any protest had to escalate to large-scale strikes before it was heard across this isolation and commanded general attention.

III Work on the Docks: The Report

The Report, then, focused on the nature of the work on the docks and what over the years had come to be regarded as normal about it. Dock workers, managers, companies, and unions, and also the families and communities in dockland had all learned to cope with it like that, and the nation at large too had grown so used to it that way that docks were normally out of mind.

Heavy unemployment in the 1930s had left workers, unions, and communities powerless to resist pressures for more continuous working, and the war had immediately ratcheted the pressures up again. As a matter of highest priority, ships that had made it past the German submarines had to be turned around fast, in all weathers and "all conditions". So also "at any cost"— that removed all fiscal constraints. Overtime work (at overtime rates of pay) and extra pay for keeping work going in all kinds of weather and all manner of irregular conditions had all become normal. When the docklands went up in flames, with many dead or maimed, and the communities had to disperse to wherever housing of any kind could be requisitioned (mostly in distant suburbs), the workers then had to add hours of commuting by public bus or underground to those long workdays, rough and dirty as they were and shunned, often rudely, by city folk. Well, these were special times and lots of other people too were deprived and in danger and having to make do. So the nation at large still did not notice anything amiss or brewing in the docks; other parts of the war effort always pre-empted attention.

Till, that is, there was no longer a war on and times were no longer so demanding without question. Exhaustion and making do had to come to an end sometime, and this was the time. The ways that "had served so long and so well" crumbled.

By now, the late 1940s, angry confrontation too had become quite normal, even over little things that made no sense to people away from the scene. The awful sense lay in the rottenness of the system, the way a wall can decay with dry rot (or, for us soon after in Sri Lanka, with white ants). In that state of near-hopelessness many attempts were made to put Humpty Dumpty together again, one repair at a time and most well-meant. They quickly perverted into yet more occasions for frustration. Every annoyance could be the last straw.

Every so often some worker somewhere on the docks had had enough and walked off, taking his mates with him. As they stalked angrily away, they cajoled others to join them, first on the docks nearby, then up and down the London Docks, and then in ports up and down the coasts. These others required no great urging; they were ready. "If we don't stop them now (doing us out of x agreement or y custom), we never will", was the common line. And joining together in strike reaffirmed solidarity too, community of sorts. Over the months following the end of the war, this readiness to explode grew and stayed high, and the processes for spreading strikes and for living with and through them became quite smooth. So the normal pattern had come to include all that too and had displaced the hobbled other.

The table of contents of the 32-page report shows this direction of analysis. It traces "the vicious cycle" of what employers, workers, and trade unions were doing to one another as it ground down into ever tighter circles of the "strike-prone situation" that had become virtually permanent now. In a brief final section we indicate "Some Implications for Management and Organization". The paragraphs are numbered, as was the habit of the day, and the instances under each indented and numbered again—107 clearly set out pieces of telling evidence.

To the body of the Report we appended a "Strike Diary", a nine page account, *staccato*, of the 1948 summer strike. It started on May 27 when Coe's gang disputed the rate of pay for loading 3,000 hessian bags of zinc oxide from barge to ship at Regent Canal Dock and ended on June 30 when all men returned to work. That was 36 hours after the King had declared a national state of emergency and (Labor) Prime Minister Atlee had broadcast "a personal appeal" to the strikers not to be misled by "a small group" holding political views dangerous to the country, and please to return to work. At its height, the strike had 20,000 men out in London—more than 80 percent of all there, 7,000 in Liverpool and 700 in Birkenhead; and in Southhampton 2,000 were debating whether to join. In London, 152 ships lay completely idle, 100 more in part and already delayed 10 to 14 days, at a direct cost to owners and employers of £800,000. That this account of ours simply reprinted paragraphs we culled from the most widely read newspapers for those five weeks probably made it doubly offensive to the authorities.

The extracts from the Report here center on "the vicious cycle" the parties had got themselves into and on its implications.

The employer: worker relationship. This seems to be the main problem area. The immediate needs of the two sides are contradictory: the employers require of their workers great flexibility and great willingness to change, but the workers...regard every change as a further threat to steady work and security. The battle over this issue has been fought over many years and with increasing bitterness; by now the two sides have become so estranged that neither seems able to appreciate the genuineness and force of the other's need; so change has virtually ceased. "Going slow" and strikes are merely the clearest signs of this situation.

3. The primary need for both sides would seem to be to come into closer contact, so as to be better able to recognise each other's problems and seek jointly for agreed solutions.

4. Neither the great variability of the work nor the lack of real contact between employers and workers present problems essentially unique to the docks. Experience in other industries suggests

that the two promising lines of development might be more permanent association of workers in gangs, and more permanent association of gangs with supervisors and employers....

5. ...the emphasis of the [Dock Labour] Scheme on the individual's work hinders the development of significant contact between employers and workers.

6. It is doubtful whether responsibility for discipline can be effectively severed from operational management. [In trying to do so] the Scheme may have merely removed the most contentious issue from the real conflict at the cost of unbalancing management.

7. .... It is doubtful whether joint [union and employer] responsibility can be a success if the real conflict between the two sides has not been faced. Trade Union officials...lose support among their members, and unofficial leaders emerge to represent the views of the workers.

8. In these respects the Scheme seems to hide the real problem area and to stand right in the way of a real solution....

14. *Not a study of strikes.* There are numerous small strikes in addition to those that make the headlines. But it is possible to pay too much attention to strikes. This is so not merely because strikes probably do not account for even the major immediate shortcomings in the docks. "Going slow" on the part of the dock workers and their resistance to mechanisation and other changes that might lead to improved performance are probably more important. The chief importance of strikes, as also of "going slow" and of resistance to change, lies in indicating that a number of things are wrong in the docks. Therefore the situation in the docks needs to be studied rather than the strikes.

15. ...many less obvious indications point in the same direction. The refusal of the workers to agree to alter long established rules seems so much taken for granted now that many technical improvements are not even seriously considered by the employers. Both workers and employers are preoccupied with written rules.... [There are] continuous requests for more detail in the provisions of the Dock Labour Scheme while there is, at the same time, regular resort to the Scheme's numerous escape clauses;...pressure from the workers' side for improved welfare arrangements but...difficult to find worker members to serve on Joint Welfare Committees; and the...greatly enhanced security of work [under the Scheme] seems to have entailed only stronger demands for more security [still].

Such paradoxes are likely to be resolved only at deeper levels of understanding....

I. *The nature of dock work.* The many different kinds of work... performed in the London docks, each with its own special [character have] one feature in common, varying only in degree: the great variability in the work and in the conditions in which it is performed.

[Ten paragraphs follow here under the headings of irregular employment, movement of workers between sites with varying conditions of work, constant changes in work teams and supervision, and leading up to the relentless pressures for "human flexibility" to cope with all this "uncertainty". That had been difficult enough earlier, the Report goes on, but then:]

48. .... Human associations at work and in the communities were largely the same [till the war]. Members of the same gang often lived in the same block or street and went and returned from work together. The pubs in the same locality were focal points [for convivial gathering] and were regularly frequented by the same men according to trade and station...points too for intelligence about the movement of ships and the likely locations for work the next day, about grievances and strikes elsewhere in the port, union and political activity, ...hop picking parties in the autumn, having a "whip round" for a mate who had an accident or for a widow for sharing earnings with less fortunate families, as they would when conditions were reversed; all this mixed in with a game of darts and the rounds of drinks in the natural social centre in working class communities....

The meaning of solidarity. To the world outside, the close integration of work and community in the docks meant stricter isolation from the dock workers and increased opportunities for misunderstanding them.... To the dock workers it meant enhanced dependence on each other, strong solidarity and greater security.

50. People without acknowledged place in this scheme of things are rigorously excluded. Clearly among them are the dock employers and their staff...promotion for a worker usually means desertion to his former mates, so supervisors...move [away]. Outsiders are highly suspect. The workers club together to protect each other....

53. In their own ranks, offences against the accepted norms, customs or social relationships are long remembered...and there is often serious and lasting social ostracism for [even] small deviations.

54. Only together had they secured the most significant improvements in working conditions, and only together could they continue to resist the encroachments of their insecure, hence hostile, environment.

55. Solidarity therefore means more than that...dock workers have little opportunity for contact with new ideas and standards

outside the docks: change in ideas and standards would endanger the established [hard-earned] order of things and [upset] the precarious balance that spells minimal security. The social pressures in dockland, alike at work and in the communities, are thus traditionally wholly and strongly against any deviation from the accepted norms, customs and social relationships.

56. This conflict, between the workers' immediate need for security and the employers' immediate need for flexibility on the part of the workers to offset the variability intrinsic in the work, has been sharpened by the numerous changes in recent years in the docks and also the communities...[the] ever higher time pressures; divisions among workers; protecting some at the cost of others; readiness of some to accept increased pay as compensation for continuing faulty and even unsafe conditions.... And, as coping has become more difficult, the workers have also learned to limit the employers' freedom by forcing concessions and getting many embodied in written agreements, e.g., minimum periods of consecutive work, vastly complex codes of pay rates, limitations on overtime, manning scales for different kinds of work, and many more.

57. The main traditional pillars of security—personal independence, social structure, trade union, community—have all been impaired...generally two things have tended to happen: firstly, the workers have resisted change, sometimes so successfully that it could not be carried out or at least sufficiently to modify and refine it; and, secondly, customs and relationships have disintegrated and left what we may call social vacua, and this has set workers searching for security in other directions.

58. Positive efforts to increase security have been concentrated on raising the economic security of individual workers: the number of workers looking for work on the docks has been reduced and dock workers have a minimum wage; and like workers in other occupations they are protected through various national social services. This helps in some ways.

59. But extra economic security does not appear to be generally adequate compensation, much less to be all that is required to reduce the workers' resistance to change. The function of customs and relationships in the docks was not merely that of providing some economic security in the absence of formal provisions: they grew, as we have seen, out of the need to limit the impact on the worker of the great variability of dock work and also provide satisfying human association. And these the drive for increased economic security has actually further impaired. The increased

resistance to change, marked on the employers' side by attempts [occasionally successful] to get *some* men to change and then use them to lever the others to change in turn and, on the workers' part, by persistent endeavour to maintain their ranks intact and bog the employers down in [ever tighter] rules and regulations, [these are telling] indication of the gaps that have been created and the even greater importance the workers attach to the customs and relations that remain.

[The next forty paragraphs, with numerous examples, then walk the reader through lists of attempts to deal with this "vicious cycle".]

The strike-prone situation. Each side attempts to drive matters just as far as it expects the other side...to go without breaking. Forcing the other side into making concessions or into eating its words becomes something of a game often played for its own sake rather than for material results.... The more out of contact the trade union officials are with the men, the more likely it becomes that the shadow of a dispute is mistaken for its substance and the more difficult to judge the precise limits to which it is safe to go....

102. Many disputes and strikes result from driving bargains too close. It is not difficult for either side to justify its actions and miscalculations in terms of actions and omissions of the other. Once started, disputes and strikes quickly get burdened with the general resentment that has accumulated [and festered] for all sorts of reasons and they are not explicable in terms of the issues formally stated; those provide no more than the occasion [and the language]. Difficult problems of face saving almost invariably emerge, [delaying] settlement and making it finally more painful. And with each the employers and workers draw yet further apart.

Some implications for management and organisation.

103. The prevailing atmosphere of suspicion and distrust in the docks renders almost any action liable to misconstruction.... The problem facing management is [how] to facilitate a change in these attitudes. [That] the two sides have drifted so far apart that real contact between them is very deficient...is probably the primary difficulty in the way of better understanding [and useful action]....

106. *Need for lasting association.* It is possible to emphasise the differences between docks and other industries; there are many. But there are also many significant similarities...research findings from an increasing number of widely separated industrial organisations may therefore throw some light on needs [and possibilities] in the docks. They all agree that for high morale and the associated high productivity, readiness to change, low absenteeism, labour turnover and strike incidence, the intimate association of workers

in small groups and a close relationship with the immediate supervisor are of primary importance.

107. ...keeping gangs together wherever possible would be... useful. [It] would affect schemes of mechanisation and other changes on the job as also the engagement, movement and general obligations of the workers....

110. Dock work puts many physical obstacles in the way of close contact between workers and supervisors. Also, a supervisor [now] is sometimes responsible for ten gangs or even more and the composition of his workforce changes frequently. Contact...is therefore largely spasmodic and lacks depth...taking greater account of this in defining the responsibilities of supervisors and in organising the movements of workers may well be beneficial.

111. [In the absence of good contact] strikes are often resorted to as an effective means of communicating with higher management...[and] the association of trade union officials with imposing disciplinary action inhibits contact yet further. [That consequence of the Dock Labour Scheme] may be its most doubtful venture.

A Flash—Then All is Dark Again

As I put the Report down I have the sort of "so there!" feeling I get when I hear or read a doctor recommend a change in lifestyle to reverse course. Even if quite logical from the evidence, it is not useful by itself. For one thing, that recommendation is usually not news; I had not come to hear it confirmed once more, nor for the detailing of troubles that further delaying fundamental change would surely entail. I had gone for practical help, even a little, for taking actual hold of one or two pieces to start with to rearrange my life. I came to learn what to look for by way of faint signs that I am on the right track and that I am not deceiving myself with my exertions. Without help on some such lines as these—and perhaps even with it, the odds are not good—my life of trouble, firmly enmeshed as it is in me and my long-familiar situation, remains intractable, unmanageable, overwhelming, and also irreversible. I just know I will fall off if I don't keep pedaling as before, trouble and all.

The built-in weakness of this study of the docks was that the workers, employers, and community leaders who produced the information for it and also discussed it at the meetings were not in positions to effect the drastic changes essential for making the docks work. They were not close enough to where those kinds of decisions would have to be taken. Not close enough even to appreciate what all got in the way *there* for people in those positions to turn their whole business around, or even (this could have been the essential first step) to identify common ground that all the essential parties could explore together for strategic direction and priorities. And then go on together instead of, as now, tripping each other up and that mostly from staying so frozen and in the dark.

Given that distance from the field of action and the players there, did the Report at least point to the kinds and order of actions to be taken, and what might be a practical first step or two the essential actors could consider taking? The Report certainly envisaged both. Noting that difficulties arose much more frequently and severely in some docks than others, all in London, and in some firms than others even on the same docks, it proposed that these differences under the same general conditions be studied and understood. It identified seven locations where dock work was organized and carried out better even now, and proposed ways to make those heartening exceptions accessible to others. And it proposed two lines of more comprehensive research, amounting to action-research: "10.1. Work with one or two firms to study jointly with them problems of dock management; [and] 10.2. Work with the Dock Labour Corporation to study jointly problems of administration and useful developments in the scope and organisation of the Scheme." These proposals were on page two, at the end of the executive summary.

In the end, the Report spoke most to the country at large— loudly—and that probably also made the end of it. After a research timetable that cautioned me for good against settling for orthodoxies in such matters, another dock strike flared up that April and spread like wildfire. So, after spending all of the previous fall to settle on the institution to anchor the study in, then the winter on the meetings (eight in all), we then had just three days for producing the Report. With the new dock strike raging fearfully, the urgings for goodness sake to tell *now*, right now, whatever we had to tell, overwhelmed good sense and proper care. A press conference already arranged for three days hence to launch two new BIM publications would launch this Report as well. Good looking pamphlets those were, with shiny covers

in several colours. Our "Interim Report", run off from stencils in
the hectic last minutes on 17 legal-size sheets front and back,
looked bedraggled next to them but took all the attention.

That it was marked "confidential" was totally ignored; the fuller
specification of it, at the end of the introduction, now appears
laughable: "The material [so, only the material!] has been cleared
with the people who provided it for the sole purpose of showing
it to the Ministerial Committee examining problems in the docks.
It is shown to them in strict confidence." The next morning, with
the dock strike still on, it made the headlines all over the national
papers. In *The Times* and others it was the lead item and mentioned respectfully in editorials on the strikes—past, present—
and future?

And that *was* its end, till now, here resurrected. That the powerful bodies that controlled onward action were not pleased we
gathered from their silence. And no champion for taking next
steps arose in the BIM, the Institute probably too divided over
so much limelight on its youngest "officers" and the solid work
of seniors neglected, pushed off stage.

Mapping the "Areas of Freedom" to Act

The stubborn requirements of a situation continue to receive my
first attention wherever I start work. What I am specifically after
is making a map, early and quickly, of the area(s) of freedom (as
I have come to call them) realistically available for making improvements and plans.

This is mapping: heady stuff, even hard-headed, devoid in the
first instance of people and personal feelings. When these get
worked into the equations, the areas of freedom may contract a
little or enlarge a little, but not very much, not "off the map" of
factual possibility. This impersonal, essentially mechanical nature
of analysis became clearest for me on a self-chosen assignment
just 10 years after the dock study. While working for some
months on developing therapeutic communities at the State Mental Hospital in Salem, Oregon, I was struck by the patent sense-
lessness of the so-called occupational therapy there and, of
course, volunteered to put sense into it. I arranged that therapeutic
staff should restrict their prescriptions to the key characteristics

of the relationships a particular patient should next experience (e.g., with man or woman or in a group, with someone else or her/himself in charge, with older or younger person[s]; also the recommended frequency of such therapy, strenuousness, attention spans and complexity, and the kind of space, [such as, confined or outdoors]). I had working staff and supervisors on the spot identify independently and keep up-to-date lists of activities categorized by these same characteristics. Occupational therapists could then do the best matching possible that day between prescription and available task. This took psychologists and psychiatrists out of assigning patients to activities they hardly knew and gave occupational therapists a much wider range of truly therapeutic assignments to make.

Soon after, I made similar impersonal mapping the basis for meticulously recording my institution-building efforts (see Chapter 3), and some years later again I proposed that strategies for community involvement in family planning programs be guided by the socio-technical requirements of the family planning methods in commonest use (Lynton, 1977).

Back in the docks in 1949, not only was our "area of freedom" for effecting change close to zero because of our meager connectedness to the strategic actors, but even a low-order socio-technical analysis like ours was bound to confirm that even the actors would have had difficulty identifying areas for possible action, never mind agreeing steps to take in common. The dominant patterns were a convoluted mess and basically self-defeating. It was the first situation I worked in where significant development was simply not to be had along currently accepted and acceptable lines. I recall the impish temptation to offer my services to the *strikers*, so that together we had the chance of making that hopeless prospect so public that major radical changes would at long last become the order of the day. Obviously, I am tempted still.

References

Deutsch, Karl, *The Nerves of Government*, Free Press, New York, 1963.
Lynton, Rolf P., 'Administration of Fertility Control Programs', American Academy for the Advancement of Science (AAAS) Panel Meeting, Denver, February 1977.

Lynton, Rolf P. and **King, S.D.M.**, *Research in the London Docks*, British Institute of Management, London, 1949.

Scott, Jerry and **Lynton, Rolf P.**, *Three Studies in Management*, Routledge and Kegan Paul, London, 1951.

Van der Post, Laurens, *Yet Being Someone Other*, The Hogarth Press, London, 1982.

Weisbord, Marvin, *Productive Workplaces*, Jossey-Bass, San Francisco, 1987.

2

FACTS FROM WAY DOWN (TO WAY UP)

Management "Science"
Organizational Fit
Oh, Where Have All the Managers Gone? Far, Far Away
An Opportunity Lost
Down to Solid Ground
Vivid Memories

*You can lead a horse to water
but you cannot make him drink.*

Common wisdom

Fall, 1987. Delhi, India. A young colleague, Deepankar Roy, stopped by for one of his occasional visits to talk about what he was doing as a freelance consultant. He was just back from his monthly visit to the coalmines in Eastern Bihar. As he spoke of his experiences and the issues on which supervisors and managers wanted his help, I asked whether he had ever seen the chapter on coalmining in *Three Studies in Management* (Scott and Lynton, 1952) about coalmine management in Scotland four decades before. What Deepankar talked about sounded so familiar to me, but I did not say that then. I simply lent him a copy of the book, with some trepidation, since it was my only one, the one inscribed to me by my co-author, and the book long out of print; moreover, my copy was very much the worse for aging in tropical climates. Deepankar promised to take good care of it and to bring it back personally quite soon.

Two days later he called, all excited. The chapter described "exactly" the situations he worked in in the Bihar mines and, even better, analyzed them usefully. Could he copy and distribute it to the managers there? Of course. In the event, for me he copied the entire book and had it bound in hard cover so I would have a working copy and spare, the precious original with the dedication.

It is this copy that I have just reread, but this time, unlike rereading the study of the London docks, for background only and without any expectation of finding there what I most want to recall for *this* book. My mind here is on our self-imposed labor over two years to show the National Coal Board, the apex of Britain's then newly nationalized coal industry, how to align the superstructure and functioning of this huge industry more closely with the needs of its production units, that is, the collieries themselves. (The industry then employed three-quarters of a million people.) I could be certain that I would not find anything about this strategic fit in the book because the Coal Board had stopped us from publishing anything about that. Any publication had to be confined to the workings of the mines themselves: not even extrapolations "upwards" were allowed, not to speak of the actual examination of the new area, division and national organization.

For this long-forbidden fruit I have therefore gone back now to the original, unprepossessing paper as we presented it at the time, first to the Information and Research Committee of the British Institute of Management and sent on from there, with only minor revisions, to the National Coal Board: 82 legal-size pages of properly numbered paragraphs and sub-paragraphs plus a four-page appendix on the scope, methods, and contacts of our study.

What we laborer–authors confidently expected to be a discussion of it (the Committee too? also the Institute as a whole?) took place at a special dinner meeting at the genteel Brown's Hotel just off Piccadilly. All I remember, besides the awsome formality and the courtesies throughout, is that the doors were locked immediately we were all in and that at the end Board members themselves made sure to collect all copies in the room, to lock them away. That ranging version of the study was never published.

Since issues of good fit are hardy perennials in large organizations of all kinds and anywhere, parts of that fearsome paper of 45 years ago seem worth recapturing—for historical record, for one thing, of how this strategic issue was formulated in earnest and passed muster in those years, and how or why it was then also immediately hidden from public view, and coal a public enterprise at that! As for the issues of organizational fit, only in focus and metaphor have they changed with time and circumstance. Contemporary versions include "downsizing" the organization, "collapsing" managerial hierarchies, and "outsourcing" functions that till quite recently belonged without question *inside* all organizations worth the name. So, achieving a fine fit across different components of an organization—production with maintenance and supplies, finance and marketing, field services with headquarters, between levels or between specialist and operating units—continues to pose important concerns for planners and executives, and also for students of organizations, no matter what metaphors are currently used for them.

Management "Science"

But first, even now, and more striking than the substance of the wilted paper, comes the question of how several man-years of effort and expense invested in that study had led to this stand-off: the august client simply refused to clear the strategic part of it for publication; and, on the other side, the BIM simply submitted to this veto, at once and without argument. The study and recommendations focused on a manifestly and universally strategic issue after all, and that was the very domain the BIM with government backing had declared peculiarly its own: large organizations. That coal was a public enterprise and the Board was here dealing with an institute half-funded by the government made the stalemate extra stark and strange.

The dominant notions in the immediate post-war years of what "scientific" research in management and organization entailed had lots to do with it, I think. They have a Victorian flavor: we researchers were pioneers, off like explorers to distant isles peopled by strange tribes. Very sober and serious, and after laborious preparation, we would proceed ever so quietly, so as to cause least disturbance in the object(s) of study. That was the way of science, and nothing could be more important than that.

Scientific Management was the title of the most recent and much acclaimed set of three pocket-size books by L. Urwick. Colonel Urwick—he was addressed by his military title—headed a renowned consulting company with offices in high society Mayfair (where the new BIM also had its first offices). His company was a corporate founder-member of the BIM and he personally "a must, of course" on its first board of governors. Like lesser lights in the field, Urwick acknowledged Frederick Taylor's work at the turn of the century on work study and relating pay to output: rate × count. He also referred warmly to Mary Parker Follett's seminal writings, in the 1920s, on the social dimensions of work and the practical importance of organizing work around groups of workers rather than individuals. Though Follett's writings would actually prove more important in the long run, it was Taylor's promise of getting at the science of it all that held the greater appeal.

On this foundation of management "science", Professor Bartlett and others had built 30 years of rigorous studies in machine design and its implications for machine operators. Laboratories with experimental equipment were the setting for most studies and the Medical Research Council funded them, itself a jewel in the government's scientific establishment. His Majesty's Armed Services were greatly interested. Ways to reduce worker (or pilot or gunner) fatigue through better machine design and the like had been discovered, and this was followed with the orderly identification of traits for selecting operators who would do best on particular machines and tasks, and of working conditions with optimal characteristics.

Into the 1930s. Elton Mayo, the father of my chief at BIM, had then securely riveted the social factors into this expanding equation of management science by carefully documenting and analyzing the influence on productivity of small work groups and of different ways of leading and supervising them. That had backed Follett's observations and insights with real science. Wider generalizations followed about informal and formal organizations and the importance of a good match between them. The Hawthorne Studies, published in the early 1940s, became the standard reference for them in post-war Britain as well as in America. The Human Relations Group at the Harvard Business School that had anchored those studies had by then studied such urgent wartime problems as absenteeism and labor turnover on the same lines. It was from that Group that Jerry Scott, my senior colleague and co-author of the coalmining study, came, as well as Tony Mayo, our chief. There was a family quality about this science. Together we took afternoons to visit Elton Mayo himself and talk about our work; recently retired and ailing, he had an apartment in a magnificent old countryhouse that looked out on handsome wooded slopes halfway between London and the South Coast.

Assembled in the Field Research Unit of the brand-new BIM, we ourselves had quickly signalled particular interest in *large* organizations and their scientific management, and that suited the BIM perfectly. Important and obviously needy clients were right at hand for the ministrations of our burgeoning new science: the dock industry, privately owned but so strategic to the country's economy that it was already subject to special legislation and government schemes; British Overseas Airways Corporation (BOAC), government-owned and then running heavily in the red; and, of course, the newly nationalized coal industry on which homes as well as factories and rail transport throughout Britain depended utterly for energy, and the Labor Government for much of its hopes for post-war Britain. So the Institute quickly signalled its interest in all three giant clients, and I recall envious glances and under-the-breath comments when Tony repeatedly flew off to distant parts of the globe, First Class "of course", or limousined to another luncheon with top officers of BOAC.

BOAC, as they raced ahead in air travel, depended directly and obviously on staying abreast of a wide spectrum of technologies and of the scientific advances that sustained them. On the contrary, an old industry like coal had to go all out to counter its image of perennial backwardness—ragged rows of baretop, brawny, sweating men underground slamming pickaxes into the black in front of them: a whole industry in elemental dark and danger. In the new era ushered in by nationalization, the Board grasped eagerly at opportunities to show its utter determination to move this industry into the mid-twentieth century. And the clearest way to demonstrate this was to back scientific inquiry and validation, and to include its own organization and management in this. The many parties involved in giving the industry new direction, with all their differing and often conflicting interests, were at one when it came to showing how very up-to-date they were in this determination to go about their task scientifically.

Directly from success at war, operational research (OR) had just arrived on civvy street. J. Bronowski, the Coal Board's top scientist, was an active instigator and contributor to the OR group's meetings in the Royal Academy.[1] There I too sat, representing research at the BIM, daunted and silent, and often totally mystified by the detailed tables and equations displaying such nationally important matters as electricity generation capacities, or options to choose from for public transport means and patterns, or urban planning designs. Organization and management, too, were mentioned there, as a perfectly acceptable area to do OR in. R. Revans, ever enthusiastic, was into work study and rationalization of work anywhere in the coal industry at all. He openly welcomed idleness, the more the better, because that showed that machines and processes were well aligned and doing the work they were meant to do: maximum output at least cost.

So science was unquestionably "in" with the Coal Board. Even if the BIM had been backward in offering its ministrations to so worthy a potential beneficiary, His (soon to be Her) Majesty's Government would have pressed us to step forward via that same committee that Home Minister and Deputy Prime Minister Herbert Morrison had tried to mobilize for advice on the epidemic of dock strikes. The studies that Eric Trist and his colleagues at the Tavistock Institute carried out in coalmines (and would craft a few years later into socio-technical analysis) had that committee's interest too Our study proceeded parallel to theirs.

There is also a personal connection. With so many forces and fashions converging on science, I myself, at 24, was suddenly and quite unexpectedly basking in scientific approval: *Nature*, Britain's leading journal for scientists with interests in fields beyond their own specializations, devoted the lead article for Christmas Eve, 1949, to a review of my first book just out (Lynton,

---

1. Also a published poet, Bronowski became most widely known, later, for his book and TV series, *The Ascent of Man*, Little, Brown and Co., Boston, 1973.

1949). So what I had written there was science, had to be, if *Nature* treated it so. The message of the review reinforced it: that studies of management were becoming scientific at last; that there was at least the beginning of that science here in England my book and others confirmed. Mine in particular, they wrote, was even "far ahead of much literature in this field [and] had the intellectual content of a sound mental discipline". So!

For me, pleasant and ego-building as this warm approval was from so august and unexpected a source, it was also confusing. How could what I had done be science, given the crude way I had done it?

The book had started in the field, and that made good sense to me: I had questions, doubts, concerns that called for answering. They had come as I worked in the factory at war, as thousands of others were then doing too up and down Britain. We worked long shifts—for my three-and-a-half years I worked 12-hour nights, 62-hour weeks. My job was to put the final outside grind on long, hollow cylinder sleeves for Sabre engines for fighter planes. I stayed on that same operation—#52—all that time, and must have completed it on something like 25,000 sleeves over those years. Accuracy was essential—to two-tenths of a "thou"—measured by hand gauge. That the pieces reached me in good shape, in particular that they were round enough even after series of heat treatments which could distort them, was very important. I had little scope to rectify earlier error, *very* little; and that took extra time I would not be paid for, except if there was a whole batch (24 in a box) to rectify and I made a fuss, successfully, about getting extra pay for it. Many times I actually welcomed the diversion from the routine that some creative fooling with the machine offered and did not bother making a fuss.

It was the many seemingly senseless misfits, delays and discrepancies in the ways we worked that had struck me in the factory—the lack of science, if you will. It began right from day one, when I was put to work on a monster grinding machine just after actually qualifying as press tool fitter, which had required the longest training of all. The misfits continued. Inspection, which existed at #51 for the very purpose of making sure that the sleeves were still "within limits" at this late stage, was unreliable, and it did not improve markedly over time, or so it seemed. That quite regular hazards, such as encountering a "dead" point of numbing fatigue around 3 a.m. every morning, led to no preventive steps for avoiding accidents to person, machine or product was strange too, to say the least. So also were the sudden flare-ups between operators which often soured the atmosphere, apparently out of the blue and without patent cause; yet this was somehow not unexpected either, just part of a charge in the air. The foreman was rarely around, particularly at those moments; he stayed mostly in his office. When he did appear on the floor, he had his eyes chiefly on papers on a clipboard, looked harassed, gaunt, and so not really approachable. Weird too was that maintenance and repair jobs on the machine took so long to arrange and get done, even simple-looking small adjustments which I could have done myself had I the tools. That the delay held up the whole production line did not speed things up as far as I could see. The foreman steered clear of the repairmen; better leave them to it, he mumbled.

Each and all had been new to me at first—this was my first real job. Quite soon the always ready excuse that "there is a war on, remember", had grown tedious, then provocative: yes, exactly, there *was* a war on! How could it be, then, that so much exertion produced so little, that there was so much fussing and so little planning, that we got into the same difficulties over and over again? At my age, 17 at the start, I was doing a job I was told I would never have been allowed on in peacetime. My pay, princely money in my eyes, with all the night shift and overtime, was less than two-thirds of the regular adult pay for that work. Why? One midday soon after VE-Day, thousands of us marched in procession through Central London with banners to protest against the idea that "shadow" factories like ours would be closed at the end of the war. Strange business.

For my first two years of war work I did little with those questions. The daytime hours, after sleeping, I spent studying for my basic degree, to be ready for better things by the time the war stopped. High drama ended the study: as 400 of us sat for the examination in a cavernous examination hall of the University of London, the first unmanned missiles fell. Again and again we ducked under our desks when the whines and crashes outside got too loud (= too close?) and sat up again when reasonable quiet resumed. But at the factory that first morning, a land-mine exploded at the entrance, killing two workers who happened to be standing there, and—this was the most direct effect on me—disturbed the machine beds inside so much that for the entire next month we produced only scrap: no finished sleeve was within limits, not one. By the end of that month I knew what low morale was like.

Till I had my degree, all I managed to do with my disquiets about the factory was to jot down brief notes about characteristic events and my abiding questions. Some of these I used soon after I was free of my studies for a piece Charles Madge asked me to contribute to the series of *Pilot Papers* he edited. I gave it the staid title—quite appropriate for "science"—of "Factory Psychology in the Transition" (Madge, 1944). In it I reproduced my mates' remarks in the factory as bases for generalizations, a way of vivid writing that a new organization called Mass Observation had popularized during the war. Oral history. Data. Science. My paper was of that kind.

But my book, half-a-decade later, which supposedly advanced science, was far from even that immediacy. With the questions, doubts and disquiets from my factory experience only raw in my head or unsorted jottings in a notebook, I had gone *reading*. All day Saturdays I spent at the British Museum Library for what I took to be the very necessary historic sweep; that became half the book. That done, I combed the libraries of several professional associations, of the Institute of Personnel Management most of all, for recent and current examples of management practice, good and bad. Out of ranging of this kind came the rest of the book. Its 200 pages of text had 512 footnotes, happily all at the back. Also many dire predictions. And this was what *Nature* pronounced science and a great advance over the prevailing level of discourse about management. The book had data identified and attributed, true, and it referred to events on record. It raised questions that were at least plausible and could be researched. And it had direction overall. But science?

So I basked in *Nature*'s commendation and also, even then, had my doubts about the stampede all around me for "science" and taking it *too* seriously. The proof is the quote I put on the title page of the book. It is from Shaw's 'Introduction' to *Saint Joan*: "...the nineteenth century, and even more the twentieth, can knock the fifteenth into a cocked hat in point of susceptibility to marvels and miracles and saints and prophets and magicians and monsters and fairy tales of all kinds." That lighthearted doubting must still be with me since I have the quote by heart.

That the new BIM would pay me to take my questions into the field attracted me very much. That is where they belonged in the first place, and that is where we "Field Research Officers" (sic!) would take our diligent but also orderly methods for studying them. What we had not yet got over and beyond, however, was the classic linear research model: first, we, the researchers, would do the studying; then, after analyzing the data and giving due thought, we would independently come up with "results"; third, present to decision-makers, as, in this instance, the National Coal Board; fourth would come presentation to fellow researchers; and fifth any more general publication for interested readers. That our client figured in the sequence at all and would receive results ahead of our fellow scientists was our step from classic to applied research. Ours and others: it certainly satisfied the BIM's Information and Research (I&R) Committee which had to approve our research plans and would be the first recipients of our reports on "results". That simply was how proper research was done at that time. The sequencing in fact—of research first and application afterwards—was held sacrosanct, for application considered too early would muddy the purity of the research. The metaphor of reference was the laboratory freed of all contamination and ready for experiments in natural science. Management science had not (yet) grown to encompass in its field for rigorous scientific attention the relationship between research and action, research and actual policy development, and research and ongoing professional and organizational practice. Maybe in place of the common wisdom at the head of this chapter about the horse that refused to drink I should have put the story of Baron Muenchhausen's horse which would not stop drinking because, this noble knight noticed only when he turned around, its back half had been shot away in a recent encounter and no amount of water in one end and out the other could quench its thirst. Management science too lacked the other half for setting itself up, deliberately, for contributing most to organizational learning and changing. The structuring and facilitating of that part of the scientific enterprise lay still ahead.

With this truncated view of science and research, several major determinants of how findings might be used passed our research strategy and plans by unnoticed. Among them were the client's own range of perceptions and agenda for improving the industry, those represented on the Board itself but also those of the many other parties strategic to any major action in the industry—a complex mix; also left out was the BIM's quite understandable and beclouding eagerness, new as it still was, and ever so eager to show what all it could do.

Any awkwardness over these exclusions had been simply avoided from the very start. In line with that English classic history text, *1066 and All That*, in which the authors thank their wives for not preparing the index wrong—"there *is* no index"—this research had no mandate. Intrepid explorers as we would surely prove to be, and armed no doubt with proper scientific standards, each party simply encouraged us to find our way "into" the industry however, wherever, and whenever we could and there start doing what researchers do: study. Good things would surely follow.

Setting out with no broader perspective and understanding, Jerry, Tony and I delighted in the freedom that simply learning all we could offered. In an "interim report" to the I&R Committee in April, which we later attached as an appendix to the report we sent to the Coal Board that September, and which I use here, we foresaw a time ahead when we would indeed be able to offer proper hypotheses for studying "crucial questions...presented by the facts themselves and not before the facts are observed." A page of preliminary, indicative questions and subsidiary questions followed, all "intended to throw light on the problems of management at [the] operational level and their relationship with the hierarchy above, up to the Head Office." "Extra caution is also required", the section on research methods reminded readers, "in order to stay in the field at all, several research bodies having been thrown out of the industry or refused admission". And then this under "Contacts":

> 7. Our original contacts were with the National Coal Board, the Scottish Division, professors at Glasgow University and miscellaneous contacts at lower levels. From the Board and the Division we have obtained and maintained permission to do research...but only informal assistance. We have been content with this arrangement as we feel that formalizing the research would tend to introduce fears and biases.

The professors have introduced us to area level executives. From there it has been a matter of contacting colliery managers and carefully "clearing" each contact at colliery, agent and appropriate area level. Only then are we in a position to spend two or three weeks at a pit "living with" various line and functional executives and supervisors.

8. From the pits we are gradually working upwards. In two cases it has resulted in our being able to "live with" agents. And one general manager has now suggested that we spend some time in area headquarters. Only in this way, i.e., by being invited, do we feel it is possible to gain access to the workings of higher level management in coal. In this way, also, we hope to gain access to statistical data which is closely guarded....

9. ...we are making Union and community contacts, attending official functions, and taking part in Coal Board and other educational ventures connected with mining. These produce not only contacts but valuable research material as such. The same should be said of our contacts with the National Coal Board.

Four of the 10 paragraphs of the Introduction to the report itself described the informality of it all and the goodness of that. Looking at them now, the exhaustive—and exhausting—explanations alone confirm that "the field" to which we had access would actually be quite limited. The main actors for ensuring the best fit of "bottom" and "top", namely the Board and the government, had quite limited stakes in outsiders coming up with findings they could actually use, we or anyone. Any findings we did come across in this informal way they could contain tightly, well short of challenging the organization at a significant level. Their parts in the "true picture" they could keep to themselves.

Given the high political risks of "the truth" about coal and government in Britain just then, these limitations were perhaps inevitable, perhaps even desirable. "The truth" as revealed by "scientific research" and made public would surely have pushed *all* major stakeholders in the industry and government toward closer collaboration than they would then have found possible. Essential safeguards *could* have been designed into the research strategy and plans. But that depended on a larger view of science first of all.

It is strange and sobering to look back now on how very severely this stunted, meager opening compromised this major study from its very inception. Were we so eager to "get in" that we could not foresee the straitjacket into which we would be strapped, and all the more tightly the more "truth" we found (out)? What accounts for our blindness to the more encompassing and more promising ways that colleagues were pioneering at the Tavistock Institute, a mere 15-minute bus ride away and at this same time, colleagues whom we esteemed and also met fairly regularly? That blindness, that compartmentalization, is troubling. We must have believed, rigidly, that we already knew all there was to be known for our purpose and the only thing needed now was to get started.

I suspect too, and this is kinder, that our view of the world encouraged the smug belief that we would be able to work things out to advantage from any start whatever. All issues, even explicitly organizational ones, had personal and inter-personal perspectives in the forefront—"where the rubber hits the road", in the Americans' graphic phrase—of that we were sure and in those we felt competent. With people of good will—and most people *were* of good will—the logics of our findings, the data we presented, and the fine order in which our conclusions and suggestions followed would carry the day, no matter over what other obstacles. Any residual hesitation our clients might still have we would doubtless overcome with our usual charm and persuasiveness in the meetings which the people who made the decisions would surely be eager to arrange, all the way to the top—the Board.

That at every level—coalmine, area, division, each of the six levels into which the industry was organized and, finally, the industry as a whole in its national (and even international) settings—powerful *organizational* imperatives were also in play fell outside this view of ours. We knew they existed, of course, but did not need to be taken account of in how we planned and worked. Nor, if challenged, would we have granted that the Board's first business was in fact to deal with those organizational imperatives, and likewise the managers at each level; nor that decisions and actions out of that perspective might quite properly cut across happy human relations. It would take yet another decade of work and several more disappointments on this score for me to be able to open my eyes at will to this distinction and use it fruitfully from then on.[2]

2. Chapter 6, "Seeing Systems—At Last", is about this shift.

Ironically, when I finally "found our way" into the coal industry, my Tavistock connections had much to do with it, the Institute where our colleagues were well ahead in designing and
managing work better. I met the chairman of the Scottish Division at a management conference that Harold Bridger of the
Tavistock Institute had organized and led; he was then working
with a branch of the Glacier Metal Company where I was friends
with several managers; at the time I was even working directly
on a Tavistock project.[3] Even so, the wider perspective did not
affect our approach to the coal study.

At the conference I so intrigued Lord Balfour with our wide
open purpose and good will that he opened the door to our quite
undefined study. By then the contacts we had made informally,
with the Glasgow University's programs of workers' education
and in mining engineering, had assured us welcome to several
mines. Now, with Lord Balfour's approval, we could go there. So
Jerry Scott went to work in the Eastern coalfield, I in the Western.
After about a month in a mine, the people there, usually the manager, would suggest a next mine or two where the order of questions we were then surfacing might be well explored. Usually
they made the contact for us.

To share our findings and plan next steps, Jerry and I met at
weekends "in the middle" or at my home in London. Presently
and most agreeably, "the middle" in Scotland became Glasgow
and a particular, handsome house of a well-established family
with a beautiful and accomplished daughter whom Jerry married
in due course. The wedding would be at her sister's house on
Tyneside, down the coast into England, another coalmining area;
her husband was a mine manager of the new generation, fun and
of great promise. I was there, of course. Not long after that, the
young husband was killed in a roof cave-in during a visit to a
more mechanized mine in the Ruhr, Germany. That was the
trouble with having all those machines going, old miners said: he
wouldn't have heard the roof giving way. Or with those
new-fangled steelgirders holding it up; he had no warning such
as you got when wooden props started straining and buckling.

3. Together with Geoffrey Ladhams, a production engineer on contract with the
   Tavistock, I was helping set up a little knitting factory in a nearby coalmine
   village. That study is the second in *Three Studies in Management* (Scott and
   Lynton 1952).

Organizational Fit

The extracts from the report included here concentrate on the implications we saw in our findings in the mines for the better organization and operation of the industry at higher levels, exactly the sections the Board decided to keep under lock and key. Of all the findings about mine management, only enough is included here to set the stage, and those come mostly from the composite we named "Burncoal" and made the first of our *Three Studies in Management.*

Pit and Community

21–23. *Conditions of work.* Coal mining has all the problems common to surface industry, plus more gratuitously provided by mother nature. Dirt, dust, danger, damp and darkness—"the five ds"—condition the job which is significantly described as "winning" coal.... Physical conditions of work are also far more variable [and] each pit has its own ever-changing problems.

25–38. *Customs and social structure.* Around the difficulties and experiences of mining have grown the habits and customs and relationships of the miners and the mining communities.... Physical isolation has added to their strength. So has the segregation, in men's minds and actions, of miners from other men.... To an unusual extent miners depend on themselves and upon each other; and they are very much aware of the fact.

Work at the pit is regarded in terms of jobs to be done rather than in terms of hours to be spent. Traditionally the collier and his mate walk out when they have completed their task. It is expected also that hours...fit in with happenings in the community [such as weddings and funerals and meetings of local clubs, Union, football, and Labor Party]. The community in turn adjusts itself to the needs of the pit.... Miners' wives are well-known for the interest they take in and the knowledge they acquire about their husbands' activities and relationships at the pit.

39–51. *Custom versus development.* .... Attempts made by the Board to synchronize [timetables, travel and other] arrangements between pits have led to grave objections and to considerable absenteeism.... In the shuffle following nationalization, many communities were deprived of leading personalities. All sorts of local pit-community arrangements were also lost and failed to be revived by the Coal Board.

The Manager

Like the captain of a ship, he is ultimately and legally responsible for a large, distinct unit closely dependent on nature [and] always on call.... Many managers regularly return to the colliery in the evening.... Like the captain again he is in intimate touch with all the varied aspects of his unit...the manager of Burncoal Colliery is more of a key figure than the works director of a factory of comparable size. In a given day he may have contact with men from the level of a picking boy up to area production manager or higher; he may deal with problems of all sizes and implications.... In addition, [he] must serve, usually as chairman, on several colliery committees...must perform many duties outside the colliery, such as calling on officials and men when they are sick or there is death in the family, visiting the village schoolmaster on community matters, acting as master of ceremonies at various social functions, even going to meetings of both political parties during an election campaign to show [his] willingness to listen to both sides.

Many matters will come to the manager simply because mining problems are so infinitely variable [and a] decision can save or lose thousands of pounds. The...essential flexibility in mining must be, and has traditionally been, found in mining men, in the support and teamwork which they give to each other, in their deep-seated habits of co-operation, and in the forms and processes of organization and management which they have evolved by trial-and-error over centuries.

127. [Now] for an increasing number of decisions the pit manager is required to obtain prior agreement from his immediate superior, the agent, and from higher levels of administration....

138. Of the new administration the manager is certain only...that his career is almost wholly dependent on it, that his [now nation-wide] employer has a monopoly of the only industry he is fit to work in, his security upon retirement is uncertain, and his very house goes with the job, which means that on retirement he must find somewhere new to live; [that] higher depersonalized levels of authority are assuming some of his former functions and exercise control over the rest; [that] his men, through their union...often obtain earliest news of future developments at the pit and at higher levels; and there is considerable stress on the need to educate him for proper management coupled with heavy criticism of his present methods by outsiders endorsed by the press. He is uncertain how higher authorities will respond when their agreement and action is required or how they will react to such variations as show themselves in the numerous and...not altogether comprehensible statistics

and minutes of [meetings] he has to send them. He fails to understand many things about the numerous specialists at higher levels. Why are they duplicating his functions, or, even worse, appropriating some functions, such as pit development, which are essential to pit management? What is their relationship to himself? Finally, some of the people at Sub-Area and Area Offices are less qualified than he; what then are the criteria according to which they were so obviously [preferred to himself]?

"Management is now more chancy", reflects one agent. "Whereas before, the manager had to deal with one set of uncertainties and restrictions—those imposed by the conditions he managed—now he has another set as well—those imposed by the structure above him."

The Superstructure

First level up: The agent

144. ...usually has charge of 2, 3 or 4 pits—aggregating about two or three thousand men....

145. The agent performs a number of specific functions, formal and informal, in his supervision of the managers of these pits. In conjunction with the manager and the Area Planning Department, [he] sets the course, for instance, by specifying in what directions development work...for future extraction of coal will take place. Keeping a check on the efficiency of the colliery is another important function.... He gets records [daily and weekly] of the colliery's accidents, wastage, absenteeism, production, consumption of roof supports [weekly], manshifts worked, sectional wages costs [weekly], face advance measurements [linear records of coal extraction], etc. These and similar details are expanded to a detailed monthly record of total cost, which in turn leads to a monthly profit and loss statement. In addition to routine records, he gets special reports and measures, for instance to help determine whether Saturday working is justified despite high absenteeism, or to check on dust and air conditions in different sections of the colliery. The agent approves the manager's requisitions for supplies—and sees that he gets them—and examines capital expenditure. He may inquire several times a day as to how things are going and may actually see the manager once or more a day.

The division of function between manager and agent is one of the chief sources of flexibility in colliery management. Often the agent gives detailed attention to long-term problems, e.g., he may spend much time on improving...air circulation in the pit, discussing the matter with the colliery engineer, electrician and with higher level specialists [and] actively direct a major operation like re-routing the pit ventilation.

He must be present at meetings to settle differences with the union as to rates, perhaps coaching the manager in facts and strategy. He may attend the joint consultative meetings and take an active lead in discussion. On some occasions he may hold special meetings with the colliery union representatives, for instance, to negotiate an agreement for limiting the areas of the pit in which the men take a day off when a mate has died underground.

In all these matters the agent is the link between the colliery and other levels of management. The manager is almost completely absorbed in running his colliery. The agent is close to the colliery and intimate with its problems, yet can stand back now and then and look at it as through the eyes of higher-level policy-makers.

150. But perhaps the two most important functions of the agent are acting as "father" and support to the manager, and being the main link between manager and sub-area or area general manager. These are extremely important functions, and it is surprising therefore that the [current] Annual Report of the Board hardly mentions the Agent....

151. .... It [only] touches on...the general mix-up of relationships that occurred after nationalization [though that is] probably the most important single effect of nationalization.

152. For the manager...it is of first importance that he has someone strong to guide him and to hold on to, and to constantly reassure him that he is not entirely alone against nature, the union and the administrative superstructure. It is relationships with those above him that managers most look to for support. They are unaccustomed to the "advisory relationships" that are used most now.

154. .... In most [cases] we have seen, the agent is the constant and friendly tutor and critic of the manager. In this sense, the agent is perhaps the manager's most effective educative influence apart from circumstances themselves [and] it is worth considering whether education for managers [a subject in the air these days] cannot be just done through the agent.

Functional specialists

[Sub-titled "Leaves from a researcher's notebook", this section of the report tells, one after the other and without comment, 35 instances of "higher officials" intruding on a manager and thus overriding the agent's efforts to protect him.]

The agent—"fathers" are weakest as guardians. The intruders come from any level "above", often unannounced, like rains in April, and they either expect quick attention or total independence on the manager's ship. To the manager it makes little difference whether the higher-level specialist comes from the NCB or from the Ministry.

195. .... [Though] many of these instances are not to be taken as "true" in the sense of giving of an accurate picture of the situation, they do however correctly represent the feelings of the managers. When nasty rumors are chronic in an organization, it is perhaps more purposeful to try and find out why they exist than to worry about their literal truth or falsity.

196. Second, remembering this point, it is clear from these examples [chosen as representative] that the usual relationship between functional specialists at above-pit levels and colliery managers are...not effective working relationships.

Two steps up: Area officials

197. *Reasons for arms-length relationships.* Undoubtedly a number of factors are responsible. First of all, the typical colliery manager's career has consisted of hard-won advances from miner to ever higher levels of management...staff relationship is not familiar to him.

198. There is moreover the emphasis in the pit on quick and decisive action, often unrelated even to lines of authority. [A manager] may therefore tend to interpret the relationship of the functional specialists "above him" in terms of authority, a mistake to which the specialists themselves...may be equally prone.

199. Third, when specialization has evolved within the pit, the tendency has been for a line supervisor to specialize. Authority, for practical purposes, depends on the situation...not on official designation.

200. Fourth, ...it takes regular and constant contact for a colliery manager to maintain his working relationships with the officials under him....

201. Fifth, ...there is the danger that the arm's-length relationship may become not only typical, as it seems to be now, but customary—which would make for a perpetually unwieldy, ineffective and inefficient organization.

202. Right now the situation is still fluid. Area specialists, at least, still like to "identify" [as the psychologists would say] with the managers and agents, i.e., they like to think, and to reassure each other, that their natural sympathies and interests lie with the manager. [Some of them have been managers.] This is evidenced by their casual conversation and is probably why they make so many jokes and complaints amongst themselves about the NCB superstructure. But this feeling is not reciprocated by the managers, and there is a danger that area people, and even more the divisional people

and HQ, will gradually form into their own 'club' and permanently lose touch with the managers. In this struggle to achieve communication with the managers, the area people need help in some form. They are now frequently in the almost intolerable position represented by a comment made by one manager: "If one of those chaps from area criticizes me I get sore; if once they praise me, I start wondering what they're up to now!"

203. Specialization is inherently difficult.... The colliery manager is accustomed to looking at his problem as a whole: undoubtly there is an underlying awareness of the artificiality of specialization, however necessary, that tends to "put him off", regardless of other aspects.

Communication and control

206. The essential difference between a disconnected group of independent producing units and a large organization lies in the effectiveness of its internal control and communication; if these are not effective, planning and the other advantages of large-scale organization go unrealized.

207. The whole matter of control and communication has been under examination recently. There has been a tendency in modern times to assume that the existence of mechanical devices—reports, memoranda, lines of communication, etc.—implies control. Starting with studies of restriction of output amongst workers and, simultaneously, studies of the nature of true authority, a substantial knowledge of the limitations of this concept has been built up. Control, some are now coming to realize, is to be judged by actual results.

'208. Let it be said that the NCB have not been as ambitious in their expectations of what can be done by paper as many controversialists imply; the average colliery manager's "paper work" is a small proportion of his job compared with the works manager of a light-engineering works of comparable size. Nevertheless, in an old established industry where personal contact and personal authority have been the traditional rule and remote control and indirect communication comparatively rare, it is extremely difficult to introduce paper controls—particularly when the organization is radically altered at the same time, ...controls are reintroduced on a blanket scale, and the industry is full of uncertainties, historical and present, and insecurities. How effective have the NCB been with their control devices?

[Here the report follows with 35 cases of mismatch under subheads such as: "Allocation of scarce materials", "Misuse of communication devices", "Misdirected or mistimed communications",

"Unnecessary bother", "Exhortation and publicity", "Forms", e.g., cost sheets, targets, cost control. Then:]

223. *Relation to flexibility*. It is an old custom amongst factory workers to keep something "under the bench" to provide flexibility…to build up a little reserve against a day when things don't go so well. The same practice has been found to be common amongst foremen. It is not surprising therefore that the colliery manager, faced as he is with unpredictable and manifold variations, should adopt similar practices as protection against unseen officials who, he believes, are worrying over things like the low output after holidays.

224. The method is comparatively simple: he simply accumulates reserves on paper on good days and spends them on bad days….

227–28. *Censoring communications upwards*. An allied protective device against unseen officials is censoring communications upwards, e.g., minutes of consultative committee meetings. It is usual for managers to make alterations or even write the minutes themselves….

These are not all new practices created by NCB administration…. But, at some pits, the practice of "censoring" reports has got to the point where there is practically no real reporting….

229–32. …meaningless uses of statistics…correlations seem quite irrelevant…figures, though impressive, prove on close examination to be self-evidently absurd…one of the results of functional specialization is that the main types of figures are asked for again and again…a recent form, to be filled up at area level, had as its purpose to find out how many forms the "filler up" had to fill up each day! This might be at least a warning signal of disease.

234. To sum up, the chief problems of control and communication in the coal industry are:

1. The reality is extremely complex;
2. Conditions are extremely variable;
3. Flexibility is at a premium;
4. Remote control is not a greatly accustomed thing;
5. The industry is hyper-sensitive; and
6. Many relationships are new and/or remote.

235. The last point—the overall relationship between the controller and the controlled—is probably the most important.

236. Clearly, a system of paper controls, insofar as it is greatly relied on and insofar as it distracts attention from control through relationships, is a dangerous delusion. For this is the ultimate difficulty: that even where "doctoring" reports…is not the rule, yet because the system depends essentially on comparisons, the mere

fact that *some* people in a group "doctor" or...doctor inconsistently seriously weakens the control device....

237. We are not saying that the NCB's problems relating to formal controls are unique, or that all reporting upwards was accurate before nationalization.... Our persistent question is whether the NCB is improving or aggravating the situation?

238. Nor are we suggesting that formal control devices are quite useless. Certainly in some cases the combination of conscience... and of the threat of being caught out are enough to give the controls justification. Second,...having to report a condition [may] make a man give more thought to that condition, no matter how much he may "doctor" the report itself. It is absolutely essential, however, that the formal paper control devices supplement and assist informal control: they cannot replace it.

239. Thus there is an essential and crucial difference between a colliery manager counter-signing stereotyped firemen reports without reading them [and] a man in London, or Divisional or even Area offices, studying [those] reports and taking decisions primarily on the basis of them...in the former case (a) the manager is under no illusions as to the value or validity of the reports; (b) he can and does readily go and actually see for himself the condition to which the reports pertain; and (c) he knows the men whose reports he receives and has a routine working relationship with them through which he exercises real control. In this context, the paper reporting device is at least harmless and perhaps of some use.... In arms-length relationships, misinterpretation is frequent and serious.

Tentative suggestions

332. As the colliery is without question *the* producing unit of the industry, the first function of the superstructure is to help the head of the unit, the colliery manager, to produce more and better coal with greater efficiency. His greatest needs of the higher levels of management are more flexibility and more security.

333. Our review of the operations of the superstructure indicate that so far it is not fulfilling those needs. The evidence is that this failure is due in part to misapprehension of the purpose of the superstructure, but perhaps more to organization and methods.

334. Specifically, the chief symptoms of inadequacy lie in failures of functional specialization and failures of communication.

The fundamental errors of which these failures are symptomatic, the evidence so far shows, stem from the prevailing attitudes and methods, from the top down, of organizing the industry on a large scale....

335. Only on the basis of such an understanding can the seeming paradox be explained that in its attempt to assist the producing

units, the superstructure has created the impression at the colliery level (and sometimes higher too) of hindering those units. By saying "created the impression" we are not begging the question. On the contrary, we have shown how:

1. Specific factors created the impression by failing their function;
2. The impression itself...obstructs the functioning of the organization; and
3. The ramifications of these situations keeps the organization at cross-purposes with itself.

336. Alongside these difficulties have arisen two problems which are common to all large organizations today, but which are acute in the coal industry and therefore should be specifically considered.

337. *The dilemmas of the industry*. The first is...providing the local units with the advantages of large organization and planning without threatening the local leader with loss of "face" and loss of authority.

338. This dilemma manifests itself in two areas particularly: labour relations, and relationships between the producing unit and higher-level specialists. In labour relations, events had already before nationalization reached the stage where labour and management were chronically hostile: any member of either "side" who showed a conciliatory attitude towards the other side thereby endangered his standing with his group and risked ostracism.

339. As regards relationships between collieries and higher-level specialists, the situation is not yet thus crystallized, but the danger is imminent: the "clubs" are beginning to form, and...misunderstanding and failure to communicate will unite the members of each group in hostility to the other; any sign of co-operation between specialist and manager will [then] endanger their standings with their respective groups. Every effort should be made towards avoiding this kind of situation. The cost of correcting it once it crystallizes is shown by the costs—in patience, time, trouble and money—of the Board's admirable efforts to correct the situation in labour relations.

340. Finally these two dilemmas, [reflecting] attempts to improve the lot of the miners, lead the managers to believe that *their* own lot is being neglected even while providing new machinery for reviewing labour disputes looks like undermining their authority as well. So that both these major problems are but aspects of the fundamental dilemma.

341. [And] each problem is strongly tinged with dilemma and difficulties of transition.

347. *Two suggestions*. Two things could be done. First, the colliery manager could be given more security, in the broadest sense

of the word. Second, he could be [helped specifically] in his dealings with his workers.

349. Briefly, "more security"...means more secure relationships with the superstructure. This would entail a readjustment of the approach to organization and administration right down the lines from the Board itself.

Concrete steps

354.1. *Functional specialists*. By way of a first concrete step towards implementing such an alteration of attitude, we suggest that the Board might give a few colliery managers complete freedom to avail themselves of specialist advice and other aid if, as and when they want it, i.e., have complete freedom [beyond legal requirements].

354.2. [In] *labour relations*. As a second concrete step, we suggest consideration of particular devices to encourage the manager to re-focus and enlarge his conception of his job, e.g., again as an experiment with a few managers, ...[recognize] community activities as part of their job and [make] an allowance of money for that purpose.

354.3. *Manning future posts in the industry*. As a third concrete step, we suggest...that in the future when formal posts are to be manned, greater consideration be given to the acceptability of the prospective executive to his subordinates and colleagues; and if a satisfactory person cannot be found, that the posts be left unmanned.

These three steps to be considered as experiments.

Oh, Where Have All the Managers Gone? Far, Far Away

The marvel is that the hard-pressed National Coal Board met with us over the report at all. It can only have been for political reasons. For the issues of organizing and operating the industry that our report focused on were already well-recognized and painful open sores, and the Board cannot have relished outsiders scratching them yet again without also helping to bind and heal them.

True, in a long paragraph in the Introduction and so right from the beginning, we had distanced ourselves from the daily sneering and sniping at the Board in the press and the running commentaries and public debates among real and self-appointed experts.

We had also acknowledged the long decline of the industry prior to nationalization and then the vast difficulties of nationalizing it in a mere few months so soon after the war. But this demonstration of goodwill and good sense could still not take our report beyond the several other reports the Board itself and/or the government had commissioned. Some it had already received, considered and also begun to act on.

By the time we offered them our report, the Board had already met *formally* 230 times and gone over these same issues many times. Its members had fanned out over the whole country for question-and-answer sessions with officials at all levels of the industry. They had listened to severe criticisms from these key insiders, heard the industry virtually writtten off by some, also been attacked personally. At its request, Sir Geoffrey Vickers, a prominent industrialist and also theorist of management, had studied the structure of the industry at the very top. His report had opened flatly with this withering assessment: "In my opinion, relations between the National and Divisional Boards are unacceptably bad and getting worse"; and he had then gone on to detail many of the same impasses and open conflicts we too had found in our research and included in our report. With many misgivings and verbal subterfuges the Board had begun to modify the top-down "command structure" set up at its birth. For instance, it newly required managers at two adjoining levels to meet and take decisions together. And it agreed to turn a blind eye to some local fudging of organizational boundaries, even at the risk of abuse and of charges that it favored some places with flexibilities that it disallowed in others. Having these and other deficiencies pointed out yet again must have been tedious at least. Worse, if our report "explained" them more fully and went on to trace their roots to a basically flawed approach to organizing and operating the industry as a whole, then our failure at the same time to move the Board closer to effective action in its actual, practical situation, would have soured any virtues in that.

In agreeing to meet with us over the report the Board must have decided that the Institute's high-level connections made it simply wiser to bury any resentments it harbored and accept the invitation, and in that same sweet reasonableness then bury the report as well. All the publicity over the BIM dock study only a few months before would have sidelined any opponents to this diplomatic solution. Its cost: yet another evening spent working.

An Opportunity Lost

Buried along with the report was further work on the list of industry-wide "Questions Raised About Organization" with which the Introduction to it ended. There were 17, and we proposed three "Concrete Steps" for researching them. That we could not, or did not, pursue them strikes me now as especially regrettable because they would have taken us, even without our knowing, to the missing cornerstone in our scientific edifice: building an effective relationship with our client, the person(s) and organization(s) who could then also put the learnings to use.

What these steps had in common was an experiment with giving "a few colliery managers complete freedom" to do some specified things differently. We would continue in our special role as avid and now locally well-accepted chroniclers of what these managers then did freely and what followed from this. For this new strategy to be worthwhile, others in the industry (additional managers, higher levels, even eventually, the industry as a whole) would have had to show interest in this experimental approach and in this initial direction. They would then also have been more likely to incorporate useful aspects into their regular practice.

The process itself, starting with the selection of the initial "few" experimenter–managers, would have aroused interest up and down the system, and this would have shifted and spread responsibility and commitment, highly desirable in any case. Colleagues who responded positively were readying themselves for learning at the same time, as in the clarification that, yes, we *will* pay attention to what Colliery X achieves and how; or, no, experiences in Colliery Y or Area (or Division) Z are not relevant for us in our conditions (or at any rate not just now). Working out such strategic approaches to fostering change in large systems by identifying and instituting it first in an "innovative sub-system" and ensuring its proper linkages with the whole, learning-organization-to-be would become a major theme in my practice and writing later, as Chapter 7 will show.

The Scottish Division would have been the obvious client with which to establish such a sub-system for a start. We were already known and working there and had active contact right up to and including the chairman. The division was large and varied enough for the learnings to spread. Quite possibly its chairman, Lord Balfour, was free and independent enough to pursue it, even off his own bat and without formal approval from the National Board. But we did not suggest it and neither did he. It is possible too, of course, that our Institute, the BIM, would have found it inconceivable to have a client even one step below the national very top.

Down to Solid Ground

What did get set up following the dinner meeting and, if my memory serves well, independently of it, was a fresh focus for our studies in coal: they should make explicit what all besides mining engineering went into managing a coalmine. The technical side included meeting the essential safety specifications required by law and the responsibilities it held the manager liable for personally. Besides these classic requirements, what did a manager have to know, be able to do, and also be able to live with to carry that job out well? And also, what had to be "in it" for him to make a career and a life of it?

That was a new question in the industry then, and an important and urgent one because "suddenly" there was a severe shortage of managers. It had crept up virtually unnoticed till it reached crisis proportions. In the past, quite distant past it turned out, enough people with the right capacities and standing had simply come up in the mines and "grown into" managers over time through accumulating and refining hands-on experience. Along the way up the ladder the best of them had entered a degree program in mining engineering. These best, tradition held, came from families of mine managers, often several generations of managers. Like army families, they were. Managers' sons followed their fathers down the pit from a young age, often without much question or choice, there being no other "real man's work" in the place anyway.

By 1950 this tradition was all talk, and not much of that. The long decline of the industry, the Great Strike of 1926 and its lasting aftermath full of anger, then the deep, world-wide Depression which in Britain really lasted right up to the war, had dried up this flow without anyone's noticing. Except the manager–fathers. They had long ago taken to advising their sons *against* entering this wretched industry and helped them get educated and into clean, safe, promising, better-paid work elswhere. Or into the Armed Forces when the war started, where again the eyes and abilities of these sons opened to other fields even while their fathers carried on down the pits. This *they* of course did "for the duration"—but not a minute longer. In wartime, managing a colliery was truly important, even essential work. The war over, the superannuated managers retired in large numbers. More left when the industry was nationalized and they did not want to change. And of those who still stayed in the industry, some hundred more left the pits for the new positions in area, division and headquarter offices that nationalization created. Experienced managers were needed there too.

At this moment then, when coal and energy production were at a premium in war-weary Britain, the shortage of colliery managers was suddenly very obvious and very severe. And, to mind-boggling horror, the quiet sliding into managerial positions in the past had left blank what this management really was—blank plus unsorted ideas, abstractions, maxims, and lots of opinions. So no programs were available for training managers either. Practical, effective, reliable programs, that is.

Our studies in coalmining were henceforth geared to this urgent national effort to develop an effective strategy for starting a reliable flow of managers and for implementing programs for this at a run. Sets of teaching cases and other educational materials, as well as major parts of two books, resulted directly from this onward effort of ours. The Board used these studies along with those of colleagues in other institutions in setting up a staff college for new managers at all levels of the industry. Soon after I left, in 1953, for work in France and America, Jerry himself went to this college for the few remaining years of his career: he died still young.

Vivid Memories

I cannot think of the work in coalmines back then without four scenes springing to mind, jostling for attention, all very vivid.

One is of Jerry, in a variety of settings but most characteristically as he leans back, his chair reclining, in thought between comments, and puffing his short-curved pipe. A second is a general sense, attaching itself here and there, of the splendid people I was with down the mines and also at the pithead, there mostly in the manager's office. These men knew who they were, quiet, tough, knew right from wrong, knew tragedy, knew, really knew, that they were not alone, ever, that they needed one another and also stood by one another. Silent much of the time (but not distant, just quiet). One scene is of me sitting in the manager's office waiting for him to say something. Anything! I did not know what to do with my hands as I sat there waiting. This is where I hatched the idea of copying Jerry with his pipe. He took his time extracting many, many matches laboriously from the box, to light the pipe, and light it again. Easy comfort it looked. Him it occupied all the while that the large clock on the mantlepiece over the meagre, smouldering fire ticked the silence. (Me the same maneuvers occupied totally, most of all feeling idiotic, and I gave it up.)

Another vivid scene, from underground, is of a miner drilling into stone straight up into the roof above his head. He is "looking for the coal [seam]", the official I am with tells me when I can make my question heard as we step away again, crouching, down the 4-foot tunnel. No one (of many) had been able to "read the fault" in the coal seam just there, whether its layers had shifted up or down. The search for it now was all cost, so drilling had to be in minimal space. The roar from the drilling in that little shaft up was absolutely deafening But the beauty of that place! Beams from the driller's lamp on the yellowish ragged rock. Beams from ours playing on patches of sidewalls through the swirling dust (what *did* that miner's lungs look like, doing this day after day, his cloth mask chafing at his skin, and hot—had he put it on just for our coming? Surely not, for he could not have heard us, through that din).

So also distinct memories of other scenes down the mines, or, indeed, of walking up to the pithead (why are they on hilltops when the same shaft at road level would be that much nearer the coal, I wonder; but then, what do *I* know!) for the start of the day shift at 6 a.m. on a black, gusty winter morning. Or a couple of miners hacking at the coal in a 22–inch seam as they lie on their

side, shoulder in water. Or—a scene that Ronnie loves to tell—
me with a team of miners sitting on our haunches munching tiffin. Theirs is a slab of something between thick whole slices of
white bread. The thick crusts are for gripping with black, grimy
hands: handles merely, to avoid munching coal dust; they get
tossed away, overhead or sideways, depending on space and, I
imagine, long habit. My tiffin, prepared by the solicitous help at
the nearby inn where I stay, who also have time and caring to
spare these winter days, is all delicate: crusts cut off, and the
slices thin and cut into the tiny triangles customary for afternoon
tea, Jane Austen style. I have little to eat, also little to throw away.
I sit where it is darkest. I can hear a rat rustling, making away
with the crusts (from the others).

Down the mine much is beautiful to the eye, and to personhood altogether, and community. Ever since those coalmining
days of mine, the wide variety of tough conditions, of straight-
talking gentle people, of beauty in surprising places, all this
should be in everyone's education, I feel sure.

Years later, in pursuit of just that, at least in a genteel, cleaned-
up version, we parents took time out on the long drive across
country with our three children to visit the demonstration mine
at Beckley, West Virginia, USA. The retired miner who took us
around, a black-lung victim as I learned afterwards, was only
minimally and routinely communicative at the start, even when
I volunteered that I too had "worked down mines" in Scotland.
Till, that is, I mentioned casually that we had once "lost a quarter-
mile of conveyor" and couldn't find it again. "You did?" he ex-
claimed. "Tell me, tell me." (The roof-fall had simply covered it
too solidly for further searching.) *That* made his day—and mine.
We talked excitedly on and on, swapping stories. In-group talk;
the family wandered off.

Finally, working and living in mining communities for weeks
on end, what a difference that makes! The dock study, though
with dock workers and managers, had been almost all talking,
and that talking often weeks apart. My war work, before that, had
extended over three years in the same place in the factory and
with the same mates; but I had lived at home, with family and
among books, and music and talk, and studied. So it was only
now, with our research in coalmines, or probably with that field
research experience on top of my factory work, that I came to

appreciate deeply how important it is for a researcher "to live with" people and their situation for a long time, to understand them as truly as another can. That, for me, is the notion of "utter familiarity", as Hippocrates termed it for his medical students. What people *say* about their situation and their activities and purposes can heighten this familiarity by adding detail, broadening it, deepening it by rooting it in history and explanation, even modifying it by highlighting some part over another or relating the parts differently. But what people tell cannot take the place of knowledge-of-acquaintance, familiarity: first-hand, all round, sustained, integrated. I retain a healthy suspicion of thought-castles built just from interviews of craftsmen and practitioners about complex tasks in real-life settings. And polls of people's opinions about them I avoid in distaste: they seem so very disrespectful of what are other people's lives.

Our method of working in the mines we described as "living with" people on the job. That phrase, already in our initial note to the Institute's I&R Committee, we repeated in the appendix to the report to the NCB:

> listening and observing in contrast to asking and seeking...questions asked, too, are a clue to the questioner's preoccupations, and tend to result in the recipient consciously or unconsciously trying to address such preoccupations rather than giving a realistic picture. Important in all field research, this is extraordinarily important in Coal...by reason of the fact that management [there] is largely intuitional, and that many managers simply cannot describe verbally their methods and problems.

> The feelings of any manager who is being observed at work for days on end demand special care. At first the research worker must be concerned almost entirely with easing and developing the relationship. This being the case, it is surprising how much useful material comes in the early stages. Nevertheless, the "per man-hour" productivity of the researcher's time at this stage is slight; the rewards come later. This is also true of all early contacts in relation to the future of the project as a whole. The grapevine in Coal is all too effective.

> Another important reason for the "living with" method is that it makes less demands upon the managers' job and time than any other. An interview takes him from his work. "Living with", if done properly, is no burden on his time at all. Lord Balfour once asked

us if we go underground. "Almost every day", we replied. "That means you have to be accompanied by an official" [safety regulations required this]. "No, we accompany the official on his normal work, not the other way round."

References

Lynton, Rolf P., *Incentives and Management in British Industry*, Routledge and Kegan Paul, London, 1949.

Madge, Charles, *Pilot Papers*, Vol. 12, 1944.

Scott, Jerome F. and **Lynton, Rolf P.**, *Three Studies in Management*, Routledge and Kegan Paul, London, 1952.

3

EXPANDING THE MOMENT

> A Four-step Progression

...it slows down moments in life sufficiently
to, as it were, catch reality....
The material here served itself alone....
All that was added later was understanding.

Ian Buruma 1995, pp 86, 112

A second book also came out of our studies on coalmining: UNESCO asked us to parley our field studies of British industries and their communities into a broader, international coverage so that credible generalizations could be drawn about good industry–community relations. *The Community Factor in Modern Technology* (Scott and Lynton 1952) was the result, an early volume in UNESCO's Tension Series. Along with our studies it reported others by colleagues in five other European countries, for a total of 12 industrial enterprises of various kinds that had either established themselves without disrupting community life in their localities or, if they had disrupted it initially, had repented of it, repaired the damage and put their relations with the communities on a sound footing. UNESCO had "non-industrialized countries and those in the process of industrialization" particularly in view for any alerting and guidance that might be gained this way from experiences in Europe. Alva Myrdal was directing the Social Sciences Department at UNESCO at the time; already internationally renowned then, she would later receive a Nobel Peace Prize.

This international work foreshadowed the exciting new trajectory on which my career was about to take off. I did not see that then—"tall oaks from tiny acorns grow"—but within the next five years I had worked, first, all over Europe from a base in Paris (on educating young people towards a more united, and less war-torn, Europe), then for two in the United States (to reconnect management education more directly with management on the job), and then, newly married, to start our innings in Asia that continues still.

The work in Europe and Asia will be primarily in focus in this chapter because my solitariness in each position spawned my life-long habit of rigorous recording. This origin for "slow(ing) down moments" and making sure I take a second look and so a better chance to "catch reality", is worth marking right here, at the beginning of this chapter. The inherent complexities of the work itself in each place—I have a penchant for going for work "well within the realm of impossibility"[1]—made collecting data for going over episodes a second time a good idea too, but that came later. My first need was to have a colleague to talk things over with; since none was right there, I learned to "talk" with myself—over the record regularly so, every morning. This regularity, of record and review, then fed into developing a sort of double awareness in habitual play. Along with its many benefits, of which having rich records for this book is one, that relentlessness, without let-up—or humour—has its seamy sides. It took me years to learn to manage the relentlessness along with easy spontaneity.

Of all this more below. The newness of people and place each time we moved urged "expanding the moment", to record it

---

1. This wonderful phrase occurred in an editorial in an English-language newspaper about the next five-year plan in Indonesia and smoothly became part of our happiest family language—so smoothly, in fact, that I failed to record a reference for it. This was while we lived and worked there from 1981 to 1986, in focus in Chapter 8.

enough to go over it again later, away from immediate pressures, in slow motion, quietly. "To make something of it", as the saying goes, give it meaning, tease out guidance, and track progress. Any sharp change of role heightened this need. The clearest example of this came when I moved into full-time consulting with a new institution after six years of creating and directing "my own".

Newness, and also my (characteristically Germanic?) strain to make sure I would do my best and not neglect anything that might help, fueled this. To excell and shine publicly has not mattered much, then or now, certainly not success: *that* usually depended on many more pieces coming together than I controlled. Just that I did my best. Then I am quite ready to let things be, to run on from there.

A Four-step Progression

The habits and schemas I have developed for recording and reflecting on my practice show a four-step progression, in line with my growing responsibilities over the years and the ever larger systems in which I worked. These escalations washed out any relaxation I may have got due to the greater ease of operation the mechanics of my recording offered. So, colleagues tend to see me as "always working". "Rather self-conscious and deliberate" is probably truer. Again and again I have straitjacketed myself into recording methods of unrelenting rigor which I am then unwilling to loosen, never mind forego. I do work best at full stretch, *feel* best at any rate, and included in that compulsion is this urge to learn the most from each passing moment. Not every last one, of course, but that's the overtone: then, and only then, have I done my part.

Done for then and there, that is. After each major assignment I take time off, for a sabbatical (with or without funding). This is for going over the same record yet again as a whole, to regain the sense of what the five- or six-year effort was for and to put it to rest before setting out on the next. That is when I learn better again, another round. One time, the learning that third time round was dramatic, a direct step up. To my utter consternation, I discovered that by only reviewing my record day-to-day while on the job, I had quite missed a strategic gap: the relations with policy-makers over a 1000 miles away. The consequences were dire.[2] Only in the overall review years later did I realize unhappily that what had hit us "out of the blue" at the time, I could—and should—have had in view and worked much better on all along. Now, with computer technology for running totals concurrently without extra effort, the huge omission would be quite inexcusable. The belated recognition of it propelled schemas and reviewing habits to step three. The other advances were quieter. But without fail, every review of data for a whole project over several years has brought learnings that immediately—and lastingly—affected my practice in important ways from then on.

One more signal, and then on to the step-by-step progression: while good order and rather dogged persistence dominate record keeping and reviewing, rather heavy, humorless, quite the opposite is the personal history of our lifelong international engagement itself—mine and my family's. That trajectory, quite indeterminate at the start, also only just skirted, fizzling out altogether several times over the next 20 years. Or so it seemed each time—most abjectly in 1961, and again in 1966—when major work finished before we had any idea what would come next. Something did, every time. But the notion of order, as in a plan to follow or even to dream of, would not at all catch how things actually came about. When, eight years later again, I undertook to start a new professional school in one of the poorest states of the US, I was quite clear that that ruled out any early return to international work. Not so, again. The next sabbatical turned into another 10 years of full-time work in Asia. By then the trajectory we were on was clear enough and doing competent work on it was what all the recording and reflecting was about.

That difference, between the good order and dogged persistence involved in recording, and the big picture made up of crazy incongruities and disjunctions, we will return to, but only at the end of the book. Intended or unintended no matter, particular moves on the trajectory set the stage for recording, and that in turn for reflecting on what all could be learned from it (and what not). Readiness and "being around" when the moment comes is all. Telling that contrapuntal story will also take any heroics out of the frequent question we get about "devoting" so much of our

2. That story is told in Chapters 5 and 6.

lives to being and working abroad, and in India in particular. "We are happy there" is the short answer (as we also are in our other home in USA). That one thing leads to another is a more reflective reply: you get to know more and are also known more where you are. So connections get made and become a dense fabric. The little steps make the direction: the trajectory.

First Step: One to Keep Company

A seminal book for me along the way was *The Creation of Settings and the Future of Societies* (Sarason 1972). Here I recreate the first setting for recording my practice.

It was Fall 1952 and I had just moved to Paris to be full-time board member at the Secretariat of the European Youth Campaign. The Campaign, set up to be the educational arm of the European Movement, was starting its second year. Its governing board of 14 had two wings: seven representatives of youth organizations in the 18 countries of the Larger Europe and seven "adults" from the original six—the Little Europe—that was then forging ahead with the Schuman–Monnet Plan for a Coal and Steel Community.

The "adults" made a formidable group of Elder Statesmen. Paul Henri Spaak, in and out as premier of Belgium during those years, chaired. Henri Philippe and George Bidault, both ministers of earlier French governments, were the members from France. All were well-known pushers for an early political Federation of Europe which the American funders also favored. Youth organizations, still recovering from the awful perversions of the 1930s and the war, rejected all political agendas or were divided over this one. But on our side of the table too, four of the seven headed the youth wing of political parties; three were also members of parliament. In most of Europe, full-time work with youth organizations made life-time careers. On top of that tradition, the war had decimated the upcoming generation of leaders, killed them, or so compromised them for their politics that they were ousted immediately after. All board members were adult then, and most were active politicians.

In that formidable setting I was an odd man out. How I, a German immigrant only recently naturalized, became the board member from Britain I will never know. Perhaps my selection expressed the ambivalences about Europe that continue there. With politics I had little acquaintance, and of active participation in it no experience at all. At 28, I was also the youngest. For languages, I did have easy English (though accented, then as now), fluent German (though often short of grown-up words), and school French. The French quite quickly became serviceable, gathering speed and gestures, and too readily accessible ever since to undo the bad habits with which I first put it to use in and around the meetings in Paris that spring and summer.

I mention all this here on the way to recapturing the welter of new, unsorted, complex, and often conflicting considerations that mattered to playing my part on the board and presently also in the additional function I assumed in the Secretariat. To contend with were the political party differences, and also the personal differences and ambitions of members on our side of the table as well as on the adults'. Then, across the adult–youth gulf, policies, priorities, and programs had to be negotiated and funds allocated. Making sure that these decisions would then also be carried out became the issue after that. The Secretariat for the Campaign was already at full force and operating by the time the board expanded to include us seven. Large enough to occupy four floors of a fine corner building on Avenue Marceau, it was directed by Jean Moreau, a career officer of the Foreign Office of France on special leave. Nothing led us, on the youth side, to trust the Secretariat to be non-political; we were on the contrary quite convinced that our partners on the board and in the Secretariat wanted us most for screening their political purposes. By summer, we were clear that periodic meetings with them could not possibly change that. To safeguard our interests, we needed a full-time presence right in the Secretariat itself.

I, unlikely as I was to be the best candidate for watchdog, took on that function. Without political allegiance, single and by then working on my own, I had less than the others to hold me back. So I moved to Paris. My salary, at the level of division director, was Fs 1,100,000 a month (the one time in my life I have been paid in millions!), my office overlooked the Arc de Triomphe, and my budget included funds for a personal secretary and for frequent travels all over Europe.

About the work and its outcome, it is enough here to tell that overseeing the Campaign Secretariat proved to be quite impossible and lasted just one year. Then, at the large 18-country conference in newly beleaguered Cold War Berlin—a location that the adult politicians had vehemently opposed—we pulled the youth organizations out of the board.

But the attempt made great learning for me! And most far-reaching was how my function of unwelcome surveyance confined me to my own counsel, and taught me how to be so alone, as well as circumspect and open at the same time. I was always on guard, watching and safeguarding. When I was away traveling, I could count on finding that the Secretariat had slipped some actions by me and the board as a whole. Usually I could then only object, but not halt or undo the actions. All was courteous, but all was devious too, and so also *very* deliberate and guarded. This had its gamy side, I recall, with highs for cleverness—clever maneuvering, trumping, tripping up, forestalling, check-mating the other, or at least taking his or her pieces—and for laughing in shared recognition for especially skillful devilry. But also, I soon realized, the better I myself became at these games and at anticipating my partners' moves, and over the months even managed to hem them in with board policies to enforce conformity with board decisions, the more adversarial my relations with them became. So also the more exacting—and that forced me back on myself alone.

There really was no one there with whom I could talk freely. My personal secretary—lovely, tall, blond, and bilingual—could not be that colleague, I judged, not even in matters in which she might have had something to contribute from her own considerable experience in youth organizations. I did not feel free to burden her with the political or the personal ramifications that my differences with the Secretariat people touched off or with my ideas about counter-moves. That she might not keep them to herself and undermine my position was never the issue; she was utterly reliable and skillfully reserved even while also being socially active and generally friendly. No, besides her necessarily more limited interests and experiences than many of my concerns called for, it *was* the burden of it all that would have been quite wrong to visit on her. I am still convinced that was right. I tend to lean far back in such matters.

With that, "talking to myself on paper" and so going over events and thoughts a second time got started. Spasmodically at first: I began with writing when I felt like it and looking at it again when I found the time. Quite soon that had two important additions which then moved my recording from mere notes in date order to orderly, albeit still very limited, monitoring of my professional practice: stage one.

I found that letting my note-taking depend on momentary inclination and chance availabilities of time made too loose a connection with my task and purpose, and so also with the complexities that I wanted it to help me understand better. Writing regularly was the answer to that: I settled for making notes at least once every day. I wrote by hand on normal size pads such as I always carried and aroused no suspicion with writing this different kind of note along with the rest, even in the course of the meetings themselves. My small and messy writing gave me extra confidence for stealing odd moments for making notes in the normal run of the day. When a sheet was full I transferred it, punched, to a binder that stayed at home. No one else has ever seen it.

The second refinement was to focus my recording on unfinished business, on relationships and situations that I had questions, ideas or even some vague residual uneasiness about. So my notes became quite specific and directly purposeful, and that sharply focused selection also made it quite possible to keep up with events—a very important consideration, as we shall see. They would get nowhere close to documenting a history of the Campaign or even of my part in it in general.

I like to think that keeping this diary enabled me to order things better in my head, so also to take in and handle more facets and greater complexities, and altogether make me more effective in action. I know that it gave me peace in the midst of all that turmoil and the relentless activities in the remaining months in Paris. I slept soundly, woke up refreshed. If I had dreams that I remembered, I recorded them too if they seemed to play around something I was working on—working through, we might say now—but I did not make dream recording into one more task. I had me as companion, that was the essence.

Step 2: Blanket Recording
The next step came so undramatically, matter-of-factly, that it did not alert me at all to the enormous amount of work it would

entail. That was in the late 1950s, when we attempted to record an entire training course at "Aloka" in rural Ceylon. Quantum jumps in recording and transcribing technologies since then and their virtually universal accessibility would make this much şimpler now. Simpler, and so even more tempting to record "everything", an aim no less Quixotic and also unnecessary today as it was then.

To this day I do not know who asked for the funding, but UNESCO offered us £250 for writing up the development and work at "Aloka", the training center for young leaders in newly-independent countries that the World Assembly of Youth (WAY) had decided to set up in 1954. UNESCO's interest in us seemed natural enough—the World Assembly of Youth had non-governmental status with the United Nations[3]—but till they asked we had simply not recorded our doings beyond the notes faculty and participants made individually, the quarterly newsletter we sent to alumni and friends, and my formal reports to Aloka's international board and funders. That it took UNESCO's request, initiative unknown, to provoke us into systematic recording and writing deflates me still, for it shows Aloka and its sponsors were just as neglectful as international agencies in general are about learning more about building new institutions, though that is a goal all profess.

As Aloka's founder-director, I was quite happy to be provoked and to let UNESCO's tiny grant stand for world-wide interest in what we were doing. Without giving it much thought in the midst of the constant engagement that a residential program evokes from the eager, I simply resolved to tape-record a 12-week program: it was the obvious thing to do. That record would make the core of a book. We decided to record Program #9, our third for leaders in educational institutions. That gave us the spring of 1958 to prepare.

A less suitable place for tape-recording discussions among 30 people could hardly be imagined. Our sessions were in the erstwhile living room in the "big house". Very sensibly and beautifully built to afford maximum exposure to views and breezes, this was U-shaped and cantilevered over the waterway below. All

---

3. Chapter 4 and later chapters will review various aspects of Aloka's structuring and workings.

this also opened the room wide to all the noises from outside, from crows all day to tropical frogs into the night. To get all possible breeze, the rows of narrow windows swiveled open, and had to stay open. Participants sat strung along the continuous table we had built to fit that same fine U. With the cacophony from outside flowing into the room along with the breeze, the members spoke in their various Englishes and fluencies and, of course, a wide range of decibels.

We placed two mikes in the middle of the room to face into the U; a third faced the trainers at the straight table facing the U. All mikes were of the basic type most commonly used then for speech-making from platforms or for broadcasting loud wedding music from a van into the neighborhood. We rented them locally, having neither the funds nor the time (nor, I suspect, enough good sense) to import better equipment. The tape recorders and the extra typewriters we would need were also rented for the three months and we hired four more typists for transcribing the tapes, all personal friends of, or at least known to, the two live-in secretaries we already had.

All in all, we ended with seven machines of four different makes, six young sari-clad women typing all day every day and into the night, boxes and boxes of seven-inch tapes filled or to be filled and stacked in various corners of the house, and growing mounds of other boxes filled with transcribed talk, double-spaced on legal-size sheets accumulated in dated folders. On any day, one or other tape recorder was out of order, and away or about to be away for fixing in Columbo, a 20-mile ride away on narrow roads winding between paddy fields. There were no earphones and only one footpedal (for stopping and starting the tape without interrupting the typing). So at all hours any available corner of a table in any room had a typist or two listening to a tape playing just as softly as still allowed hearing, typing, or reaching over to stop the machine when it got ahead of the typing, or to reverse the tape to replay and catch more of it on second or third hearing.

Those long days of always near pandemonium the typists navigated with apparently indestructible goodwill and cheer, and often boisterous fun and games, even as the days turned into weeks and the weeks into months. Maybe the task and situation had immediately struck them as so outlandish that laughing and keeping on laughing was the only sane response. More likely, they had no more idea what they were heading into than we did. Whatever the explanation, giggling good cheer held steady across wide differences of intelligence, competence, speed, and good sense. For most of those young women, this was their first "job", so the possible craziness of it had no pre-fixed limits. That our two permanent secretaries had found these recruits in their own neighborhoods and networks of friends was probably enormously important. In this suddenly escalated and pressureful situation these two simply assumed their supervision, allocating tapes, machines, and space, and helping sort out no end of queries and technical troubles. And they turned to transcribing tapes themselves whenever their usual office work allowed.

More about how those six *really* made it through those three months, kept smiling, and protected me and the other trainers so that we could carry on running the program—the very one that would make it into the permanent public record—I will never know. To this obviously-telescoped account of what resembled nothing so much as a wildly uproarious skit if we had designed it for presentation, I will only add two further notes. One is about our power supply: the only electricity we had at Aloka was generated by a 3 Kw engine which I had bought and installed for all needs. A huge machine by today's standards, it thumped its revolutions throughout the day—to pump water, run our freezer, give us minimal light for reading in the evenings, and now, of course, set us up for tape-recording and transcribing—till I turned it off at 11 p.m.; it too, frail lifeline that it was, failed us occasionally and needed regular servicing at the best of times. The other compelling memory of those wondrous, absolutely exhausting weeks is of my occasional attempts (against all odds) to retrieve and haul back into crisp awareness the rapidly escaping notion that Aloka was in the business of training community leaders and not a factory for manufacturing information. The scene itself came alive again years later when Art Buchwald made the case in one of his columns in the *New York Times* for developing factories that could produce enough data for the quickening rash of ever faster computers around the world to chew on.

At first glance, what this prodigious recording effort at Aloka churned out was utterly discouraging: piles of paper—an inch or so per session—with many blank spaces, haphazard punctuation, paragraphs unattributed to any speaker (we *had* from the first settled on starting a new paragraph whenever the voice changed) and, here and there, jumbles of many voices at once. And, of course, only barely into the program the transcribing was already far behind the recording. The strategic decision, right then, was to settle for recording just as much as we could, so as to lose least of the actual discussions, and to transcribe sessions in rotation from the several parts of the program. Tapes waiting to be transcribed we could store, at least as long as we could protect them from milldew and had enough blank tapes as well. We also decided to rotate transcribing sessions from the several parts of the program.

Thus, pared to practicalities, we got an average of two hours per day transcribed over the 12-week program, and they properly sampled all aspects of the program. Then, brushing disappointment aside for the dismal look of the pages and the piles, we on the faculty kept pace with the transcribing: we quickly edited the transcripts of sessions we had led (or co-trained) and, putting recent memory and personal notes to use, made a particular point of revising and attributing what we recalled as especially telling parts. It was hard work and came on top of an already exacting schedule, but those rules made it manageable. Further, this going over the record right then produced exciting contributions to faculty meetings about the ongoing program. So long term and short term interwove. That we were putting the transcripts to use so quickly no doubt also encouraged the laborers in the office.

The further work of writing it all up extended over a couple of years. Those years also included moving Aloka from Ceylon to Mysore (now Karnataka) in South India, and continuing programs without interruption. The book about Aloka, *The Tide of Learning: The Aloka Experience* (Lynton 1960), is based on these recordings and quotes from them at length.

Step 3: By Matrix and Metronome
The next step in recording my professional practice was again unplanned and again took me leagues beyond its original and quite personal and immediate purpose. I wanted to manage with maximum sureness and responsibility my transition from founding

and directing Aloka—that full, direct responsibility of a CEO, the lone, "buck stops here" kind—to working as a consultant to a new institution with someone else in charge. I would moreover be in a team of consultants; later I would also lead it. Ronnie cautioned me that this transition would be dotted with potholes and temptations. Keeping track of my thoughts and actions would keep me wide awake and alert for them.

Without further thought (again!) I went for broke: I set out to record *everything*. I kept *all* documents on file, of those I sent I kept a copy, and made notes on *all* contacts I had with colleagues, Indian and foreign. That chain of notes would be complete, way beyond my Paris diary of a decade before.

I started this regimen even before we landed at Delhi on December 1, 1961: by then the exchanges of letters to cover the contract and institute plans at various stages of development were on record. Note-taking began with meeting the institute's director at the airport, as he welcomed us in true Indian fashion, even at 4 a.m.! Over the next few days, he and I spent many hours planning together. He also took me to meet officials in the union ministry. Two days on we flew to Hyderabad, saw the buildings and met state officials. By then, team leader Joe had returned to Delhi from abroad, so, again back there, I had notes to make of additional meetings with him and with officers of the foundation which funded the consulting effort. Each event had *some* record.

Most notes I made in the little breaks that even the busiest days provide. I recorded people present and order of speaking, main themes and thrusts, a telling phrase or a perplexing omission or delay, an onward question I had at the end. These jottings sufficed to set off the fuller record I wrote the morning after—first thing, at home; that became my habit. With that start I cleared the decks for the new day. It was also, I soon found, excellent preparation for it. Only when troubles came many months later did I stumble on to the seamy side this had: the fact that I arrived for work day after day so very ready and bushy-tailed made some colleagues very uneasy.

When we settled into our permanent site in January, in Hyderabad, a 1000 miles south, meetings multiplied there—with colleagues (Indian and foreign), with officials, with local industrialists to plan field placements for participants, with foundation staff in and out, with applicants for positions, with visitors. The sheer volume of contacts threatened to overwhelm my simple plugging away at narrative recording. For an increasing number of contacts, text became unnecessary: I already knew the people, and many contacts concerned routines. For them, soon to be the majority of contacts, simple scoring could keep my record complete.

I made myself a matrix: the people to meet with across the top, the day divided into half-hours down the side. With simple red lines made during the day, I could keep score of every contact I had. A long line showed a long meeting. Lines down several columns at that time showed that those several people were at that meeting together. In the margin I numbered any contacts I wanted to think about more, and it was about those that I made myself notes the following morning. That streamlining amounted to shifting gear: my recording could again keep up with the fast-flowing events.

Of far greater, even strategic, importance was the choice I faced in detailing the list of contacts for the matrix. Easiest and also quite in line with my record keeping this far would have been to list all the colleagues, officials, and others I had met already and give them a column each, and then to add columns for new contacts as they occurred. I do not know what alerted me not to settle for that or with what certainty I knew what to do instead. I know for sure that it made all the difference to what I had routinely in view from then on.

I decided to build the matrix on the contacts my task and position *required*, that is, required of the consultant to the Small Industries Extension Training (SIET) Institute in extension education, no matter who it was. The setting too was fixed—it was *this* location, site and set of buildings—and so also were the time and the means available or to be secured. In short, I based the matrix on a socio-technical analysis, the approach I had adopted years earlier for the study of the London Docks. Since then Eric Trist and his colleagues at the Tavistock Institute had worked it out and named it; and they were currently using it to reorganize a textile mill in Ahmedabad.

I grew to think of this matrix as my map for relationships. I had the day's copy of it before me on my desk all day, all cells blank at the start, marked with red lines as the day progressed, and many cells blank still at the end.

I took two cuts at getting the matrix right, in the second and fourth months into the project. The February draft was based on the projected faculty positions and departmental organization, and on the obviously required contacts outside with union- and state-level officials and with the foundation. That identified 38 relationships to keep track of. The April draft differentiated key individuals in agencies and cohorts I had only as one unit in the original, e.g., some specific industrialists and not just their association. That increased the number of columns to 46. Columns here and there for "others" allowed for later additions and still finer differentiation without having to change the matrix again all over. All fitted on one legal-size sheet; one sheet for scoring each day.[4]

Over the same two months I found that I could also keep score of some additional information about each contact. Who had initiated it interested me as a consultant eager to see Indian colleagues initiate more; so I added a column for that. In further columns and through simple letter coding I could show the main purpose of a meeting, my assessment on the spot whether that purpose had been met, and also if the meeting had noticeably strengthened or weakened the relationship(s). The distinction between the last two could be important, since I (by some initiative of mine, or insistence, opposition, enthusiasm or whatever) sometimes carried the issue, but at the cost of cowering people and increasing their reluctance to do things on their own, whereas working our way through a tough spot together could leave our relationship strengthened. Many cells stayed blank, as I noted only clear indications one way or another.

Figure 3.1 reproduces extracts of this matrix as I constructed and used it when I became dean of a new professional school 10 years later: this is how it looked marked up at the end of one pretty typical day (except that the lines were in red and stood

4. The next time I again took charge of developing a new institution some years later, as dean of a new school of public health, the number of required relationships rose to 148—*two* sheets full. Ten years later again, when I worked in Indonesia to help decentralize the official health services and the team I was leading worked in eight provinces as well as with the central ministry, the daily matrix spread over four sheets. Even that I found quite manageable, though having to turn the sheets while scoring aroused curiosity more often.

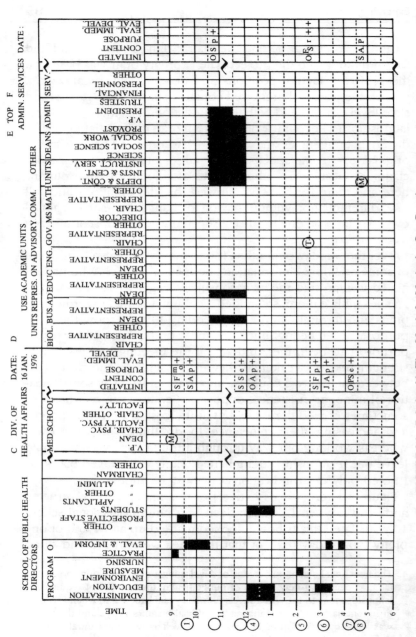

FIGURE 3.1 Relationship/Time Matrix for Monitoring Own Practice

KEY TO FIGURE 3.1
Classification of Personal Interactions
(Five right-hand columns in matrix)

Initiated
 self = s
 other(s) = o
 joint = j
 unclear = blank

Content
 Program Activities = A
 Administration = Ad
 Colleagueship = Col
 Confrontation, conflict = C
 Diffuse linkage = D
 Future, scanning, long-term = F
 Normative development = N
 Organization structure = O
 Other Resources = OR
 Policy = Pol
 Relationship building = R
 Sanction, support = S
 Student Selection = SS
 Faculty Selection = FS

Purpose
 allocate = a
 advise = ad

confront, for example,
 differences = c
develop = d
explore = e
firm up, set = f
inform = i
implement = im
maintain = m
monitor/evaluate = mo
obtain = o
plan = p
represent = r
scan/visualize future = s
teach = t
think = th

Evaluate: immediate
+
–
blank = no comment

Evaluate: developmental
+
–
blank = no comment

out). The communities and the offices in state and other agencies outside were set out similarly on a second sheet. The five columns for quick and ready categorizations ran next to the columns for people and institutional units. The key shows the categories I used (Lynton 1992).

I think of this matrix as the "map" of the relationships I need for a particular work at a time and place. After testing and a little fine-tuning over a couple of months, it serves me unchanged for my whole tenure. For tracking and reviewing my five years' work with SIET Institute, I have 1,080 sheets scored day by day. The contacts especially numbered for diary entries the following morning make 4,500 typed pages, double-spaced. Throughout I kept on collecting all documents, in and out, and all reports and publications. They fill most of a large filing cabinet.

Pros and cons: Recording this comprehensively takes prodigious effort. Ignoring the mere moments spent in marking the map during the day, an hour or more the next morning went into reviewing it and making notes, a total of say 1,200–1,500 hours at least, the equivalent of over 30 normal working weeks or well over a half-a-year's work, i.e., 10 percent of the contracted time. True, the working days and weeks were not normal, and nothing shows that other work was short-changed because of these hours I spent making notes and reflecting on them.

On the contrary, though there is no assessing might-have-beens, I feel convinced that the mapping, scoring, reflecting, and eventual reviewing benefited the work both immediately and in the long run. To spend extra hours on this was my choice and I have found it worthwhile to mount similarly exhaustive and exhausting efforts in later assignments. I treasure the critical awareness that meticulous recording calls up for better action. The map is a craftsman's tool in the first place, a researcher's only in the distant second. Extrapolated from the task in its full scope, it guides me to the best work I can do under the very exacting conditions I choose to work in. I could not live with myself if, seeing the high risks that go with building a new staff college in India (or a truly community-oriented school of public health in the USA or decision-making capacities at the provincial level in Indonesia), I did not do everything I could to sharpen my perception of events around me, use the best conceptual formulations for what to anticipate, and monitor my own behavior, all in a very orderly fashion. Usually I do it together with close colleagues, members of my "core group", and sometimes with an outside consultant hired for just that purpose as well. But much of it is also inward, to stimulate my reflective self and also nourish it. The responsibility I carry in an innovative enterprise rests finally with me, and spending a tenth of my time on keeping that critical awareness alive may not be too much.

Differentiating the world set by task and setting from what I personally see and want is quite essential for keeping both parts in clear view. I record both, side by side: two worlds, separate but related; matrix and notes; overlapping moment-by-recorded-moment. That clarity is a direct benefit of this way of recording.

Both worlds would have benefited even more if I could also have simultaneously done comprehensive analyses of the daily recordings, specifically if I had kept an eye on running totals and noted trends. Only technologies readily available now would have made that possible.

Three examples from the comprehensive study I made of the data after I finished working with SIET can indicate the kinds of strategic learnings that I would have eagerly put to use on the spot had I been able to gain them right then (Lynton 1970).

The first strategic learning confirms that in shifting initiatives to my colleagues I was indeed on track. The fifth quarter, that is the first of Year 2, was in fact the first in which I *had* colleagues in "my" department (of Extension Education)—hence its significance here.[5]

Initiatives: Mine to Faculty Colleagues

	Quarter 5	Quarter 6
Formal structure and administration	1:0.8	1:6
Policies and plans	1:0.5	1:2
Current programs	1:1	1:2
Personal and professional development	1:2	1:1.5
Relationship patterns	1:1	1:2
Relationship quality	1:0.5	1:2
Evaluation and other	1:1	1:10
All items	1:0.8	1:2

My initiatives increased again in the seventh quarter and on, but this marked a shift to other, fresh dimensions of the work: from work on starting programs and recruiting colleagues I moved to capacity and longer-term organizational and policy developments. The frequency counts of contacts bear this out. Whereas in the fifth quarter each of these items accounted for 8 percent of all contacts, that proportion doubled in the next and thereafter, and in absolute numbers trebled. The diary also confirms this shift of priorities: of 94 entries about extension, 63 are about these fresh emphases.

The second extract shows the multiplication of contacts the consultant had with the principal director and the departments as the Institute expanded and as he assumed leadership of the consultant team (by the beginning of Year 2, i.e., the fifth quarter).

5. That story is in focus in much of Chapter 6.

My Contacts with Principal and Departments: Totals

	Quarter 1	Quarter 3	Quarter 5	Quarter 7
With principal	140	195	250	230
With departments				
Area development	110	145	335	335
Management	40	115	225	185
Extension training	0	35	515	490
Communication materials	0	65	45	100
Total	290	555	1370	1340

The sharp increases do not denote briefer contacts, but more contacts with *groups* of colleagues meeting together. Comparison *between* departments at the time should have alerted me to my neglecting the management department before that led to repeated difficulties. And yet finer analysis would have confirmed what I only suspected: that organizational development within departments was lagging behind and diffusing energies away from developing the Institute as a whole: "When contacts with department *heads* are also separately identified, a second problem area emerges: contacts with faculty other than [department] heads remained high, which suggests little progress with internal differentiation and organizational clarification [in the departments]" (Lynton 1970, emphasis in original).

The last example documents our—my—truly appalling neglect of SIET's sponsors and funders in distant Delhi, which came to haunt and harm SIET soon after. We will reflect on the substance and implications of *this* neglect two chapters later.[6] The point here is that the fact of it escaped us totally, so relentlessly busy were we all with current programs and with the *internal* development of the institution (or, more precisely, our various parts of it). A mere 1 percent of my contacts were *outside* the Institute and that minuscule percentage did not change even after I became team leader (though the absolute number of contacts doubled); and even of that anaemic attention I gave to the world outside, most contacts were local and did nothing for our strategic relationships with the policy-makers on which the Institute so

---

6. Chapter 5 on "Seizing the Moment", and Chapter 6 on "Seeing Systems—At Last".

largely depended. I am sure I would not have remained blind to this virtual void and its growing dangers had I seen these summary figures and trends at the time. Programed on to a spreadsheet, they would have been easily available now.

Even then, maximizing my learnings from such comprehensive data gathering as I did at SIET Institute and in major institution-building efforts later comes only in the spacious context of a sabbatical afterwards. Only when I have experienced that, to my limits, to be sure, am I then ready to start the next endeavor. Each time I am freshly clear about what in particular to try to do better. Blindness in future will come around new corners.

As I persist with it, comprehensive recording and its benefits also spread. At SIET in the seventh quarter,

> four colleagues [two consultants and two faculty], and a fifth in a sister institution, told me they were making their own notes...of both content and relationships, [with the] most elaborate and formal arrangements for recording and for securing agreement from the head of department. [Yet] I made a point of not...making this type of recording an integral part of institutional activity... (Lynton 1970, p. 40).

What did become a norm from early on, perhaps encouraged by my diligent recording, was that all major program activities should be recorded, reported, and reviewed, and this set high standards of accountability in the Institute generally. To warrant continuing, activities had to be worthwhile, openly so. Most remarkable on this score is a series of 15 reports, each of 20 or more single-spaced typed pages, which documented the three weeks of daily sessions on inter-personal skills and team building which SIET Institute included in every program. Meticulous recording also anchored the training of additional faculty for this work. As they dispersed, later, they then took those standards and methods into still wider use, e.g., for developing and admitting members to full professional status in the Indian Association for Applied Behavioural Science.

More personal constraints: There are seamy sides too to such pervasive and continuous recording, and they are serious enough not just to pare it down and so lessen the effort but, more basically, to set the lesser recording up differently.

Even if it is well-meant and eventually more widely beneficial, carrying on a private purpose in public and acquiring for unknown uses information about other people makes for trouble. The matrix always on my desk, on which I made little marks throughout the day and every day, attracted notice and mixed feelings. I thought it best to deal with those as and when colleagues asked. On several occasions I showed and explained the matrix. As for its use, "No, only mine", the diary reports me saying in the seventh month, "these are all devices which help me be reflective about how I spend my time".

Two events coincided when I was just into the second year at SIET. Pandi arrived to be the new principal and I became leader of the consultant team. I had met him several times before; I liked him and liked his coming to direct the Institute. Pandi was nothing if not meticulous and exhaustive; he labored over every detail. We met frequently those early days. The diary records:

> Pandi asks about the notes. I tell him that I have a visual memory and that I profit from writing down the notes afterwards.
> P: Yes, I can see that. This would be helpful, but how do you find time?
> I: I don't. It is a real chore sometimes, but I find I am far more efficient when I live through the situations again.
> P: Do you ever read the notes?
> I: No. Maybe when I retire I will read them.
> P: Will you then write a book?
> I answer in the same light vein as the warm atmosphere of the whole meeting has encouraged.... (I) enjoy this great freedom and relaxed feeling.

Only later did I learn that the warm relationships I generally enjoyed with my colleagues could also contribute to keeping issues and challenges about my recording under the rug that would have been better dealt with early and openly, or better still avoided. Sure, I *meant* no harm, and seeing me "always working" and so not wanting to add even one more thing for me to worry about, they kept their disquiets from me. Commenting on a draft of this chapter now, 20 years after the event, one colleague and dear friend from my deanship days writes:

> I do think many—students and others—found your meticulous discipline [obsessive recording?] intimidating. I was in awe. It was a

standard I felt I could never meet—and yet it seemed, by your very devotion to it, to be an *essential* standard that I *should* meet.... When I tried it, I felt in a straitjacket.... And, yes, it *is* inhibiting to be always "on record"!

That my recording made logical good sense made it also no easier to talk about the disquiets with it, so the exchanges invariably ended with the logics. Only 40 entries in the diary for the five years' work at SIET (.05 percent) deal with recording, and of those only 14 mention colleagues' inquiries about it. Clearly I worried little about mixed feelings and perhaps doing more to unscramble them, never mind putting them to rest. Postponing recording till *after* a meeting was about the extent of my accommodating, even when conflict was in the air.

The disquiets must have festered. It took only a secretary's "small chance error" (oh, *really?*) half-way through the fifth year to touch them off in a loud explosion. By then I had gotten into the habit of dictating my diary notes—it was easier and quicker, and we had the equipment and used it quite routinely for correspondence and drafts. My very competent and trustworthy secretary readily used gaps in her day to transcribe my dictated notes and returned those tapes and transcripts all to me. That day, she had left one of those tapes out; another secretary picked it up in error and, as she began to use it for something else, heard my private thoughts. Flustered, she alerted her boss, one of my colleague consultants. Many fires smouldered just then—divisions among consultants, disaffections with and among some Indian faculty colleagues, jealousies involving the Institute's director, confusing signals from the Foundation—and this spark ignited them into an impressive conflagration. By the time they were banked, the consulting team was leaderless and SIET's principal close to throwing in the towel. So the "small, chance-error" that day was costly. And it was altogether mine in making this convenient but risky arrangement, however often and readily my secretary agreed that it would work fine. My recording was, of course, merely the spark to ignite the many smouldering fires, not the cause of them. If the recording had not provided it, something else would have, in time.

Most subtle and insidious were the effects this relentless recording had on me personally. It made it all too easy to express on paper, to myself, doubts, conflicts, and angers that needed dealing with on the spot and with the people directly involved face to face. Appreciation and enthusiasm I expressed readily. How very much I had drained all other feelings off into my notes became clear only some weeks after the crisis of the misplaced tape had caused me to make my recordings "less regular...." (I quote from the diary.)

> Perhaps for the first time I find myself lining up with some people against other people! The pressures and feelings apparently have to come out *somewhere*, and the detailed diary served part of this function for me. Is that what gave me an appearance of distance from others...that I had so much equanimity, that "I did not express my feelings" while they expressed theirs? Perhaps I *had* them, but I seemed always so even and task-centered....
>
> I am now expressing my frustrations in words, balanced, also reasonably circumspect—and certainly to no great disaster. What interests me is that I feel like doing this much more than I have been used to—and I am anxious about it. And, self-praise aside, if this happens to me, with my interests in analytical methods [even] in the midst of "ecstacy", what about others less disciplined and experienced?

Along with all its values for me (and also for others, I do believe), recording had accentuated my tendencies to introversion. One consequence I now see is that it was not just feelings, and negative feelings in particular, that I held back from expressing, but that *understanding* things, seeing how some situation would develop, was a steadily intriguing alternative to taking action. By little steps, studying can take on a life of its own, *become* the action, as it were, and this temptation is magnified in innovative enterprises that have many riddles professionals are eager to sort out.

Least dramatic but most far-reaching of the troubles that exhaustive recording over long periods can lead to may be the most insidious of all: it inhibits playfulness, the ease and fun among colleagues that frees relationships and helps one over rough spots. I tend to be very purposeful anyway, and in each institution-building effort there were always more things "I had to get done". That combination may well have made me fretful and impatient to end small talk or unfocused togetherness.

It has certainly seemed that way, as several colleagues have confirmed. The record itself suggests a more complex connection. My "contacts [with them] were numerous, close and often confrontative" it says and also shows. For I also enjoy fun and fooling, easily pass the time of day and readily compliment and recognise achievements. The discrepancy suggests that it was not just my holding back or my impatience to return to work that became the severest barrier to simple good fellowship. My colleagues themselves may have talked themselves out of confronting me with *anything*. In sum, my matrix and all it symbolized made contacts *heavy*. Even at dinners in each others' houses or at other social occasions I was seen as "sure to" tag conversations and all manner of details in my mind, to make notes of in the morning. All this is very discouraging of play.

Step 4: Open and Shared Recording

Taking all pros and cons into account, in the next major institution-building effort, in Indonesia, I shed recording "everything" and also my privacy with it. Episodic recording took the place of the first; open participation of the second. For the duration of each episode, my matrix and my close-to-total coverage remained unchanged. The matrix I constructed as meticulously as before (and still do in the first weeks of a new task). My recording continued to be a craftsman's tool, not a researcher's: episodic recording was not my attempt to achieve, by judicious sampling, what had so far required total coverage. While it lasted, my recording was utterly full and regular as before.

What the episodes of intensive recording marked were periods of unsureness on my part, when I did not know who and what would come into play, how untried colleagues would match up and what backstopping they might need from me or from others, how the central government would respond when Province X fielded a new regulation, policy or way of working, and vice versa, and the like. These were times when events threatened to exceed my competence or augured some other disaster. I became like a conductor of an orchestra who concentrates his energies (and reviewing) on just the trickiest and perhaps most contentious passages of a piece. With greater experience in building institutions and longer acquaintance with colleagues, these episodes of anxiety became fewer. So my overall effort towards recording has decreased sharply.

That parsimony then also made it feasible to encourage colleagues to identify the episodes *they* saw as warranting special effort. Initiatives, framing an issue, putting time and other boundaries around recording, sharing results, and planning interventions—all became joint activities.

This openness of the whole process and the clear focus it put henceforth on particular parts and the transition between them dissipated the constraints and festering suspicions of earlier times. Together these changes amount to a reversal of direction: from using recording for individual learning and improvement to using it for improving the functioning and prospects of team and institution. So I moved from however righteously private to usefully and safely public.

What remains unresolved is how this craft of full, meticulous recording is best learned, and in particular how far my eight plus years of recording "everything" helped me learn it. The five-finger exercises on the way to learning to play the piano may be a useful way of thinking of what this mastery requires, and that must be followed at once by the sobering thought that virtuoso Arthur Rubinstein kept right on practicing two hours or more each day till he died. So limber did he need the fingers to be and so practiced the runs, that the *technique* of playing would take no attention at all during the performance; only then would fresh meaning and refined interpretation have his all.

In my humbler station, I had become utterly familiar, during those years of intensive and relentless recording, with my instruments and their construction, and with incorporating their use and reviews into my everyday habits. Over the succession of highly varied institution-building efforts and roles, I had become thoroughly familiar too with the basic processes and sequences of institution development, with the indicators by which to recognize its stages and dilemmas along the way, and with what I could and could not reasonably hope to contribute and how. I had even acquired some of the elegance as well as the economy that marks an experienced practitioner in any field.

How important that earlier total effort was in familiarising me with these complexities—the necessary stage of journeyman on the way to mastery—I can only hazard to guess. Very important, is my guess. I would continue to err, if error it be, on the side of fuller recording. Initially at least, to allow liberally for the unexpected and the serendipitous, and for firming habits, exacting ones in particular, into ready personal discipline. Even stronger is my belief in the importance of basing any recording on the most careful and circumspect map of task requirements, separate and in addition to recording what is personal—feelings, ideas, hopes, and plans. For building something that lasts, what matters is the personal in the service of those requirements, and it is the essence of mastery not to mix these up.

References

Buruma, Ian, *The Missionary and the Libertine*, Faber and Faber, London, 1995.

Lynton, Rolf P., *The Tide of Learning: The Aloka Experience*, Routledge and Kegan Paul, London, 1960.

———, 'Institution-building and Consulting: Complexities in Development Assistance', Ph.D. dissertation, State University of New York, Buffalo, 1970.

———, 'Boomerangs and Alligators: Professional Education in the Public Interest', Unpublished manuscript, 1978. Reproduced in Lynton, Rolf P. and Pareek, Udai (eds), *Facilitating Development: Readings for Trainers, Consultants and Policy-makers*, Sage Publications, New Delhi, 1992, Section 4.8, pp 136–41.

Sarason, Seymour B., *The Creation of Settings and the Future of Societies*, Jossey Bass, San Francisco, 1972.

Scott, Jerome F. and **Lynton, Rolf P.**, *The Community Factor in Modern Technology*, UNESCO, Paris, 1952.

4

"LYNTON'S CROCODILE" AND OTHER COMPANIONS

Colleagues and Better
Creme de la Creme: My Twin-like Colleagues
With Much Playing Come New Tunes
Support in Turbulence and Chaos: Crocodiles don't
   Sparkle

> *Walls good neighbors make....*
> *Something there is that doesn't love a wall,*
> *that wants it down....*
>
> Frost 1964

Aloka in Ceylon was on a 6-acre pineapple plantation in the low country, by a small, placid waterway; a crocodile or two would swim into view on the first and last day of each program—that became the legend at least. In the program itself, the diagram that has served and spread and lasted best looks like a crocodile. It carried important meanings for all fighters for a better world, and the community leaders assembled at Aloka from newly-independent parts of Asia and Africa certainly meant to be that.

The wall-to-wall chalkboard at Aloka was ideal for drawing the crocodile: 16 feet of clear space. Starting at the far left, I drew a single line to 2 feet or so of the other end. That point I marked "A"—for today, now, this moment. The line represented a life to this point—a person's, a family's, an NGO's, a factory's or trade union's, a community's, a country's. So the line also represented traditions and culture, the roots that newly-independent people sought to connect with again. It is one line, unbroken, with only minor waves in direction; in retrospect, even events of high drama at the time had receded into one remarkably consistent flow. A decade later I would meet that line again, in Herb Sheppard's "Life Planning Schema", and use it to open a graduate course on stress and support.

The crocodile only emerged with what followed Point A, the point of choice. If I, or my organization or community, did nothing new, life would flow on much as before, for the past invests the present with momentum toward the thoroughly familiar, and the familiar is also what others expect and are prepared to retain—neighbors, colleagues, communities nearby, other countries in the region. If instead I strike a new direction—say to a Point B—that would make a new line, off at an angle. The whole now looks like a crocodile with its jaws open (Figure 4.1). This stayed in the participants' minds as "Lynton's crocodile", traveled home with them, and lasted. I met it again recently in Bangalore, at the Annual Seminar of India's HRD Academy.

Point A then—now—is the time to pause and take thought, to reckon the costs and risks along with the attractions of changing direction, and to decide whether one has access to all that change would demand. At the very least, opening the crocodile's jaw would take extra time and energy. And it would also spell danger.

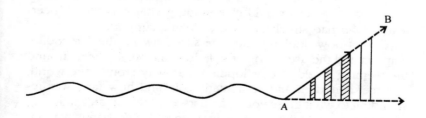

FIGURE 4.1   "Lynton's Crocodile"

What the open jaw was particularly good for teaching, and is still good for even now, is the strategic importance of shoring new directions with supports. And none is more important than having one or two companions to check with and round out the vision, to help sort out what events along the way might mean, to lend a hand, to comfort and cheer on, to guard the rear—in short to turn to in *any* need. That vital companion is best right on hand, but can still be a live and sustaining presence even when personally back in the village or office. For a brief time, even an imaginary person can provide important companionship, as our son Devadas created Mangoot for a friend during his first few days at playschool.

The jaw helps teach another important lesson right at the joint: estimating needs for support requires foresight and determination ahead of setting out, for way ahead in the new direction. At the junction itself and the first few steps after, any new direction differs from the old by very little, so little in fact that it might be just another little meandering of which any lifeline has many and which simply self-correct. The tendency to minimize change and its demands is extra strong in people already beset with great changes, as Aloka's participants and their countries certainly were with national independence so recent.

We maintained it was essential then that the leaders not delude themselves or mistake any initial downgrading by others as sufficient backing. The upper jaw will slam shut on the lower as surely as night follows day unless it is propped open—and kept open—with strong enough supports. Just as girders held the roofs up in the coalmines I knew. The wider the jaws opened, that is the more radically new was Destination B, the sturdier the supports had to be to do their job, longer and also stronger. Otherwise, the jaws would close shut, perhaps on the pioneer-leader who had struck out with too little support.

I cannot now, looking back, be sure how far the "crocodile" diagram and the use we put it to helped me get my head around the teeming world in development half-way around the world, and feel confident and competent in it, and how far I was responding to what those young leaders and their organizations really needed at that time. For me, pairing with a colleague was anchored deep, simply a rule of life. It did not stem from danger or even call for explanation. To be in company was the natural state. I had a brother ahead of me, later a younger one as well. By then, I had a personal guardian angel working overtime to get me out of scrapes. I had friends, made them easily anywhere we alighted, even in a strange language. From Creation on, human-kind went in twos. Jesus sent his disciples on their missions in twos. When I later pursued my interest in the epidemiology of support, I found many expert studies to support this sensible rule. As far as I was concerned, the questions were only how to implement it; how to make sure that the leaders at Aloka too would accord it the *practical* attention it deserved—enough, good enough, and soon enough—in the midst of their busy days; how to make support into the squeaky wheel that got attention, and also keep it squeaking—these were the issues. Maybe it was caution on this last score that had induced me at the last minute to write into the resolution to establish Aloka that "to ensure minimum support, participants will be selected in pairs". I could not have trusted all others around me to guard what was so ob-vious to me.

The young leaders certainly bought it enthusiastically, hook, line, and sinker—and it did have a sinker that studies of turbu-lence and chaos would surface, but only years later.[1] Meanwhile, the crocodile found its way into many speeches and publications as "Lynton's crocodile", the way a new star in the sky or an island in the sea gets named after its discoverer.

Colleagues and Better

What constituted support, what made it so vital, and how it was well offered/accepted/shared, none of this was very clear; only that support was a general good and that it was important to en-sure this were in no doubt. Whatever it was, at Aloka it was in-cumbent on the faculty to demonstrate it in the ways they be-haved with each other, and with the participants and staff over the 12 weeks of close cooperative living and working together.

The Aloka book describes the colleagueship among the faculty like this (Lynton 1960, pp 182–96):

It was common for two faculty members to be at the same ses-sion...to use the break-time and after class for checking with one

1. See the last section of this chapter.

another how it was going...to go in and out of each other's living quarters, sharing ideas, talking of some experience they had just had, expressing the feelings they had controlled during contact with the members, exchanging written assignments, and enjoying the close personal relationship. Traditions grew up according to which faculty members congregated in the office or had tea together regularly, without necessarily anything specific to talk about. So with their very different backgrounds and varied professional training, and their different styles of teaching, they yet achieved a consistency in their orientation and in the kinds of cues they used and their reactions to them.

The consistency cut across the...different parts of the programme. All faculty members taught some case sessions, and several took turns with the work programmes and field visits. But for the most personal discussions...the same faculty member stayed with the group. That was one important division which faculty meetings needed to bridge. A second division existed between those faculty members who lived very closely with members...and those who lived in separate cottages with their families. This division was not just one of convenience...faculty who lived most closely with the members were junior faculty, people who had been outstanding members of (earlier) courses and been brought back to develop further their considerable promise as trainers... age and recent experience as well as living arrangements and professional assignments put them nearer to members.

[These] faculty were in positions of particular stress since they were closer to the members but not of them, and at the same time members of the faculty but apprentice members, so to speak...we learned the value of bringing junior faculty in pairs [too] in order to give them a colleague with whom to share continuously their questions, their anxieties, and their moments of triumph.

Faculty meetings [of all faculty] put some certainty into the picture of spontaneous consultation and exchange. They ensured that enough time was indeed set aside for discussing everything necessary [and] also protected faculty members from each other....

There were six faculty meetings in the days just before the course began and forty-two more during the three months, lasting an average of an hour and a quarter each...in the first four weeks [almost] daily and each lasted longer than average. During the second four weeks there were twelve meetings; during the last four weeks, nine.

Though scheduled in advance and all faculty expected to take part, the meetings were quite informal...usually in the evenings over after-dinner coffee in the director's cottage. They had no set agenda. Faculty members spoke about what was important to them from the day's work and for looking ahead.... The atmosphere of free talking and listening, some of it in disppointment, some of it in joy, much of it in fun, and all in close and growing fellowship, that was of its essence. Here was the professional base of operations; the emotional base too, where faculty members found support and encouragement, tried out first thoughts, and relaxed. And from which they emerged refreshed and reassured....

In these meetings the faculty members stretched and exercised their capacities, explored and examined their own limits and practiced their ability to work as equals, as cooperative people, as people able and inclined to reflect and learn from their experiences. Essentially, the only way they could communicate to the members the value of care was by themselves caring; of cooperation by themselves cooperating; of learning and developing oneself by themselves learning and developing as persons. In the faculty meetings, faculty members had the same unified experience that they sought to provide for the members in the course.

When putting a book of readings together 20 years later, "a live example of reflective practice" clarified what support needed to do (Lynton and Pareek 1992, pp 79–80).[2]

Over a period of four years we had helped get under way a provincial strategy of training system development...the Central Ministry [was] beginning to participate significantly [and] the final year of technical assistance was just starting. At this moment it became clear that the funding agency, though warmly supporting these developments and forewarned about the high cost of delaying, did not have the necessary funding mechanisms actually in place.... This threatened...the immediate abandonment of some inputs and fearsome losses of momentum and credibility for the whole effort.

I had three long-term colleagues.... What, I asked myself, did I expect from them by way of colleagueship and support in this predicament?....

2. To a fuller account of this work we will return in Chapter 8.

An opportunity to air my frustration and my anxieties, for one…to avoid their bedevilling and short changing my assessments of the complex situation and its prospects and so limiting my options for action. An understanding person was required for this in an open, unguarded relationship. My local colleague filled this bill admirably.

Then, secondly, in the ensuing moments of calm, I needed help with assessing the situation most fully and truly and identifying "all" possible options for actions. Additional pairs of eyes, in short, and additional assessors and creators of possible scenarios.

Thirdly, I needed a sense of togetherness in what we—together, out of this joint assessment—decided it was best to do: what, with whom and by whom, and so on. We would proceed together, supplementing each other's strengths…and also communicate appropriate sureness to all with whom we needed to deal.…

And fourthly, I wanted an honest feed-back about my part in it all. Retrospectively too, what had I missed doing that this impasse had come about at all? And also, how I was to play my part from here on.

Creme de la Creme: My Twin-like Colleagues

At every major assignment and everywhere we have lived, I have had close colleagues and friends. Ronnie (also my wife), Udai Pareek, and Michael Merrill were the three long-term colleagues for helping me most to deal with this impasse (in Indonesia). And, over a lifetime, a very few of these also have become the closest and most precious. Five, for me. These twin-like companion brothers and sister of choice are on their life's journey right next to mine, and to them I dedicate this book. We live and think and work on similar wavelengths and rhythms, and with similar temper—mostly even. We each strike our particular notes and together sound chords and harmony. Each is there for me any time, the first person I turn to, no questions asked.

Udai has been my virtual twin brother from SIET days—35 years to date. At first we were just colleagues, he the "counterpart" whom I, the consultant, had found in a year's searching. Within mere days we did everything together. Formally our joint domain was just the Department of Extension Training. By day three, the diary tells joyfully, we ranged widely. Everywhere we saw common ground. Each new discovery was very exciting. Not quite trusting our good fortune at first, then with abandon, we let our fellow feeling have free rein. Within weeks we worked closely together on fine-honing the Institute's programs and on expanding collaboration between departments. We phased in strategies for developing applied social science in India and the personal and institutional capacities for work in it.

Role clarity and acting on it, even with regret, was one of Udai's strengths. He would remind me of mine, such as team leader in one situation and faculty in another, but not hold me back from exploring. We would soon see what happened and learn from that. Essential for Udai was only that we recorded it all in detail: setting, circumstances, options considered, our feelings, steps, consequences. In recording such things, Udai was at least as good and quite as persistent as I, and he was much more creative at devising simple schemas for it and at analyzing the data afterwards. Statistical data and testing them for significance and validity, etc., were second nature to him. From the time Udai and I first worked together, we recorded and prepared reports for each program we involved ourselves in—and they were continuous, and sometimes side by side—for the record, anyway, and for sharing with participants and whoever else might be interested.

Holding ourselves accountable was basic to our notion of good practice. We held our immediate colleagues to it and encouraged it in other departments. Quite as fanciful and playful as I was intellectually, Udai was far better read; he brought to our thinking together nuggets from his many years of disciplined, wide, and up-to-date reading, and also fine rigor of method. He continued to put together the annual Psychological Abstracts for India and to contribute frequently to professional journals.

At first I thought it wise—role clarity!—to keep my recently assumed leadership of the consultant team aside, but we were too close to persist with that and nobody else would have believed we did anyway. So Udai became *my* consultant for that in well-known fact, if untitled. By that time we had become close personal friends as well and our families were in constant touch. It was at the birth of Udai's and Rama's son that we first witnessed *hijras* dancing in traditional celebration, which Ronnie described years later in her first book about Hyderabad (Lynton and Alexander 1991). When that son, Anu, married 20 years later, Ronnie and I were of course among the honored guests, and Udai himself tied the turban on my head, the signal to others who might not know me that I deserved special recognition in his eyes.

By then, Udai and I had worked together in three countries, had co-authored a book and several papers, and had got utterly used to keeping in touch and consulting each other about most aspects of our lives, no matter where we each lived and worked. When my consultancy with SIET ended and I left for a sabbatical in North Carolina, Udai soon followed on a two-year appointment of his own. It was in Chapel Hill, then, that we finished our first joint book, on training. Others would follow. Still in Chapel Hill, it was Udai who broke the ceremonial coconut on the threshhold of our new house before we moved in. When he and his family returned to India, we stayed in touch by letter and visited yearly. And when, a decade later, I went to lead a major project in Indonesia and put together a consultant team, I overcame local aversion to consultants from India and had Udai invited to join me there. Now, yet another decade on, we still move in and out of each other's houses, with children and their families when they are along. We both sit on the Board of the Indian Society for Applied Behavioural Science, which has many roots in our work together at SIET in the 1960s. And we continue to work and write together whenever we can.

How this wonderful, heartwarming, ever-sustaining closeness began, blossomed, and spread, my detailed record of the SIET years enables me to trace, as also the occasional doubts and hesitations, differences, and even periods of drought along the way. To tease the most out of that record, for guidance about what support is, practically speaking, and how to generate and sustain it, I want first to broaden the focus to encompass my other twins as well, two from before Udai and two more later.

From Being Mentored to Being Mentor
Jerry Scott was the first. He joined the Field Research Unit at the British Institute of Management just after me. From the time the work in the coalmines started in earnest, we worked together

ever more closely.[3] Personal friendship grew along with the work. I return to it now with a good deal of pain. For that so-close colleagueship and friendship vanished fast when I left the BIM in 1952 and then almost immediately England for France. It ceased altogether a year later when I continued on to America to work with Jerry's own erstwhile group of colleagues at Harvard. They were his homebase, and it was he himself who had warmly recommended that they invite me. I can only imagine how he felt when, a year later, I married the young woman in that group whom, I learned in due course, he had wanted to court years earlier.

By then I had long given up writing to him, for he had never replied to my letters or himself written. Only from others and years later did I learn that Jerry had left the BIM soon after I had and joined the Coal Board's new staff college for its managers, and that he had then died suddenly, young, leaving Valerie with the still small twin daughters.

I don't think Jerry ever forgave me for leaving our very close partnership. I think now that neither of us had acknowledged how very much he too had come to depend on it professionally, and, since professional prowess and recognition was so central to his self-respect, personally too. I think, further, that he probably had at least an inkling that (even if I had recognized it) it would not have deterred me from leaving and moving on. That fear of his my departure had then fiercely confirmed. Only many years later did it dawn on me, and then only along Ronnie's insight, that Jerry had probably experienced my departure as desertion. I had then followed that briskly with usurping "his" place in the department at Harvard and married Ronnie. To him each step must have been a slap in the face, a shameful return for all he had invested in me as apprentice and his protege. I had left him to soldier on through his life quite on his own and bare to a harshly peremptory world.

With that sad thought, I remind myself of the sharp pangs of grief each time some other close relationship ended just as abruptly as mine did with Jerry and as "without reason". Barring one, these have all been relationships in which I was the elder

3. This work and second thoughts about it now are Chapter 2.

and, in hindsight, the mentor. Over the years I have grown to recognize such sudden breaks as the handiest way for each next
generation to cut loose from the trammels of mine. But even with
that, grief and lingering regrets still follow each time. To this day
I continue reluctantly to accept this scenario as the only and necessary way for young colleagues and friends to grow up and feel
free: Shiva's two sides of creation and destruction in the running
of this world. Happily, when I have yielded center stage and
avoided aggravating the unspoken conflicts inherent in this elemental drama, friendships have also been re-established.

In Jerry's case, looking back, I can now identify warning signs
of the break to come and also of the unhealthy dependencies
that led up to it. For the first two or three years of our getting
close, any idea that *he* might depend on *me* was simply out of
my range of thinking, absurd. He was eight years older than I (32
when he came to my 24); came from—was deputed by (for all
I knew)—the famed Human Relations Group at world-class Harvard with *the* Elton Mayo as head and *the* Hawthorne Studies
(quoted by everyone) its product. He looked ever so professorial
rocking gently and smoking his pipe as we sat talking in the office, in my home, in his home. He quoted from memory from all
over the literature I had not even read, and there were all those
rows of books as backdrop and yet more to be unpacked from
the boxes stacked in the hall.

I was perfectly happy to be Jerry's young, inexperienced colleague. I teamed up with him to lasting profit—a privilege. I felt
buoyed by our friendship as it grew and encompassed seemingly
all. Valerie I met soon after Jerry did, and liked her well. Weekend after weekend we converged on her parents' large house in
Glasgow, Jerry from the mines on the East Coast, I from mine in
the West. There, in comfort beyond any I was accustomed to, we
shared notes and made plans. He and Valerie must have been
courting then. When the wedding came, Jerry had Roger Tredgold
for his best man, not me, and that was only right since Roger was
his senior at the first institution in England that Jerry had worked
in, was British-born and sabre champion, went to the same
church, and was altogether a splendid person indeed.

What gives me pause now are recollections from quite early on
of qualms Jerry had about letting me be in the lead as much and
as often as he did. We would sit discussing something—a next

step in our research or, later, in a piece of writing, or even an idea before any concreteness to it. Long pauses. Reactions from him more often than leads. Many restatements of what I had said, encouraging me to continue. That was the Rogerian way, I knew: "non-directive interviewing". I also enjoyed being in the lead so much. I must not overdraw this aspect. If I remember rightly, for our first book together, Jerry drafted most of the chapters of generalizations from the *Three Studies in Management* which gave the book its title and incorporated in them learnings from the management literature. The first study we wrote together. I had done the research for the other two and so also drafted them for Jerry to comment on, which he did very fully. So he contributed plenty. And in the course of it all, we laughed a great deal and had much excitement and fun.

But I also remember that things seemed never to come to an end with Jerry. What I had first admired as thoroughness, I then grew weary of. And wary, especially when I realized that more and more of the ideas and drafts that Jerry commented on and elaborated so endlessly were ones I had started off and put forward with a finite concrete purpose.

The watershed for me came with our second book together. I fretted over doing most of the writing as well as the managing. Jerry was simply not pulling his weight, certainly not as the lead author which I assumed he would be again. I said none of this and Jerry never voiced his fears of my leaving him. It was easier to carry on without telling, and became easier for me still with each day closer to leaving.

That internal wrestling over the second book came alive again a quarter century later when Udai and I were finishing the book on training, our first together. He had arrived at SIET only as I was putting the finishing touches to a volume of training materials, too late to be its Indian co-author as I would have preferred (Lynton 1964). For the new book, for its best use as well as for signaling the proper relationship between its authors, I would have pushed hard to have Udai the lead author. But when the time came to decide, I had drafted about half the book while still in Hyderabad and now, in the fall, found myself writing most of the rest too. On those drafts Udai commented continuously, and often with quite startling expedition. His own drafts were mostly sections and additions to mine. Most special were the marvellously creative diagrams and tables he orginated which made the book clearly practical. But I obviously led and worked on the book most. That L precedes P in the alphabet made the decision simpler. But I was anxious even about raising the matter, and still regret losing my wish.

Composing a Life—Together

Long before this, almost a decade before Udai and I first met, came Ronnie. I had met her briefly at the very end of my first visit to the US in Summer 1951. From England, Jerry had arranged that I spend an afternoon with the Human Relations Group at Harvard, and Ronnie had been there. Paul Lawrence had insisted that we three meet again in the evening, at least briefly. That was all Ronnie could manage as she already had a date.

When I returned two years later as full-time Training Fellow, Ronnie was one of the three faculty we five Fellows met with as a T-Group every morning. She also was the one to make sure that the Fellows were comfortably settled and received what help they needed, on and off campus. I doubt she was allocated this function in any formal way. She probably assumed most of it from habit and personal inclination; that would certainly have been in line with the whole School's expectations at that time. As the member lowest on the totem pole in the department, as a woman, and like the other two women then at the Business School on only single year appointments with no hope of tenure, for the eighth year by then, it was entirely "natural" that she would be the one to take care of us Fellows. Kind person that she is, her care included occasional invitations for dinner and the evening, most particularly for the two Fellows, Tommy and me, who lived in the dormitory and would surely tire of cafeteria food.

All was so new to me that few specifics stand out about the initial months. There was a set program, but it took up only a few hours a day. After 12 years of tightly scheduled activities ever since leaving school during the war, I was here responsible for nothing other than my own learning. My room was cleaned regularly, a check (for $62.50) turned up in my mailbox fortnightly without fail ("every two weeks", I learned to say), the cafeteria was just a walk down the tree-lined street on campus. Quiet, beautiful. I had free run of the university's facilities, also those across the Charles River. Well, there were charges for some of them, but the stipend allowed for paying what I wanted. I resumed playing squash. Not only my colleagues—the other Fellows and the faculty—but also people generally were pleasant and helpful, if also often a little strange. For instance, they seemed determined, several times that first fall, to use every possible occasion to celebrate America's independence from *my* country across the water, with Boston and its miserable Tea Party in the lead. Thanksgiving for *that*? So each holiday I visited friends in New York from my first US trip. By the time Christmas came, I left behind as a present for Ronnie, Hilaire Belloc's *Cautionary Tales*, adding a suitably hesitant dedication. It was a prescient title. But it would take me most of another year to throw all caution to the winds, while Ronnie too was dealing with hers.

The Fellowship Program has been described in a little book by the faculty (Roethlisberger et al. 1954). For my part and preparation, I had come with at least passing acquaintance with observing and recording as well as working in small groups and, through Jerry, also with case research and writing in which the Business School was then leading. And my experience of field research and even action research was rich. Working further and more systematically on these, and with such illustrious colleagues, was bound to be great.

The part that intrigued me most was the work that all eight of us did together as a T-Group. Studying personal feelings in this "here and now" and the group as we developed it in actual fact, this was quite new to me. Newest of all for me was *expressing* my feelings openly. That I had never done, and it actually went quite against the grain of all I had grown up with in Germany and then in England. Here, in the T-Group, personal openness was not merely encouraged; developing the group depended on it. And from this shared experience, we then also drew implications for group development in general, for planning and facilitating it. Heady stuff. Senior and renowned as they already were, Fritz and George shared the headiness of it. They had just returned from spending three weeks of their summer in Bethel, Maine, experiencing and learning about this then still novel orientation and methodology of training. They were determined to make full use of it, at least to give it a good try.[4]

To me, Ronnie stood out for her steady competence in the small group sessions, as also in the other settings in which we worked together. The truly remarkable capacity she had for precise recall of dialogue showed keen attention and mindful order. I also liked her firm work habits and solid responsibility: when she undertook to do something, that item could go off the list. I first became crystal clear that she expected me also to meet her sterling standards of character when I told her that I had decided to stay away from the T-Group in the morning. I would simply not go.

We were eating by ourselves, having decided on the spur of the moment to talk over a plate of spaghetti near Harvard Square. It was February and our T-Group sessions—three hours every morning since I had arrived in mid-October—had become sheer grind, grimly uninviting like the grey ice-cold evening outside. Nothing new had happened for *weeks*, just the same people saying the same things over and over: an absolute refusal to budge. No intervention, not any of the "leaders'" nor any I had tried, had loosened this stalemate. So there simply was no point in going. I wanted Ronnie to know, that's all.

Well, all it was not. I couldn't do that, said Ronnie, certainly not. Not if I was the responsible person she thought I was. She had no problem with my leaving, but my leaving unexplained was simply, well, out. Coming to tell the group what I was doing and why was essential. And that, of course, made my walking out in the morning into a powerful intervention.

We became each other's counsellors that spring. In April, paired up on the staff of a workshop for administrators of New

---

4. That their book nowhere uses the terms "T-Group" and "sensitivity training" by which this work later came to be generally known, confirms how radically new its personal approach was at that time; and also the doubts and discomforts it has continued to raise, rightly I think, when used perversely and in the wrong hands. As for these terms, from Aloka days on we changed "T-Group" (for Training) to "L-Group" (for Learning) to avoid the association of "training" with telling and with the instructor's power over (lesser) participants. When, two years into Aloka, we went on to base the small group part of the program on the psychoanalytically-based work that the Tavistock Institute in London was pioneering and modeling, we followed them also in calling them "S-Groups" (for Study).

York's vast municipal hospitals, we scared the sponsors so thoroughly with our daring interventions that we left for the weekend break not at all sure they would want us back for the second week. They did, and we two were doubly impressed with our rightness and with each other. That summer, Ronnie had had her fill of the insulting position the School had held her down to now for eight years and accepted the position a fine consulting group with School connections held for her. And I accepted to stay for a second year as research associate, and so came to occupy the very position and salary slot that Ronnie vacated.

Back from Singapore and the resolution to set up Aloka and me at the head of it, drafting and redrafting of plans and numerous meetings in New York filled much of the fall. All of it we did together. When we announced our engagement that November, our colleagues presented us with a book of poems they had composed to document our oh-so-slow progress to this easily predictable end. We married in April; left for Asia in May. The morning of our departure, Ronnie's aunt Henrietta Larson, of business history fame, read the 23rd Psalm over us, tearfully, unconvinced that she would see her favorite niece ever again.

I, quite regardless of how new Asia and married life really were, and Ronnie also newly pregnant, simply assumed she would keep pace with me however hectic that was. It took me years to become a little more thoughtful and respectful, and also a little more flexible. The other side of that over-full life was that Ronnie too found at Aloka full scope for just about all her wide range of interests and abilities, professional as well as personal and social. Starting from scratch, even finding a site to replace the unsuitably located and vastly expensive property the World Assembly of Youth (WAY) had identified, we planned, initiated, and developed all aspects of this brand new, multi-cultural, residential training center together. Together too we dealt with its numerous crises, along with the excitements that come with a first baby and being a young family. Between programs we traveled throughout the region, visiting the organizations which sent participants, recruiting more, finding locations for our urban programs off-site, and making arrangements for them; so our three children were born in three different places in South Asia. In every program we took some sessions together. In management circles in India, stalwarts recall the stories Ronnie told about the nursery school we started at Aloka around our own children and about "Timmy's blanket", which was a priceless treasure to a toddler when singular and, contrary to commercial maxim, became despicable when augmented with an identical (clean) second.

What we could each do well and how we could help one another the most, both became clear and clearer in the doing. Many more Alokans went to Ronnie than to me for comfort and counsel, and some became her proteges for years and decades. She comments fully and helpfully on all written work—participants' and mine. I am often the one to do first drafts, sometimes even of small pieces for Ronnie's own books where she feels stuck. I can comment usefully on her drafts overall, much more rarely on detail. In reverse, I can depend on Ronnie to find sentences too long and unclear in all my writings, and altogether to repair my wording and even make it elegant. We have written whole books together, four to six depending on how to count them, starting with *Asian Cases* (Lynton and Lynton 1960).

In the introduction to the book about Aloka itself, I mention that though, in addition to all the planning, developing, and running the center, Ronnie "equally fully shared the authorship of this book, [she] resolutely refused to do the same on the title page" (Lynton 1960, pp 1–2). So, contrary to authors who thank partner and children for their patient forbearance over the many months of silence peppered with ill temper, I could quite realistically thank "my wife...for being in my way the whole time" (ibid, pp 1–2). In the Spring of 1959, when I went off to Tanzania to run an off-site course without Ronnie, having with rare consideration discouraged her from joining me with the two small children on the grounds that the facilities there would be unfamiliar at best and Dar-es-Salam at that season hot and steamy, I also persuaded her to organize a second course at the same time. After all, she would be at Aloka anyway and could do it with the remaining faculty. She still likes to tell, with wry amusement, how we in Tanzania then moved the course up-country and I wrote her about the view of the snows of Kilimanjaro.

The counseling and co-authoring—acknowledged or secretive—have continued. My consultancy in Hyderabad excluded Ronnie from working directly with me at SIET. So she developed tasks of her own, including professional contracts, for some of which I joined *her* later. During our years in Chapel Hill and then in Indonesia, she was again "on my team" along with other colleagues, for a special part. Through those years her income contributed essentially to the extra we needed for unexpectedly many years for our family as a whole. As the need for that declined, she turned her research and writing in a new direction: nineteenth-century India. First came a pair of books about Hyderabad, our city, then one about dance in contemporary India and dear long-time friends who have strategic roles in it based in our second city in India, Ahmedabad (Lynton and Alexander 1991; Lynton 1992, 1995). No matter what the content—past or present, fact or fiction—I am her first reader and she continues to be mine.

When, during our stay in Delhi in the late 1980s, the binding of a much earlier book came undone with age and much moving between climates, Ronnie and I decided to have it rebound in leather (which, in India, we could afford). Liking that well, we went right on binding the rest thus luxuriously as well: past, present and in future. Now in our house in the North Carolina countryside near Chapel Hill stand two strikingly handsome rows of books we have authored: six jointly, six jointly with others, 10 individually—22 in all. So far.

Vital Thrusts Must Make Big Sense

John Thomas came to India in 1964 in time to join the interinstitutional faculty development program that Udai and I had organized for the following spring. Warren Bennis and I led it. Warren and John were in India under the Ford Foundation grant that had enabled the Indian Institute of Management (IIM) Calcutta to link up with MIT's Sloan School, just as IIM Ahmedabad linked with the Business School at Harvard. Warren headed the MIT consulting team that year and had included in it his young colleague and former student, John.

John does not stand out in my memories of the faculty development program itself. Only recently arrived in India, his relations with Warren and the two Indian professors from Calcutta in the program were still to be worked out—whatever the reasons, he must have been quieter there than is really characteristic of him. He pushes for things "to make sense", quietly, steadily, and with dogged persistence when necessary. Somehow he stays wonderfully well-read, up with a wide range of literature of both content and method. To meetings he comes with thoughts clear and a fine economy of expression. For me, John is formidably intellectual, and takes care of that flank along with Udai. Happily, he combines this with an equally matter-of-fact and liberally available practicality, and an eye to what is feasible and promising, also politically. And warm caring for people, present or distant, underpins it all.

All this and more I would see flower and come to glory only later, and most clearly from the late 1960s on in America. At that time, we began working together closely and regularly, first in the new Program in Policy Science in Buffalo and then also in South Carolina in connection with developing the School of Public Health and, unorthodox as it was, getting it accredited. By then we usually stayed in each other's homes, part of each other's families. Our Nandani became their particular friend.

Of that Spring in 1965 and our first meeting then, my memories highlight three quite disparate parts. Readiest and almost overpowering all else looms the recollection of how miserably cold and uncomfortable Dalhousie high up in the north was that April, and how that inescapable misery became mere background, hardly an eyelash in my awareness, when I caught sight of the elemental, breathtaking loveliness of the immense snow-covered Himalayan range across the valley, stretching along the whole horizon without end. At no time was it more lovely than when very early on crisp mornings the still-wintry sun moved slowly down the white peaks with faint pinks and blues, then over the valley still dark with night or hidden under a thick fluffy blanket of mist.

The most vivid second memory of these years really crystallized only after the Dalhousie program was over and had shed its immediacy and pressing demands. It is of marveling and looking back that the program had taken place at all. In sheer logic, the idea of it was impeccable: faculty at SIET was expanding so fast that the rigorous and effective, but also time-consuming, arrangements for taking in newcomers threatened to break down; the pressure was greatest on the three weeks of daily sessions for improving inter-personal competence; at present and for some time to come, only Udai and I could lead those and we could not accommodate more people.

A larger program, focused wholly on this component, just for faculty, but those from several sister institutions, could break this deadlock and have some other advantages as well. But prospects of moving the idea forward were surely dim. These inter-personal skills sessions were the most controversial component of the intake program; Indian institutions had no great reputation for collaborating; and, not least, Udai and I had really no extra time to give to its preparation. So, the fact that we mustered the nerve to propose this far-out and controversial additional program and that it then actually took place is sheer wonder. Though Udai had been in on all stages of it and helped set it up, he decided against going to it himself to safeguard his relationships with the five SIET colleagues who were in the program.

The third memory brings John and his importance for me into clear focus. During rare off-hours in those two weeks in Dalhousie, Warren also shared with John and me his idea to develop a program for policy sciences in the United States: at MIT (or somewhere else, if MIT didn't want it); no, not political science under a more snazzy name but oriented to putting fresh policies actually on the books. That was doctoral-level work and required mid-career people to do it. Rare people had to be found—and funded—who, at this mid-point of their lives, were still eager enough to fashion their years of practical experience into directions for public policy, and able as well as ready to learn up-to-date methodologies and the new and fast-developing technologies of the computer age to equip themselves for making that contribution.

Sitting there side-by-side on a boulder brushed clear of snow, and the majestic scene before and below us, I first saw John use his head with the great zest and creativity characteristic of him, his dogged persistence, and also his personal warmth and readiness for fun. Along with that first inkling of John's ample capacity for close colleagueship and friendship, I sensed also John's private side, his determination to be his own man.

I liked it all. We stayed in touch. At the end of the year, Warren and John returned to the States. Warren moved to Buffalo as provost of the state university there. He got the Doctoral Program for Policy Sciences funded and recruited John for it. When I reached the States a half-year later, ostensibly for my year's sabbatical, I also had a standing invitation to visit them in Buffalo, and these

visits led to attempts to work out some way in which I might join
Warren and John in Buffalo. Those were expansive times for universities, disturbed as they also were with students protesting the
Vietnam war and, only a little less dramatically but also more per-
sistently, protesting against the older generation and the life they
led. Warren asked me to take on the School of Social Work as dean,
no doubt regarding my lean academic background combined with
my long hands-on experience in community development in
various cultures and in building institutions just right for pioneering drastic innovation. But that was too far out even for me—
with my doctorate still ahead and that School and traditional profession then angrily divided. That winters in Buffalo were endlessly grey and dank helped me turn down the challenge.

But two years later, when my doctoral studies at Duke reached
a dead end over my unwillingness to return to the field to collect
data for a properly hypothesized dissertation (such as consulting
at SIET Institute could not offer), Warren invited me to transfer
to Buffalo and pioneer in the new program itself the dissertation
I wanted to do. So, beginning Summer 1968 I flew to Buffalo for
a week every month. In lieu of paying fees, I taught a clinical
course in the program and earned enough and more to cover my
travel. I always stayed with John or Warren, about twice with
John and Susan and the children for every time with Warren and
Clurie and theirs. (I fear I contributed more meagerly, certainly
to the Thomas household, than I should have, even for those
tight days for us.)

My dissertation was the first in the program and so also the first
opportunity to display the norms for doing this. The defence,
when the day for it finally arrived, was public, medieval-fashion,
that is with the whole Program present and encouraged to be active. Committee Chair/Provost Bennis walked in with large bottles
of champagne. My dissertation was no doubt quite acceptable, he
declared, but, just to open the discussion, what pointers did it
contain for dealing with the conflicts in *this* institution (where students had just occupied the administration building), and specifically for steps he himself might take as its provost. I remember
nothing of what I said (beyond that I did speak), or of the
two-hour discussion that followed (beyond that I continued to be
active in it). And that at the end of the afternoon I was indeed declared passable and drank at least my share of the champagne.

Through staying with John, Susan and their two small children so regularly for a week at a time, and also leaving each morning with John for the same work in the same place and then usually returning home together with him for those evenings, John and I became very close. Those were the times when just about *any* idea could be shared and were, and into which we also drew others as they showed up, certainly Warren. After Summer 1970, when my regular visits to Buffalo ceased with my "crowning", I went right on with the good habit of sharing and checking with John any idea of more than ephemeral order. That continued even after John expanded his special interest in public interest law and regulatory matters and buckled down to add a law degree to his degree in management; also when his interest in small group processes faded soon after and he ended his active involvement in the NTL Institute in Washington, DC, whereas I continued mine.

Institution-building continued to be an interest we shared, especially in building those with innovative purpose. When my work on contributing to a general guide for team leaders of technical assistance projects (Rigney et al. 1971) led me to doubt the adequacy of prevailing taxonomies for institutional linkages, it was to John that I turned to work out collegiate linkages as the fifth classification. New institutions, and innovative ones especially, needed sister institutions to support them. If those collegiate linkages also opened them to opposition, it was better to have that opposition out in the open, where proponents could seek common ground, than hidden and surreptitious. When John in turn invited me some years later to co-author a chapter in a book on consulting, we included in that the augmented five-fold taxonomy as well as our updated understanding of the two-way nature of the relations between organizations and their environments (Sinha 1979, pp 80–100).

Organizations *made*, indeed *were*, the environments for one another; so waiting to accommodate to environment in the abstract was bad strategy. Co-authoring again, we developed our thoughts on institution-building into a "theory", properly so called in the piece to be used as a "diagnostic framework for organization development" (Lynton and Thomas 1980). For that we used university population programs as an example; I was in one, in Chapel Hill, and was then developing and coordinating an international network for sharing practical experiences with building them (Lynton 1974).

Soon after, I went to start the new School of Public Health in South Carolina as founder dean. Besides Ronnie, John was one of the two persons with whom I discussed my ideas and strategies for developing it. Racine, my latest twin, was the other; with him I could talk right there. Even so, I still mailed John the major proposals to comment on and knew I could count on hearing his reactions by whatever time I needed them. When the School neared accreditation, I engaged John formally to consult with me on structural and process issues. When I resigned as dean, quite in character he encouraged me to write about that too.

After 1981, when Ronnie and I moved overseas again full-time— first for a year, then for indefinite time ahead—my contact with John thinned out. Our interests diverged. For months we did not talk, and only our annual Christmas letters kept him and his family acquainted with our news and plans. Months turned into years. Yet John continues to be "always there". I sent him end-of-assignment reports and, true to my picture of him, he kept on responding with comments and encouragement, as if we had met just yesterday. To the report on the five years of work on helping the Indonesian government decentralize its health services, which had also engaged Udai and several other Indian colleagues he knew, he marveled at (my/our) "getting my arms around vast systems like that, again and again". And when Udai and I put together the book of readings to accompany the expanded second edition of our training book, John suggested several readings we used. So, of course, he has also seen and commented on parts of this book.

"This Above All: To Thine Own Self Be True"
Racine is a *talking* person. Racine's slow-paced resonant drawl— a Southern trait—is a fine match for mine in low voice. His unhurried sentences take yet longer for the long pauses in them while he marshals his thoughts to continue speaking. They do not invite interrupting; he is quite evidently working out onward thought and its best uttering. He smokes a pipe or a cigar, less now than he used to. He is a man, a person, of ample space inside and out, solid and tall, with a broad brimmed hat that rarely

comes off his head. Ample also as dear friend and colleague ever since the late 1960s.

I don't recall what first brought me to his attention. Geographical proximity, perhaps, and the members list of what is now the NTL Institute. He often came to Chapel Hill or nearby to join another NTL member for programs in schools and social services. They drew me into their work. Racial integration of schools and large scale transfer of mental patients to community care multiplied programs for easing relationships and for updating organizations. Racine was assistant (later deputy) commissioner for mental health in South Carolina.

Soon Racine and I paired up regularly for staffing such programs. We hit it off all round. We thought and worked on similar lines; had similar styles and pacing; found each other "utterly reliable" (as Racine put it), adding that, no, he would not necessarily handle this or that person or event quite the same way I had (or would), but he understood "where I am coming from"— a favorite metaphor—and "knew, just *knew*" with absolute certainty that I had given it "my usual careful consideration"—another.

For me, what he was referring to (certainly what I saw in him) was not primarily his intellectual acumen and enough stamina and persistence in putting it to use, but the deep roots these qualities had in sound, solid, personal integrity. When, as native son and the long-time and well-regarded deputy, he was a shoo-in to succeed the state commissioner in the 1980s, he removed his candidature so that the legislature would end its long invidious battle over abolishing the restriction on considering non-physicians for the post. He then also left his department, the arena of his career, so that the new commissioner would have clear charge and would also be seen to have it. I was moved but not surprised by either action. I have seen Racine challenged many times and in widely different situations, even heatedly, but never over integrity. That is rock solid and patent to all.

I have also known him when *he* examines this or that part of his integrity for possible soft spots or fault lines below the surface that some spontaneous reaction of his or some dream hinted might be there. He checks it out, reads, meditates, attends to bodily signals, and dreams about it; goes for professional help and tests for it in personal discussion; studies, clarifies, and fine-hones, all with an eye to repairing the least possible chink in every which way till he feels again true, aligned just as smoothly as he is able to make himself be. But he does so kindly, gently; no obsession here. He is after "enoughness", not perfection (even if we could recognize it, I suspect). In turn he relies on me ("can depend on" is the phrase he uses) always, "anywhere I have chosen to be". He only needs to rein in my inclinations to go too far and too fast.

That easy congruence quickly led to staying in each other's homes and the families too becoming friends. We included each other in celebrating milestone events of life and death, often also in preparing for them and helping each other attend to their echoes. So at Racine's first wife, Mary's, specific request, I was a pallbearer at her funeral. A year later, in Bogota, I used my doctoral title as if I were a physician to secure a seat on a plane back in time for Racine's wedding with Louisa. To us and also to our children he is "on call" and has taken our place in many a crisis when our own far-flung life and work has kept us thousands of miles and dollars away.

It was Racine who told the then president of the university that I would be a good person to start the new School of Public Health in South Carolina. I stayed at his house during the brief exploratory phase and discussed with him first my ideas and plans. He agreed to help me and the faculty with weekly consultation as well as ready access on the spur of the moment; he included both in his normal service to the state. He and John got to know and like each other while working with the School. It was for Racine and me, in fact, that I heard the word "twin" first used for a pairing this close. We complement each other and are also alike in many ways. Summer after summer we have arrived together for NTL's summer program in Bethel, Maine, after the two-day drive up; shared an apartment there; and emerged from it for the same sessions, also for many meals. We have separate activities too; but last thing, before turning in for the night, we walk in the center of the small town. With this much time together for talking, the proposals we make for programs sound already half-way worked out (and often are), and we approach and speak about issues as if we had lined up in advance. Others find this eery on occasion: two of us for one of them; they make us even more alike and aligned than we are. And twinship this close *does* become closer still, even more encompassing, and confirms itself over and over. Like a marriage has and does for an old couple.

With Much Playing Come New Tunes

...a small group of people from a large population suit my needs at a particular time. My support system to deal with family stress is quite different from the support system I need on the job.

Seashore 1976

Without any inkling in advance, in Chapel Hill in the late 1960s I found already assembled all the intellectual backing to be had then anywhere for treating social support as very important indeed: epidemiology in UNC's School of Public Health led the way in studying and teaching social support, and also in zest and high reputation for influencing public policy; my department (of mental health) was its offshoot. My own "support system", even of twins, quickly enlarged: Udai joined Ronnie and me there, and then Racine too, who turned out to have trained with Udai five summers before.

By the time Udai arrived, I had also started doctoral studies at Duke which, thanks to my wonderfully responsive advisors there, focused on *structural* interventions, and would make my life-long interest and practice in the multi-storeyed architecture of support altogether respectable.[5] But, despite my Duke colleagues' good efforts, for me the structural did not replace the personal dimension of support. I have kept it side-by-side with close, deep, and deepening personal companionship.

With Udai, two aspects of the personal dimension stand out in my full record of how our twinship first developed in the years at SIET. Neglect of them, anywhere, makes me uncharacteristically anxious.

High density of contacts is the first: in the four years we worked together there, they averaged four a day, even across all his and my separate absences, including too the one month's family leave a year. We met 1,300 times. Most, but not all, were at work and about work. Some days we were in and out of each other's offices a dozen times.

5. This story is in Chapter 7.

High frequency of contacts makes for closeness—and also signals it. It creates room for more and more facets of each person to come into play, just as diamonds get to shine when turned. Multiple opportunities make spontaneity easy whereas any one or a few would flatten under too much weight. Ideas can bubble, of many sorts and even from bare hunches. Our conversations were soon studded with kidding and leg-pulling, and that warmed the contacts more. Differences and their exploration were worked in, finely nuanced, and worked out with relief. At the end of Udai's very first week at SIET, following my delight in instance after instance with his "obvious competence", his "splendid ways of involving colleagues from early on", the way he had of pulling a little pad out of his shirt pocket to make a note and how fast he worked, the record also tells that "I suddenly wondered what will be left for me to do when he really gets going. I immediately went on to think there was plenty for both of us to do."

By the second month, the notes mention times when I "held back" and remained "silent, eyes downcast" so that Udai would take the lead, and when I declined accompanying him to a meeting. In one I reflect how two of my characteristics—pushing for truly fresh ideas and working all hours—cut across my wanting Udai to take the lead, presumably in *his* ways and at *his* pace. When I summarized my contacts with Udai for our first year of working together, I noted at first, with dismay, that I had continued initiating the contacts at a high rate, and then, with relief and pleasure, that the contacts I had initiated had shifted to asking his views about things on *my* plate, for instance, as team leader of the consultants. When, two years later, I resigned the team leadership, made my recording less comprehensive and regular, and noticed myself "slipping into making negative comments [when I hear others making them]...for the first time I see Udai openly antagonistic to others and in a fighting mood". By then Udai had become the safe listener to my feelings of pressure and frustration. So, when he then in turn "lost his cool, he ceased to be able to help me keep my balance".

As this twinship with Udai developed and, also, as the Institute incorporated Udai's coming, hitting his stride and working out his roles and accommodations, the dominant themes in the record change. From lively apprehension that Udai might depend on me too much in dealing with the principal director, for instance, or in divisive situations, the major themes move on to straightening out relations in our department, then to Udai's promotion to director of extension and on to the wider responsibilities in the Institute and with other institutions this invested him with, so also newly legitimating what he had so far influenced informally.

Compared with this intense and much reviewed experience of mine with Udai, I watch with anxious disbelief when others lessen personal contact. Two fashionable developments threaten this. One is the rapid spread of regimens for self-improvement and stress management for individuals, to practice mostly alone. The self-reliance and personal discipline that the best regimens encourage turn into perversion when practitioners pursue them as alternatives to ensuring social support and close colleagueship, even (in fact all the more so) when today's society discourages personal contact. Quiet reflection and disciplined meditation can deepen true colleagueship; they do not lessen, never mind do away with, the need for it.

The other dead-end, as surely bound as the other to distract, delay, and mislead, is any idea that "virtual" colleagueship between people, as in exchanging information over computers, can be the real thing, and perhaps even better because it is more readily accessible. That would confuse knowing about with *really* knowing. Relationships can begin with exchange of information, but making some of them closer and more lasting comes with changing to a different wavelength, essentially different even from putting more personal items of information into the exchange. Even as "virtual" seeing and hearing get added to technologies, support and colleagueship will still depend on frequent, free-ranging, face-to-face personal contact and will require nurturing in person. "Before I built a wall I'd ask to know what I was walling in or walling out.... Something there is that doesn't love a wall, that wants it down... (Frost 1964).

Little Attention Still

In Indonesia 10 years on, when Udai and I were again working together and preparing a book of readings to accompany a new edition of our stalwart *Training for Development*, colleagueship and support surely warranted a major section in it. Finding items to include became itself "a live example of reflective practice"—a discouraging one as it turned out (Lynton and Pareek 1992, pp 80–82):

> In the set of ten folders in which I [had over the months] accumulated readings and references to consider including, the folder for this section was very slim…. This struck me doubly hard because it was so contrary to my long-time interest,…I had a fair library in the matter, had continued reading, and had gone right on accumulating cuttings and references, and also acquiring new books. Worse was to come: as I read the few items,…I discarded them one after another as too general, too academic for practicing trainers and consultants, or as belonging more properly to other sections….
>
>   Back I went to my shelves, to scan *all* books with "support" in the title…. The result is still thin and disappointing…. Preoccupation with pathological situations and therapeutic encounters continues to dominate the literature…. [In] the special issue on support in the *Journal for Social Issues* [1984, 1985] not a single piece is on support needs in developmental situations or on collegiate support. A second [preoccupation is with] situations of high stress…as on a battle-field; special, extraordinary events….
>
>   From scanning a broad range of professions, another study [Kirschenbaum and Glaser 1978, p. 2] concludes that 'the piece missing for all of them is some mechanism for providing on-going learning and support to the individual…embarked on humanising his or her organization'.

Support in Turbulence and Chaos: Crocodiles don't Sparkle

That book of readings was published in 1992, just when India liberalized its economy. Many organizations suddenly faced what they termed "a new world" and asked for help with that: it called for creating a drastically different "organizational culture"—their word. With that I woke to the unhappy realization that Lynton's time-honored "crocodile" was simplistic and misleading. While it may have helped visualize the nature and functions of support, it did so for just one change at a time, and was not at all geared to working in volatile environments and with the multiple *flows* of decisions they called for.

At issue was not whether to change or not to change to a new direction, B, at successive points A. Rather, it was how to take in and also create fresh directions to go in, doing this not just occasionally but constantly, and refocusing resources at short notice. "Transformation" replaced "change", and that was not a mere escalation but a qualitative difference. The whole organization, township, public service, or state administration had to transform itself into a "learning" system. With dismantling protective walls, turbulence—the permanent state of low predictability—had also come to India.

And to me. For real, that is, in a conceptually demanding, upsetting, transformative way, beyond the *idea* of it all with which I was quite familiar. I had read Emery and Trist, Lawrence and other seminal works of the last two decades about turbulence, contingency management, and, the recent escalation, chaos theory. Helping institutions become learning systems and develop their capacities to stay in that mode even identified my actual practice. I even concentrated on working with institutions, to the virtual exclusion of all other organizations, since institutions were specially charged with changing societal norms. How then had the crocodile diagram survived this long as my always ready image for change?

Long habit and mindless repetition account for some of it; personal temperament for more. One step at a time, changing incrementally in logical order, suits me. That it mattered enough to blind me to the actual state of the world is intriguing. My own lifeline, after all, had had at least two rude disruptions in it (emigration and war), each so shattering that life could never be the same again, mine or others'. Yet change strategies that jumped disjunctions or made their ways through chaos as through a jungle had lodged in my mind as virtuoso intellectual displays, like a kind of circus of the mind, out there, not something to work directly and explicitly into my mental constructs and imagery and so also align image with my actual practice. I preferred to continue regarding the disruptions in my life as aberrations, freaks away from normal. Similar discounting of cataclysmic events will occur again in these stories,[6] notably when I was without companions to challenge me to look again at those events and also the resolutions I came to.

6. Especially in Chapter 6. The clarifications had to be personal as well as professional, and that probably delayed them for me.

Even now, for a book on transformative social change in the late 1990s, the best image I could come up with was a crocodile with sparklers bursting in many directions ahead of it—many Bs, like this (Figure 4.2):

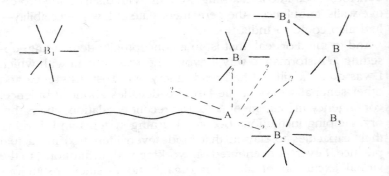

FIGURE 4.2　"Lynton's Crocodile" Dumbfounded

This image, and also the forlorn thought behind it, I made the title of a chapter in a book on transformative change, "Crocodiles Don't Sparkle" (Lynton 1997). Crocodiles were simply not made to cope with volatile change without end.

Till the 1970s there were few colleagues anywhere who might have prodded me into including disjunctions and chaos routinely in my sights, for the professional world generally shared my preference for the gentility and good sense of incremental change. Certainly there had been none at Aloka, or at SIET a decade later. There was no colleague at SIET to help me see the upsets only just around the corner then and to help me replace my worn-out image of change. How to find and keep reliable colleagues under chaotic conditions and ensure sufficient support generally calls for fresh creativity and a stout heart. Confirmed it is that steady working in chaos makes colleagueship and support more necessary than ever.

References

Frost, Robert, "Mending Wall" in *Complete Poems*, Holt, Rinehart and Winston, New York, 1964.

Journal for Social Issues, Special Issue on 'Social Support: New Perspectives in Theory, Research and Priority", Vol. 40, No. 4, 1984 and Vol. 41, No. 1, 1985.

Kirschenbaum, Howard and **Glaser, Barbara**, *Developing Support Groups*, University Associates, La Jolla, California, USA, 1978.

Lynton, Harriet Ronken, *My Dear Nawab Saheb*, Orient Longman, New Delhi, 1992.

———, *Born to Dance*, Orient Longman, New Delhi, 1995.

Lynton, Harriet Ronken and **Lynton, Rolf P.**, *Asian Cases: Teaching Cases from the Aloka Experience*, Aloka, Mysore, 1960.

Lynton, Harriet Ronken and **Alexander, Mohini**, *The Days of the Beloved*, Orient Longman, New Delhi, 1991.

Lynton, Rolf P., *Agents of Industrial Development: Cases, Readings and Assignments for Managers, Consultants and Extension Officers*, SIET Institute, Hyderabad, 1964.

———, *Building Population Programs in Universities: A Brief Guide for Policy Makers*, UNC at Chapel Hill, Chapel Hill, 1974.

———, *The Tide of Learning: The Aloka Experience*, Routledge and Kegan Paul, London, 1960. Extracts reprinted in Lynton, Rolf P. and Pareek, Udai (eds), *Facilitating Development: Readings for Trainers, Consultants and Policymakers*, Sage Publications, New Delhi, 1992, pp 84–87.

———, 'Crocodiles Don't Sparkle', in Klein, Donald C. and Diamond, Louise (eds), *Transformative Social Change*, Sage Publications, Thousand Oaks, 1997.

Lynton, Rolf P. and **Pareek, Udai** (eds), *Facilitating Development: Readings for Trainers, Consultants and Policy-makers*, Sage Publications, New Delhi, 1992.

Lynton, Rolf P. and **Thomas, John**, 'Institution-building Theory as a Diagnostic Framework for Organization Development: The Case of University Population Programs', in *Southern Review of Political Science*, Vol. 3, No. 3, pp 303–23, 1980.

Rigney, J.A., Baumgardner, Harvey L., Ellis, Walter, Lynton, Rolf P. and **Jung, Christian W.**, *A Guide to Institution Building for Teamleaders of Technical Assistance Projects*, North Carolina State University, Raleigh, 1971.

Roethlisberger, F.J. with **Lombard, George F.F.** and **Ronken, Harriet O.**, *Training for Human Relations: An Interim Report of a Program for Advanced Training and Research in Human Relations, 1951–1954*, Harvard University, Division of Research, Boston, 1954.

Seashore, Charles, 'Building Support Systems', in Caplan, Gerald and Willilea, Maria (eds), *Support Systems and Mutual Help*, Grune & Stratton, New York, 1976.

Sinha, Dharni P., *Consulting and Consulting Styles*, Vision Books, New Delhi, 1979.

5

JEIZING THE MOMENT

Idea, Enthusiasm, Escalation—And Exclusion
The Offending Monograph
"After the Ball was Over"—A Sober Assessment
Preparations for Meeting the Moment

...the richest experiences of life, from birth onwards, come by chance, and if they come more deliberately, they are rarely worth seizing....

Lewis Mumford 1979, p. 86

Out of a lifetime of moments to seize—or not to seize—I want to focus on the decision Joe and I, consultants with the Small Industries Extension Training (SIET) Institute of the Government of India, made to go ahead with publishing a monograph that was bound to raise a hornet's nest. The monograph was concerned with developing employment opportunities in small towns across India. The need exceeded 100 million new jobs a year.

Friends and colleagues in high places within and outside the government warned that issuing this monograph would make lots of trouble (including for us) and urged us not to do it. We chose to go ahead; we regarded the warnings across the board as confirmation that we would certainly be heard. The Ford

Foundation, who funded us, forbade all reference to it if we were indeed foolish enough to go ahead; but nothing was ever said about firing us if we did.

So we went ahead and ran off 2,000 mimeographed copies with only our names on them and with no institutional imprint. With text on both sides, spiral bound and a two-colour cover, it looked more like a small book than a draft to invite discussion. We sent it, single copies and by name, to key persons all over the country: in the national Planning Commission and in all concerned ministries in Delhi; also, in particular, in the Khadi Commission which was against all power-driven machinery in principle and carried the still powerful legacy of Gandhiji; in state governments; in the wide range of autonomous and also private institutions that concerned themselves with "rural uplift"; in educational institutions at all levels and research institutes; and in the media, of course.

So there! With *Industrialisation Beyond the Metropolis,* Joe and I set about challenging, as publicly as we knew how, the ways India was developing mechanized industry and non-rural employment nation-wide. A quarter-century later, Indian colleague and friend Vijay Mahajan recommended including the monograph in this book since it described how things still were, and also signalled the direction in which he hoped his own new, dispersed, small loan financing scheme for the same purpose would help the entire country move.

Back in that Spring of 1963, SIET was barely into its second year. The Institute had been set up to upgrade the government's consulting services to small-scale industries. These services were in the Ministry of Industries and employed some 600 officers at that time: engineers, accountants, marketing experts, and some economists. Along with their particular expertise they offered entrepreneurs access to banks and to a set of government subsidies and public services. Except for the few in the office of the Small Industries' Commissioner in the Ministry in New Delhi, they were based in offices in the state capitals.

In batches of 30 they came to the Institute for a 12-week residential program in production management, finance, marketing, economics, and extension training. The Ministry expected them to emerge up-to-date and more competent for their continuing work with small enterprises, motivated afresh, and also more inclined and competent to "do extension". By this was meant that instead of merely responding to requests for assistance, they would reach out more and stimulate additional people to become entrepreneurs; also, that they would offer help to existing units through training, demonstrations, tours, and other public programs.

This last was one of the shifts of emphasis that the team of international experts had urged on the Ministry. Success with it would, over the years, lead to the multiplication of entrepreneurs and employment in small units all over the country. This solid emphasis on extension then gave the Institute its name. I was the consultant for that, but the first year had ended with faculty still to be found for that function.

Co-author Joe had been with the project from its very beginning. A member of the high-level international team that had recommended it and then helped convert the idea into the plan for funding, he had then stayed on in Delhi to nurture the plan into fruition and had selected the initial set of five international consultants, me included. Then, as team leader, he had moved the 1,000 miles south to Hyderabad. There, unattached to a department, he consulted with the principal director on the Institute's overall development.

At the Foundation, support for small industries development ranked high: an important, even strategic, piece in India's development, and likewise in the wide-ranging view its by-then legendary representative took of the Foundation's contribution to it. After several years' active encouragement to the government, the Foundation had funded the expert team, also Joe to stay on, and the set of international consultants (up to eight at times) for the Institute's first five years. It had not replaced Joe when he moved to Hyderabad; he simply flew back when needed. And now he, team leader, had co-authored this very upsetting monograph.

Formally, SIET was free to publish it. With Foundation encouragement, even lobbying, it had been set up as an autonomous society precisely to escape bureaucratic rigidities and manage funds more flexibly. But the funds still had to come from the Government of India and the change of governance left the key persons unchanged: the small industries commissioner was a member of the board and the deputy secretary to whom he reported chaired it. In this institutional independence, Joe and I now anchored our challenge. The Foundation did not like it at all, and the Institute backed off.

Yet we persisted. Team leader Joe of all people and I, the consultant for that amorphous field extension (with no clear limits as in, say, marketing) were going public, quite on our own. Here, as if all controls were off, we pushed ahead publicly with a severely critical assessment of small industries development to date country wide, and with the prognosis that significant progress depended on making radical shifts in overall strategy and national policies, also in funding. While services to individual small units would have to continue, more important was to concentrate efforts and funds on developing industrial employment in whole areas, notably districts (each an administrative unit of 1 to 2 million people) and small cities (of about 100,000 population). The kinds of enterprises most worth encouraging there would use technologies which, though power-driven and as modern as possible, required little capital and only local maintenance, and employed many hands: "appropriate technologies".

This prescription was guaranteed to cause maximum offence all round—to the small industries commissioner for proposing that decisions, action, and funds be shifted away from the center to the states; the established state cadres of district and area development officers would take the lead. That several key members of the Planning Commission, most scholars and professional bodies of public administration and, less openly, many senior officials in Delhi itself favored such decentralization made the recommended direction even touchier. An unsolicited monograph like this could cut the fine mesh of intricate maneuverings to smithereens.

In his own Ministry the Commissioner faced angry criticism. SIET, however autonomous, was still in his domain and these were consultants to it. What was this "appropriate technology" anyway! (The term had hardly yet been coined.) How dare these foreigners propose that independent India use anything but the latest technology! "Second best? Technologies that they, in the rich West, have discarded! Maybe even second-hand machines—throw-aways? Good enough for *us*?!" But the opposition the Commissioner minded most (a notation in my diary records Joe telling about it) was the Khadi Commission's. Prominent Gandhians seized the opportunity the monograph offered to urge once again that mechanized power be kept out of development altogether, and certainly away from India's villages. Small industry development and getting it funded were quite difficult enough without additional trouble from the Khadi Commission and its allies.

For the Foundation from abroad, of course, any political infighting of this sort was quite the thing to stay away from. So, like Koko in Gilbert and Sullivan's *Mikado*, it admitted only to not having been there when Joe and I concocted all this trouble. The absence of any mention of the Foundation on or in the monograph surely proved it.

Idea, Enthusiasm, Escalation—And Exclusion

So this was the setting when Joe and I were ready to publish. As an idea, the venture had appeared first in my diary for January 13,1963. SIET was between programs; the next would start its second year. That morning I had returned from Delhi. When a program was on at SIET, my duties there were constantly pressing. A week away, at Erik Erikson's first seminar in India on psycho-social history, had been good for letting my thoughts range more widely.

Surely, surely, putting so much effort into servicing small entrepreneurs one by one could not possibly be the best way to achieve a rapid increase in employment. Even at best it could only amount to retailing, when nothing short of a wholesale effort had any chance of multiplying jobs into the many millions the country needed. The present strategy would not do. It had to be changed, drastically. At the seminar I had also met Udai, and he looked like the key person I had been seeking to give the extension faculty a proper start.

With these thoughts about development ringing in my mind, and my elation at Udai's possible coming to SIET freeing me for fresh things, I clocked in with Joe. How would it be if I wrote up some ideas that were forming in my head about the strategy for what we were trying to do here at SIET: overall strategy?

I had read Everett Hagen's (1963) book on economic development on the plane, and that could give us a neat handle on where to look for new entrepreneurs: not among the poor, but among the recently dispossessed—those who had lived at higher standards but had lost them for some reason and aspired to regain them. Hindu refugees from Pakistan were obvious candidates. Resettled in many parts of India but owning no lands here, they had to regain their accustomed standards in other ways. Industry! In India's own landowning families too, many second or third sons were looking for fresh things to do and could become entrepreneurs.

That set Joe off. Joe was ever ready to top an idea: *they* (these second and third sons, and the refugees too) would enhance their entrepreneurial capacities and inclinations marvellously if they did some work with "Achievement Motivation". David McClelland at Harvard had formalized that quite recently. He had also developed training and research programs for it. The thing to do was to get McClelland to come and set up a program here at SIET.

Joe, himself entrepreneurial through and through, also had special interest in new, low-cost technologies. Here was another piece for the equation we were looking for. (By this time it was clearly "we" who would do the writing, together.) Trained in both engineering and economics, Joe had wide experience with industrialization from the grassroots up—the technologies of it as well as the economics. He had been in China with the United Nations Relief and Rehabilitation Agency's (UNRRA) post-war relief operations. He stayed fascinated with all local enterprises, however weird and improbable, if only they promised employment and earnings for even one—the owner—and perhaps his son too, and, still better, three, five, even 10 people more. Over the years he had collected hundreds of slides detailing technologies of all sorts and people working them, and kept on adding to his collection on every field trip we took. I can see him now: tall, slightly stooped as he walked and talked, slow-speaking, emphatic, earnest, insistent, relentless, rather like a general disposing troops to their stations, his manner conveying that he would carry the day, no question.

That morning of my return from Delhi and as he heard the suggestion that we write something together that had this broader view and cut through all the detail, he offered to get going right away with his part. He would begin with something on the economics of it all, which, God knows, ranged from disquieting to hopeless on the current bases. And, of course, linked closely to the economics, something on the technologies that would "add up" in India: minimum capital per workplace, i.e., the opposite of Western, labor-saving technologies; only that way could enough workplaces be created. Fritz Schumacher too should come to India and start up the work on appropriate technologies that Joe had wanted from the very beginning. SIET was the right place for that. We could organize a conference for him here; doing it jointly with India's Planning Commission would be best.

Right through that spring, as we exchanged and discussed drafts, and coalesced and shaped them into the monograph, our enthusiasm with it escalated with just about every step. And as opposition to the idea of going public with it also crystallized in the course of our checking here and there, our work on this one item (out of the many that Joe and I were working on at SIET at the same time) took on a conspiratorial flavor. Yes, we would ask (faculty colleague) Das to design and "look after" the cover design and printing, but better not tell much about the controversies around the contents and risk getting him too into hot water. No, there would be no safe way to acknowledge the various contributions by other Indian colleagues, of data and of ideas. If someone had to take on the world, it had better be just us.

That Joe let my name stand first on the controversial monograph should have alerted me to storms likely ahead, for in age, experience, prominence, and position Joe was well ahead of me and also normally disinclined to take second place. Yet, here was the monograph, *Industrialisation Beyond the Metropolis: A New Look at India*, with my name above Joe's on the light blue cover, strikingly laid out, the subtitle in red for emphasis. Nothing else on it: no imprint, not even a date.

Only inside was its appearance quite humble: text typed, mostly single-space on both sides, the two full-page graphs obviously hand-drawn. All of it was roneoed on duplicating paper of the most ordinary quality: off-white describes its color most charitably; it was porous enough to absorb enough ink for clear reading, that's all. Appropriate technology. For all I remember, it was run off by hand. Our bow to the Khadi Commission.

The Offending Monograph

Any humility stopped with appearances, as these extracts show:

The monograph has been written primarily for administrators willing to undertake experimentally a new approach to rural industrialisation.... We are concerned that present rural industrialisation programmes tend to *become* rather than to *stimulate* the economy, with the result that many individuals remain unmotivated to help themselves....

[Here follows a listing of our "concerns"]

— that in the highly desirable effort to help the lowest economic groups by direct action, resources are dissipated with no permanent gain to them or to the economy.

— the over-tendency to carry industrialisation to villages and the very small towns before an industrial base has been established in rural towns of 20,000 to 100,000 population.

— that present programmes tend either to encourage traditional technologies, which are not yielding a surplus for reinvestment, or to encourage quite modern technologies which, because of an overall lack of capital, cannot provide adequate employment.

— with the growing unemployment problem in rural areas and the frustration we find among officials and private individuals who are endeavouring to tackle this problem.[1]

— with the failure to realize fully the need for very high-level technical, managerial, and administrative skills among the individuals, private and public, who are to take the initiative for rural industrialisation....

— that enterprises in rural areas be made "management-intensive", as well as labour-intensive and capital saving, to reduce the requirements both for raw materials and machinery.

1. Recently we visited a district where an intensive industrialization campaign in 1959 was followed by an industrial estate and other major investments by state government agencies. The increase in employment through all these efforts was found to be not quite equal to the new labor force which was generated in this district during the four-day visit. In other rural areas, the annual emigration to a metropolis appeared to equal the net annual population increase.

We sense a growth of population in many areas similar to water building up behind a dam. When all employment opportunities have been exhausted, the population spills over the dam into the nearest metropolitan center. "Massive Rural Industrialization", a phrase used by the Planning Commission, properly describes the dam building required to check this population flow.

— that it is practical to increase significantly the "intensity" of management through specialised courses designed for enterprises in rural areas.

— to conserve management and to allow for its more intensive use, the number of workers in each unit can be increased well above the present average.

Among the policy changes required for realising the latent potential for development in rural India [are]:

— minimise grants and give priority to the supply of highly skilled and motivated individuals, to technical and managerial training and to the supply of certain key raw materials....

— "Specialisation": ask modern industrial enterprises to concentrate on products which only they can produce, to use "intermediate" technologies for manufacturing products for which high quality and the lowest possible price are not absolutely essential.

The most difficult policy change would be the reorientation of government officials towards an attitude that people by and large can be trusted and, if given encouragement and skills, will do far better on their own than spoon fed.

Roots in Recent District Studies

From studies carried out by faculty members and participants at SIET Institute in 14 districts (and two more at a three-week Seminar of Senior State Officers from eight States in November/December, 1962)...agreement at the Seminar was very close [and] one general conclusion stands out: attempts so far to promote rapid industrialisation outside the major urban areas are not merely inadequate in execution but seem to leave out of account some major determinants in the process. Indeed, many times they hinder the very object they are meant to promote. Specifically:

(a) Government finance has not stimulated the productive investment of private funds in rural areas to anything like the amounts expected and available. The most favourable ratio we have found has been Re.0.75 private funds for every Re.1/- from Government.

This ratio is impossible to sustain...the ratio has to become Rs.4/- private to Re.1/- from Government, or higher still. Studies show that this is quite possible...e.g., a 10 to 1 ratio in a rural area of Andhra Pradesh. ...officials' very eagerness to spend Government funds has driven underground any inclination [of] local people...to invest their own funds. In short, except perhaps in the large towns, industrial development is more and more a Government programme when it needs to be a people's programme.

(b) Present assistance is capital-intensive. It needs to be skill-intensive.

(c) Present governmental practices, whether official policy or not, favour distribution of...funds and other assistance to the largest number of possible receivers, e.g., technical advice is counted in number of units visited and people seen, not in terms of results. This is driving the quest for quantity too far,....

(d) Though stated policies clearly favour strong local organisations, present official practices in fact ignore and weaken them. [They] focus either on individual, unrelated applicants—an artisan, a potential entrepreneur or a small industrialist—or on the promotion of certain specific forms of co-operatives which have no roots in the life of the community, only rarely call forth adequate management and often lend themselves to abuse. Either way they cut across and damage existing forms of local organisation without, moreover, promoting any effective new organisations.

[All this adds up to] a far more serious and immediate charge than is the similar one often levied against the very establishment of factories and modern employment: that it destroys local community life and even personal freedom. The emigration of the ablest young people due to lack of satisfactory employment now maims many villages and any efforts at development. It is not factory work as such that destroys personal freedom or a community, least of all in the small town or large village where people still have their roots. As for the inherent nature of the work and its setting, most factory work is less monotonous than transplanting paddy and more social than most agricultural and artisans' occupations that are characteristically lonely. It is negligence of the relations between people that destroys freedom and the community, inside or outside a factory. Present practices do just that by failing to promote the social objectives that general policy emphasises. Instead, the focus of programmes for industrial development needs to be existing groups and groups which may form in the processes of social change: associations, partnerships, societies, people in relationship, in cooperation, not individuals in isolation.

Four Areas of Opportunity

[Attempts to deal with] officials' present problems and preoccupations...only lead to just the endless frustrating repetition of the problems that people talk about....

Four crucial areas for action are now generally clear...also some of the steps to be taken:

A. *Industrial development: A district responsibility.* In the total panorama of industrial development, the assistance available from the Government is actually quite small.... [All] officers engaged in industrial development in India might all be employed in one large-scale enterprise. The funds at their disposal during the Third Five-Year Plan would not build a major dam; they may amount to as little as Re.0.10 per villager....

The pervasive preoccupation of everybody with the Government's part [has] probably something to do with the ease with which personal responsibility and commitment to action can thereby be avoided...an escape also hallowed by tradition, including two centuries of colonial rule. But it has something to do also with some other very real facts: the Government can certainly mar, or greatly delay, new industrial activity...people may well give up, [even] in anticipation...the overemphasis on the Government's part tends to perpetuate itself: the local people hesitate, hold back or do not persevere; to the official this looks like the lack of interest and local initiative that he had been led to expect even before he came to the District. Little does he realize that he may be party to the process....

The officer's concept of his job and his superiors' evaluation of him—at present. Though the original intention may have been to the contrary, the District officer now sees himself as administering a governmental programme. This error is supported pretty consistently by tradition as well as by the signals he gets currently from the Directorate. For instance,...half or more of his total work time...places him in a position of having to judge between entrepreneurs, suspect them, and be open to persuasion from the more powerful ones. The reports he has to send to the Directorate concern themselves largely with the progress he has made on governmental programmes.... The last thing he wants are funds undisbursed at the end of the financial year. That would count against him.... Impressive in the officer's reports is large numbers...no matter to what use.

The evaluation, therefore, gets slanted heavily towards judging the officer's standard of orderliness...[It does] not even include the officer's working time and how he spent that.... The opposite, [giving it] importance, would be more appropriate.... For the working time of skilled officers may well be the most valuable asset that the Government can place at the disposal of the District.

...—*in future.* The best use the officer could make of his time and other governmental resources would be for stimulating and supporting the mobilisation and investment of key resources already in the District: of capital, technical and managerial skill, and local organisation.... We are suggesting [that] a second, new man be [also] made available: a District Consultant.

The district's part—in future. In future, the District would take responsibility for its plan of industrial development and for mobilising resources for it…. The first connection in which to exercise this responsibility is one readily to hand: to study the District's potentialities and resources and pull them together into estimates and models of development. The result we call a District's profile. Local people know their own and their neighbour's resources. If they do not, they can find them out better than any outsider. The Consultant (and perhaps outside specialists to whom the Consultant can be the channel) may well be needed to process the information about resources into a working profile of the District, and the District Consultant may draft the plan. But all papers will be subject to discussion and agreement in the District. This procedure itself tends to encourage local commitments to action.

B. *Moving high-grade technical skill into the district.* The problem is…how to find sufficiently competent people to live and work there, even just one [Consultant] per District. Rare qualifications are required for the work. The Consultant needs not only high technical qualifications, but also substantial work experience with modern technology. On top of these, the stamina, initiative and creativity of someone able to keep going without much day-to-day external support are essential….

There may well be Districts for which no such consultant can be found from outside or where no outside consultant will stay for a sufficiently long period. Local technicians may have to be involved to an extraordinary extent, perhaps offered special opportunities for advanced training and then be requested to function as part-time consultants with Government backing and official funds. There may be no precedent for allowing suitably qualified and experienced people to be on the Government rolls and also continue running their private enterprises, but this may be the only way of drawing in for wider service…entrepreneurs and technicians whose personal interests already keep them in the District.

Already far more technical skill exists in many Districts than is used for spreading and accelerating industrial development…. One of the first tasks of the Consultant may be to locate and contact [them]…and help them organise themselves into some kind of panel of technical advisors to whom he can refer….

C. *From district profile to district plan.* The profile differs in two essential respects from the kinds of surveys now carried out. Firstly, it includes as major items estimates of four key resources: the amount and location of local finance and entrepreneurs and local groupings which may play an important part in accelerated industrial development. Secondly, the profile is more than a list of resources. They have to be weighed, given priority, related one to another in a frame of time, perhaps worked out in a series of models based on different sets of assumptions. Even where the profile can be no more than a sketch, it has to be that, not a set of unrelated points and lines.

The district plan…is essentially a projection of the profile into the future, describing what the District would look like one year, five years, fifteen years from now. Several models are possible, embodying different values and aspirations, but all using the same data. It is for the District planning machinery to decide between them [and] to go ahead.…

Both the profile and the plan will deal with the whole District from the beginning, not with a series of requests from different Blocks, because the District seems now to be the proper unit for industrialisation.

D. *Industrial development through local organisations.* Construction of the profile and the plan will engage formal associations and informal groups of people which already exist in the District and are interested in [promoting] industrial development or likely to be affected by it. New groupings may form during the process itself.… It is not only convenient for the Consultant and the District Officer to work on problems with a local organisation rather than with numerous individuals, it is of primary importance that they do so. For the individual potential entrepreneurs and industrialists belonging to such groups will not go grossly counter to the standards and ways of working acceptable to others in his immediate circle of family, friends and associates and…in the District generally.

To many officers, "group" and "association" denote primarily "factions" and "power groups". At all costs he will avoid them and the danger of getting sucked into local community and political divisions.… The present reluctance to get involved may explain best the great distance that seems to lie between most officers and people in the Districts we have studied. And this distance in turn keeps the officer back in his office; a vicious circle.

On no account must the Consultant allow such distance and misunderstanding to develop.

[The monograph identifies four areas of "Questions calling for Answers", but by "action research (which) can proceed alongside development. No further study is required to launch the strategy." Then comes the most controversial section.]

Choice of technologies. The great weakness of [village] technologies is that they usually do not produce a surplus for reinvestment

and additional employment, and therefore no "take-off-point". After an initial spurt, employment hits a plateau and stays there. India's population increase makes this pattern an utter disaster, not
only economically but socially and politically. At the other end of
the scale are the advocates of highly productive factories for rural
areas, at costs starting at about Rs. 5000 per worker.... In the long
term this approach offers good prospects [but] immediately it
would leave unemployment of such staggering dimensions that
some kind of violence is likely to disrupt everything....

The action area, certainly the area for urgent research, is...the
area between Rs. 500 and Rs. 5000 capital per worker [and estab-
lishing] break-even points for different kinds of manufacture....
There are many isolated examples in actual operation, only the results are either unknown or their implications not worked out for
general use.

In a small town the manufacturer of truck drive shafts, tired of
waiting for a Rs. 35,000 forging hammer from Germany...invested
Rs. 200 in locally available capital equipment and started producing the shafts by hand. The shafts are higher in price but of acceptable quality. Above all, they get made and are a straight gain to the
economy.... A second proprietor is using hand looms to manufacture wire screen....

Managers who have reacted to the equipment shortage by em-
ploying less-than-modern technologies are quite numerous.... For
instance, a modern piece of equipment, used multi-shift, is sur-
rounded with more simple, locally fabricated machines. By careful
planning...a high output to capital ratio is obtained.... There is
room for a large number of quantitative studies and some imaginative simple operational experiments.

Industrial organisation. [The kinds of] enterprise [to] encourage...would combine a minimum of the two scarcest resources,
capital and skilled management, with the maximum of the largest
resource, unskilled workers. By this standard, several forms of organisations which are now encouraged do not in fact fare well....

...to conserve managerial talent and capital...suggests larger initial units than are common at present, e.g., of 20 workers or more,
preferably on two shifts. [Also] associations operating common fa-
cility services, e.g., tool rooms or foundries....

An Action Program—Some Guidelines
Many implications of this approach...will only become clear as industrialisation gets under way [on these lines] and experience begins to act as a guide....

In the District, [with] involving key people and organisations in the construction of the full District profile...many of the present industries officers can make a start as soon as they have had special training.... The second step, that of securing the services of a Consultant would ideally follow hard on the heels of the first. The third step will consist of the local people, the District Consultant and outside technical specialists co-operating on [making] the industrial development plan.

A continuing flexible process. Current developments in the District need not come to a stop.... Existing governmental schemes, too, will carry on, though those still in the planning stage had better be delayed [to] fit well into the new context.

The Prospect and the Price

The difficulties we anticipate with this "New Look" loom very great, but the prospect of accelerated industrialisation in the Districts overshadows the difficulties. Overcoming them is the price that will have to be paid.

The first obstacle will not be lack of agreement with the premises and direction of this paper, controversial as they may appear at first reading. Rather the opposite: agreement will come too easily.... Self-government, democracy, Panchayati Raj, all spring from the identical premises...as this paper. But the plans have not worked out that way. [The] coin has been tossed many times, and with increasing regularity it has come to fall truth down, perversion up. [It is] as if we did not really mean the philosophy we feel and proclaim.... That is the biggest problem.

"After the Ball was Over"—A Sober Assessment

In terms of seizing one of life's moments for making a difference, was our headstrong decision to publish the *New Look* that April a *good* moment to seize? Even if it helped nudge industrial development and employment creation toward a better course, even then, there would still be the question of whether the decision was reasonable, all in all, given the risks. Or: in similar circumstances should we do it again? If yes, there is then also the question of whether we could have reduced the risks by managing it all better.

In being entirely our decision, this moment presented fate's face of opportunity, not that other, imperious face when it simply

takes over and takes a life in hand—of which my forced migration as a child had been one example, war and war work a second, and, on the benevolent side, the quite unplanned ways
work has *always* "turned up" when I needed it, and ,a string of
others. Each of those times I had nothing to do with the moment
or its momentum or how it was done. The moment simply seized
me—a God-send, sacred. The go—no-go decision about publishing the *New Look* was different to the core: it was a moment *we*
seized. And with that willful choice we also put ourselves to test,
ours and others, and to possibly learning better for another time.

Results "In the World"

On the plus side of the balance sheet came some large successes,
large by even the most exacting standards. They were of two
kinds.

One, the quieter one, was confirmation that our mapping of industrialization as it was going on and of the opportunities for significant moves ahead was broadly correct. On a canvas so huge
and with a multitude of intrinsically complex elements to document, that was itself no mean achievement. Major developments
in policy and practice have confirmed it.[2] What the *New Look*
contributed to actual take-offs in this or that subsequent development is beyond me to assess.

Except in one case—the finding and training of new entrepreneurs. There the connection is quite direct. Within mere weeks
of publication, not only had the tentative offering of a first, experimental program for district development officers been firmly
established as a second line of programing at   SIET, but Joe had
also succeeded in including achievement motivation in it for major research and entrepreneurial training. David McClelland came
to start that work in India with us and returned from time to time
in later years. Two of his colleagues at Harvard came to work

2. In India itself, the determination of several states to build planning and implementation capacities in their districts and the creation of novel financing
   mechanisms for leveraging non-farm employment are examples. Our numbers were too small: the aim now is to create 50 million jobs beyond the metropolis alone when 30 years ago we pushed so hard to make the case for
   5 million by the end of the current five-year plan. Also, the trends we wrote
   about, both pro and con, have come to be recognizably true across the globe,
   for developing and also for industrialized countries.

with SIET long term; David Winter did his dissertation there and went on to make it into a book co-authored with McClelland (McClelland and Winter 1969). Its preface consists largely of long extracts from the *New Look*.

More striking still has been the spread of this seed to all regions of India. Manohar Nadkarni, then in SIET's Development Department, nurtured it right from the start. Udai Pareek, my closest colleague in Extension, joined him in it; he became the mainstay of the research side of achievement motivation work in India, adding it to the lead he had already given for two decades to applied behavioral sciences in general. Nadkarni followed through with, first, a year with McClelland at Harvard, then, upon his return, starting off what has become a set of six national institutes for entrepreneurial development.

To the development of "intermediate technologies", which had threatened to set off the greatest uproar, publication may also have made a quite tangible contribution. Fritz Schumacher too came to SIET and the conference with the Planning Commission did take place there. The commission set up a permanent cell for supporting work on low-cost technologies in several major research institutes as well as in voluntary and public organizations, and it spread.[3]

Wisdom prevailed against developing the technologies themselves at SIET. SIET's particular genius would be to bring the several streams of work together into a second line of programing for "area development". By the summer, a department had been created with that name, with Chebbi, SIET's most senior faculty member, in charge. Several others moved over to it, and new faculty were added. Harry Wolfe became the consultant there, and later George McRobie, Schumacher's close colleague (and later successor) at the Intermediate Technology Group in London.

The Seamy Side: Splintered Institutional Development
The doubts then—the risks to review—focus much nearer, namely, on the development of SIET itself. And it is here that for

3. That there was nothing in the monograph about environmental safeguards is a reminder that these concerns surfaced strongly only a decade later. Nor did it stress the heartening implications of keeping economic enterprises anchored locally; only now are the social and public costs of making employment and livelihoods increasingly footloose, to shift about globally for quick gain, revealing themselves as quite horrendous.

the first, but not the last, time it is essential to re-enter the flow of events and the context they had created for the moment of choice when it came.

Even before our writing the *New Look*, the Institute had pulled away from its Ministry sponsor and primary client. Our decision to ignore the opposition of high officials in the Ministry, step outside our role as consultants and go public with it in our professional capacity, was then one more step in the distancing already well under way.

In my doctoral dissertation seven years later I used orchestral imagery for this distancing. "Separation: The New Generation" was the opening theme, and "Solo: The Institute Off on its Own" its confirmation. Publishing the *New Look* belongs here, and is followed by the ministry-parent fighting back: "Point Counterpoint—A Confrontation". This builds up to the "Crescendo: A Mighty Embrace", after which all goes quiet with "Lullaby: The Good Neighbors". Shades of Brahms, but the Institute was then past new-born innocence.

Here is the theme (Lynton 1970, pp 71–78):

Pandi's taking over as Principal Director was the latest in a long string of milestones which marked the separation of the Institute from its sponsor, and a large one.... The original set up was simple: the Institute was the staff college for the small industry services of the Government, both to expand and to improve them. This blueprint therefore had it wholly within the existing governmental service organization.

Phase two came almost unnoticed. Two months after starting operations, the Institute was incorporated as an independent autonomous society. This was administratively convenient and a quite common form for new institutions receiving Foundation grants....

The six months following incorporation, however, revealed sharp differences between the Institute and its original sponsor. One arose over attempts to expand the Institute's interests and clientele beyond those of the service organization. Formal provision for this was included in the original working papers which enjoyed active approval at the highest levels of Government. But in practice the issue was joined only with the *New Look*. In the absence of a publications policy, the chairman of the Board [and the director of the sponsoring organization] pronounced against issuing the monograph as an Institute publication. Privately issued, it still provoked both interest and anger. That interest speeded the addition of State officers as a new regular clientele, and they were beyond the sponsor's direct control.

...this addition [then] set off new research interests and contacts of which one developed into a major project and a third program of courses [for Entrepreneurial Motivation]. Next, the Institute began to solicit applicants from private industry for the courses originally confined to Union Government officers. [This] precipitated the issue of participant fees [and these brought SIET] additional income, independence and outside support.

Country-wide shortages of qualified personnel accentuated the differences between Institute and sponsor. *Both* were trying to expand. For the Institute's original faculty members, all officers on deputation, attractive positions opened in the service organization in line with their seniority. When they left,...the Institute looked for replacements and additions in private industry and other organizations. This made sense [for] continuity of service and stability in the faculty and also avoided competing with the service organization for the same scarce people. But inevitably this move also led to increases in salary scales and other conditions of service to the disadvantage and envy of the service organization.... Pandi's own recruitment for principal [from private industry] topped this change, and negotiations concerning his salary and conditions reverberated in the top levels of the Ministry and beyond.

Figure 5.1 shows this step-by-step structural distancing between the Institute and its sponsor.

In itself, this structural distancing of the Institute from its original sponsor acknowledged their different objectives, needs and preoccupations. SIET's task was...helping participants emerge from training so changed that...they would create improvement in the service organization, e.g., collegiate relationships irrespective of hierarchy, open expression of feelings, and new attitudes to authority,...[and] consulting in teams.... In many cases, they did just that. At the Institute these onward effects were rated as successes and...stimulated faculty and consultants to intensify this kind of effectiveness.

Self-appointed critic to the Ministry. This circular dynamics, involving participants, the Institute and the sponsoring organization, had two further effects on Institute faculty and consultants. One was to assume the position of general critic to the sponsor and others and to offer *them* consultation. The *New Look* took off from this assumption.... In similar vein, only more sharply focused on the sponsor, came a second report six months later.

This second report was the Institute's response to a request from the Institute's Board Chairman to share with the most senior

Phase 1: Institute as
staff college

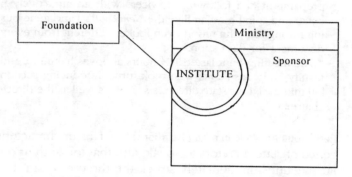

Phase 2: Institute as
autonomous society

Phase 3: Institute with
some independent income,
clientele, professional
contacts and staff

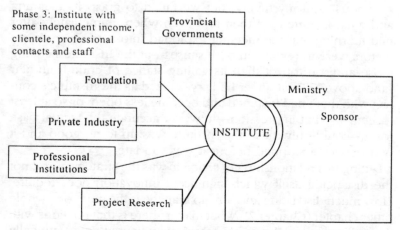

FIGURE 5.1 SIET's Structural Distancing from Essential Supporters

officers what it had learned during the first year's operations. It was presented at the half-yearly meeting of the directors of the State branches [which, this time, was located at SIET itself—*sic!*]. Though in language collaborative, and in places even deferential, 25 of its 30 pages set out the main issues currently obstructing the *sponsor's* operations and blueprinted directions for coping with them, including estimates of cost. As the introduction indicated, these were extrapolations from getting "to know well" the 60 officers who had so far participated in the Institute's 12-week residential programmes and the Institute's own growing understanding of "the tasks they face and the personal and organizational resources they have." The last five pages then worked back to how the proposed changes in the sponsor's operations could be supported by the Institute, through, e.g., selection and placement strategies, pre-training preparation and follow-up services. With an attractively printed cover and spiral binding [like the *New Look's!*] and generous spacing throughout, the report even looked different from every other document for discussion.

The meeting on it lasted 1 ½ hours and was halting. Besides the faculty and consultants who took turns introducing sections of it [40 minutes], four state directors spoke, as well as the director and chairman.

Pernicious Anaemia in a Key Relationship: This uncharacteristic reticence of state directors to speak, and that too at their own regular meetings, immediately struck the three of us in the lead as "ominous" and mystifying, but we failed to grasp its meaning and what it portended then and even when, immediately after mid-morning tea, the meeting exploded into acrimony: the directors were in revolt—in both senses—at the Institute's cutting loose and, on top of that, its galling stance of critic from afar (and above?). Their anger had crystallized as the Institute's contact with them had lessened and become less open, or so at least it seemed. That impression—however accurate the factual base for it—could only mean the Institute was up to no good and it had better be stopped before it was too late.

Letting this relationship get anaemic was the strategic error, not the distancing itself which significant innovation does require. How much distancing and how to manage is the core for a whole other chapter (Chapter 7). What matters here is that relations with these directors and the parent organization figured only marginally

on the busy agenda of the Institute even when SIET's radical innovations required their great strengthening.

"...Moment to Moment Clings; the Things Thus Grow Until We Know and Name Them" [4]

Having run the story six months beyond the decisive moment in
order to show how it unfolded, I now also want to go about that
far back of it and with that also to discard the language of
decision-making for understanding what really went on there.
For all along and without checking with each other Joe and I
never doubted we would publish if we came up with something
we thought worth publishing. Focusing on *the* moment is like
looking at a snapshot: true but without explaining anything. In
this instance, the very notion of decision would mislead: so thoroughly was forging ahead with what we wanted to do enmeshed
in the "flow of things" Lucretius reminds us of, that the "flow"
simply swept the moment along. Come hell or high water, to
publish did not take even a moment to decide.

Listening to Joe and me talking can quickly convey the flavor
of that flow. Here are a couple of extracts from conversations
while the *New Look* was taking shape.

Joe (just back from Delhi): I had the strongest instruction ever
from C [prominent member of the Institute's Board] that he
wants us to have nothing to do with Gandhian members of
the Planning Commission.

I: Will you accept this? It seems to me that our more important
job is in the Districts. If necessary, surely,...go to the Minister
or the Planning Commission directly, and force it?

Joe: Yes, sure.

I: This emphasizes again that we need a governing board of
greater weight.

(January 15, 1963)

4. A paraphrase from Lucretius (96–55 B.C.). His version:
...all things flow.
Fragment to fragment clings; the things thus grow
Until we know and name them...
and are no more the things we know.

Quoted in Curtis, Charles P. and Ferris, Greenslet, *The Practical Cogitator*,
Houghton Mifflin Co., Boston, 1945, p. 531.

Joe talks enthusiastically of his District work and choosing [means identifying?] three managers from four Districts as possible district consultants. S. *had* brought it up at the Planning Commission meeting [with Joe's prompting?] and C. had had to agree to look at it [according to an Indian colleague's report who was there].

(January 23, 1963)

Joe [ringing at 8 p.m.]: C. has bought the whole program! "Why [start with] only four Districts? and why two Ceylonese only, why not ten?" So our holiday is over! C. did suggest we consult with State Governments first.

We joke a few exchanges.

I: It sounds as if he abdicated control.

Joe: Yes, that's just it. We can do what we like now.

I: That's a fine position to be in, to have so much freedom. Now we have to be wise.

(February 12, 1963)

Neither in tone nor in content and direction do these conversations stand out in my diary. Joe and I talked possessively about all kinds of ideas and intentions we each had. We stimulated each other. Again and again Joe topped my latest excitement and I topped his. Like teenagers trumping each other's far out hopes. Fun. But wise?

Focusing on the *New Look*, on March 6 Joe "proposes, then insists, that I be first author, he second. I did not press him, suggest an Indian faculty colleague for the third. 'No, we'll take care of him in the preface.' We kitefly a plan by which our paper would start off a controversy in which very high people from the USA would also get engaged.... I propose [the Foundation representative] as third member. Joe welcomes the suggestion, is evidently excited by it all."

In the three months of drafting to going public—550 pages of diary—there is just one mention of a possible qualm on my part about possible repercussions on relationships, and that was about my immediate relationships in the Institute. Not a word about my role as consultant to the Institute and what *it* might require, or the Institute and *its* essential relationship. And the one personal qualm I kept to myself, "wondering". What figures in the records instead is Joe's and my escalating excitement as authors, with what all the *New Look* might mean and what all it might touch off by way of desirable further developments.

And—of all things!—the promise it held of making the Institute more independent still of the Ministry and of Delhi generally, that figured largest and most often. By which we most surely meant being free to do what *we* wanted to do—Joe and I certainly, and the consultant team by implication.

Preparations for Meeting the Moment

The likely effects of our decision on the development of SIET should have been a major consideration, but was not. Safeguarding, even strengthening, the Institute's relationship with its sponsors and funders became even more important as we cast the Institute as a major national resource for making radical shifts in strategy, policies, and practices. We simply missed these dimensions, they were absent from our thinking: my exhaustive diary has not a word about the risks to SIET. Yet, developing the institution was our primary task at SIET; for that we had been placed there (along with the other consultants), and in that the relationships Joe and I were endangering yet further by our contrariness had to continue to play an essential part. It was not that we tried to assess the risks and decided, all in all, to take them. They simply did not figure in our planning before or accounting later. We did no planning for any of it and this, now, is the first accounting.

My understanding now of fateful moments for choice is that they touch only actors who are prepared to go either way, even against the flow. The unready are in no condition anyway even to notice that moment as it flashes by. The readiness that matters here is *prepared* readiness, however deliberately or intuitively arrived at. There *is* no chance, just as in Jungian perspectives nothing is accident.

As I scan for indications of what proper preparation for such moments might consist of, I come up with four rather different kinds, all important.

"Utter familiarity" with the scene is the first: with the setting, the craft, and also with oneself as practitioner of it. This is familiarity as Hippocrates uses the term for the first condition for good medical practice: utter familiarity with people, signs, and things in the sick room.

Second, a "sense of direction" seems also important: to know where to look for a strategic opening to occur. This is not a precise "where", for an exact point could only have been extrapolated from some constellation known from the past, thus blocking out anything radically new. For this purpose then, "direction" means over there rather than over here, the quarter on the horizon ahead which is the most likely to open up for a leap I want and am ready to make.

It is particularly on this dimension that the story recounted here, specifically going public with the New Look, shows unpreparedness, an unreadiness to look again at what had become routine. That this flow had built such pre-emptive strength in one direction in less than a year of the Institute's existence and our working together, I find awesome and sobering. I like to think that going public with the New Look was all in all beneficial. But I like to think too that I would now notice inclinations to slide into proprietary determinism and the narrowing vision that comes with it. Under similar conditions—yes, I could choose to go against the flow.

That requires "inner work", as Fritz Schumacher in his simplicity and other more explicitly spiritual guides advise: the constant need to clarify and to keep clear my part in my views and transactions, and to do that with enough precision and constancy to build understanding and avoid patches of fog.

There is, third, advantage, actuarily speaking, in having my practice over time be diverse in settings, tasks, and roles. That way many sides of me get exposed and stay most alive, also to fateful moments when they come, no matter from where and in what guise. So that I will notice. Practically that means having several small fires already started at any time and quietly sizzling along. Herb Shephard recommended consultants do this, so that one or another ember may catch a fresh breeze whenever and from whatever quarter it comes (Shephard 1985). That is the very opposite to having all eggs in one basket.

And the fourth line of preparation is to let one's inclination to playfulness have plenty of room in one's life. There must be the room as well as the disposition to allow rearranging time, effort, things "at the spur of the moment". So that one can seize it, lighthearted and lightfooted, the way David danced before the ark.

The last thing to do with rules of thumb like these is to make them rules in the usual strict sense; that would pervert them. No determined waiting for the moment, as if it were an opportunity to pounce. That readiness would be brittle, and the longer the watch, the stiffer the hunter would get and the more harshly determined. Seeing becomes staring, and staring shades into "seeing things", things that aren't really out there but spring more from narrowed anticipation. Patience that feeds on brittle determination stifles playfulness, and prompts "taking the chance" at a wrong moment.

Rather, risk letting a moment sweep by which would have been worth seizing after all. That makes what is a virtual rule in therapeutic encounters into a good enough rule of thumb too for larger settings: an issue that was important enough to surface will come by again if still unresolved. Only registering the fact of missing it is worth doing as well as doing some inner work with that fact.

And finally playfulness, so as to be ready to jump into streams and eddies in the flow that carry promise beyond any intent or responsibility, i.e., learn to go with serendipity.

SIET's emergence as a rich seedbed for applied social scientists all over India now is a good example. Neither as function nor as outcome was this projected in any prospectus or mentioned in any report. Yet, half the first generation of applied social scientists in India grew at SIET, and grew to enough strength to take the lead in the whole field. The Indian Association for Applied Behavioural Science now has over 80 professional members and sound procedures, and a functioning regional organization for developing more; and several sister associations have also developed to like purpose.

References

Hagen, Everett, *On the Theory of Social Change: How Economic Growth Begins*, The Dorsey Press, Homewood, Ill., 1963.

Lynton, Rolf P., "Institution-Building and Consulting: Complexities in Development Assistance", PH.D. dissertation, State University of New York, Buffalo, 1970.

McClelland, David and **Winter, David**, *Motivating Economic Achievement*, Free Press, New York, 1969.

Mumford, Lewis, *My Life and Work*, Harcourt, Brace and Javanovich, New York, 1979.

Shephard, Herbert A., "Rules of Thumb for Change Agents", in *OD Practitioner*, Vol. 17, No. 4, pp 1–4, 1985.

6

SEEING SYSTEMS—AT LAST

*...like giants we are always hurling experiences ahead of us
to pave the future with
against the day when we may want to strike a line of purpose
across it for somewhere.*

Robert Frost 1964, p. ii

Here now comes the watershed of my professional journey;
so also in this book. This far, immediate relationships and
hands-on practice with persons face-to-face (or thought about as
if they were) occupied center stage. From here onwards, the cutting edge of my interest—recording, study, and writing—shifted
to developing institutions and larger social systems, and this was
increasingly true also of my practice.

Two questions immediately intrude. Aloka and SIET were institutions, and docks, coalmines, and districts in India were larger

systems still, so if that work required a different perspective, what took me so long to see it? And, second question, why now, and how? Both are worth pursuing because of the enormous difference that change made in my seeing and thinking, and so also in what I did.

The first hint of it came nine months into the work at SIET. My record for September 11, 1962 ends on a note of weariness—no particular provocation, just an overall feeling that things are not making good sense and I don't understand why. Nine months later—what could be a more proper span for a rebirth—is the last note showing any doubt about the rightness of taking a new position and putting the radically fresh perspective it offered to use. Seven hundred and thirty-five typed pages of diary (out of 4,300 for the five years I worked with SIET) cover those months of toing and froing and my attempts to shift my focus and my colleagues' as well. When I then took over as team leader that summer, I worked with them quite directly on helping build SIET into an institution and on modeling institution-building in the ways *we* worked ourselves, as a team and with the principal director and faculty colleagues. Perhaps together, with our sights raised to that same purpose, we could build the institution intentionally, step-by-necessary-step.

Even though SIET was only beginning its second year, the essential unlearning and undoing of working habits that harmed this larger purpose proved already very difficult. The experiences consultants had come with, and then the faculty too, biased them heavily toward individual working and gaining competitive advantage; so these had also come to dominate the Institute in that first year. Nowhere, not at the Institute or its clients or the board, was goodwill lacking; only old habits did not match the brave aspirations for it. Even after I sensed the mismatch, certainly by that first September, I did not see it clearly enough to act otherwise with reasonable consistency. And even for this erratic little I seemed to be on my own. The world over, institution-building efforts continue to fail on this same score: inability to walk the talk, certainly to walk it steadily enough and together.

SIET and my work there looked *very* different when my perspective on it changed, like seeing a long familiar face truly for the first time. SIET's development as an institution, sound and permanent for its task in its particular place and time—*that* was our core task as consultants (not starting up programs and myriad activities). Until the consultant team made that perspective govern its priorities and efforts of persuasion and modeling, we condemned ourselves to, well, mere pottering. This pottering yielded some fruits, but erratically so, and of those so many were then spoiled in delays, confusions, and back-biting that only months into the effort we were already coming to regard high wastage as normal. With my fresh perspective on system development, it now looked at least worth testing whether much of the waste was caused by faulty development strategy, policies, structures and priorities, and that repairing those faults and filling these gaps should have the highest priority. Traditional ways were fast eroding SIET's mandate to pioneer significant improvements, and we consultants, proud gung-ho innovators as we were, were party to this perversion.

My own learning, on the spot, came piecemeal and early steps were erratic; how very much I was on my own will be part of this story and makes a cautionary tale itself. Quite possibly, time out at that juncture with suitably experienced colleagues could have helped complete the new vision and rehearse its implications sooner and more surely. This opportunity, and intellectual clarity and surefootedness in practice, would come only with the next institution-building enterprise I involved myself in three years later, so the patterns I will presently describe for my onward work at SIET are hindsight. Then, seeing the next institution threaten to impale itself on the very same dilemmas I had not foreseen at SIET and then exerting my best efforts to extract it from them in the remainder of my innings there, provoked me to rough out a schema for institution-building and put it to immediate use. No success there, but I then used that schema to analyze the record for the two years at SIET following my awakening.

Over the months that took, I also gained a very healthy respect for the great effort *any* first-time leap takes to get from one basic position to another, to the next stepping stone, created, in poet Frost's graphic metaphor, by hurling experience forward. Only a truly startling surprise of potentially fateful import is apparently enough to provoke it. When asked nowadays what I do professionally, I usually fib that I make trouble and I make courage. Identifying the ingredients for the sufficient provocation in my case, and mapping how they mixed together at SIET, should

máke courage. So this is what this chapter is after: courage to be
quietly attentive to what's coming in the first place, and then also
to leap resolutely when it comes.

Developing New Institutions:
Crises, Dilemmas, and Resolutions

Fall 1966. Here, barely four months since the Carolina Population
Center started actual working, it was already displaying the same
kinds of enthusiasms and hectic individual activities that I knew
so recently from SIET, and was also heading into the very same
major dangers. As there, prodigious effort unrelated to building
the Center as a whole bred little empires. The director and one
or two key people hurried between no end of meetings all concerned with expansion: recruiting more staff, securing funds for
yet more staff, persuading regular schools and departments in
the university to create academic positions that the Center would
fund, recruiting a creative and so also motley assortment of prospective newcomers, and finding additional space for them on
campus or, more and more, in the town. Many corners were cut
and arms twisted to make fast headway with these agenda,
within the university and also with funding agencies. The rest of
us tried to keep up with getting new proposals and revisions "in
on time" while also doing the research, training, and writing to
which the Center was already committed. The new and additional had priority, for expanding the Center depended on more
funds, always more, and for those our Center had to win out over
the half-dozen population centers in other US universities which
competed for the same funds from the same agencies quite as
eagerly as we did.

In this ceaseless scurrying, longer-term developmental dimensions got short shrift. Those ever-tempting funds, for instance,
were almost all for particular projects or for building specific ca-
pabilities committed to identified activities; they would therefore
run out, whereas most obligations the Center entered into with
faculties and departments ran on and so had to be "covered" with
more funds.

In the hothouse atmosphere that prevailed, even hazardous
discrepancies like this gave the main runners hardly a moment's

pause. Nor was there time for building coherence in staff and efforts, though there was much talk about how very important that
was. *Manana*, sorry, but not now. Day-long meetings in UNC's
handsome continuing education center over an hour's drive
away brought all of us together once a month. But those rare and
ever larger meetings invariably went in introducing newcomers
and bringing them on board, updating information, and voicing
the latest administrative difficulties and ideas about overcoming
them. And in reiterating how very important and also how very
difficult it all was.

Two general conditions in fact raised my anxiety even higher
than I had experienced at SIET. The "population problem" hit
disaster status on the world's development agenda in the mid-
1960s and newly commanded large funds to solve it; thus tempting the Center to expand urgently to no foreseeable limit and also
making it look possible. Yet, academic traditions and organization made rapid expansion particularly hazardous, and the un-
orthodoxies invoked to pursue it laid the upstart Center wide
open to withering attack. On current lines, the more the Center
"succeeded", the greater the risks it ran of splitting into many
pieces, and the long-established units of the university which
went along with this craziness as long as it was funded well
enough would do little to hold it together.

Self-destruction disguised as development—that, in system development terms, was how the Center's direction struck me that
fall: SIET's hazards multiplied. Ronnie remembers my coming
home evening after evening despondent: first with "not learning
anything", the main purpose of my sabbatical, since I had seen
it all before; then with whether and how to intervene, and with
what promise. A foreign non-academic newcomer on a one-year
appointment, I was hardly the best candidate for prophesying
doom and expect to be heard. But these patent disqualifications
also freed me: nothing much could happen to me and the family;
at worst we would bide out the year. I would at least point out
the dangers I saw ahead—some only just ahead—and all getting
worse. This much I owed myself. Further, it had been for my
institution-building experience that the director had asked I
choose Chapel Hill for my sabbatical and help him build the new
Center. So, here was my mandate.

That resolved, the paper took only two days to write and give the director for the next monthly staff meeting. On five pages it laid out, in a tabulated schema no less, the "crises, dilemmas and resolutions" institutions faced at the stage of development the Center had now reached (merely the second of five) in my estimation. It still had to establish its identity. That work had three parts: getting agreement among Center staff about what the Center was to be (and thereby also what was outside its interests); gaining acceptance for that identity outside too, with such modifications that it would receive continuing support; and, third, balancing and melding this mix of considerations into one plausible whole.

For good measure, I presented the whole five-stage schema (presented here as Table 6.1), adding that future stages would only matter for us if institutional development were indeed properly pursued, stage by stage. For that the Center's leadership was utterly responsible; it simply had to choose institution-building options over others if the Center was to make sound headway. The time for full growth was *after* the Center had established its identity, i.e., not yet. If it forged ahead with growth now, it would remain stuck in its current dilemmas and head into worse and worse storms.

The notion of stages and most terms I used I transposed from Erik Erikson's acclaimed work on the life cycle of individuals. "Cycle" I left aside, since institutions did not have to die, but otherwise his terms suited me very well. Not problems to be solved but dilemmas to be understood and resolved at a deeper level were the milestones also for developing institutions. The need for "moratoria" (the term Erikson used for times to step back from day-to-day pressures in order to discern the deeper level at which a current dilemma could be resolved) I made the main text to follow the schema in my staff paper, and I peppered it with a whole series of specific suggestions for guiding the Center's affairs from this October day on.[1]

---

1. Having through our good friends in Ahmedabad become personally acquainted with Erikson while he worked on his Gandhi biography, I wrote him about this transposition and what he might think of it. He replied simply that he had not thought about this possible use of his formulation.

TABLE 6.1

Crises in the Life of an Institution

Crisis	Characteristic Features	Dilemma	Resolution
1. *Birth*	A few individuals full of ideas and zest. Frenzied activity. Attention oriented outward—power points, sister institutions, customers.	When should the institution be born and how large? Planning for every contingency or have a crash program?	Strong continuing leadership.
2. *Identity* a) Seeking identity	Search for main focus or foci. Conflict and uncertainty. Internal competition for attention.	Perfection of one thing or value all comers?	Clearly explicit long-range objectives as a priority system for decision-making.
b) Seeking acceptance	Search for relationships with existing systems. Inter-organizational jealousies. Attention outward.	Stress likeness and conformity or stress novelty and differences?	Moratorium to establish standards, largely in isolation.
c) Seeking balance	One or two activities have made a quick start, now threaten to dwarf or belittle others. Jealousies within.	Curb fast starters or let them run loose?	Focus on lagging functions to encourage their momentum.

Stage		
3. *Growth*	Great demands for services, mostly short term. Temptation to take on too much load. Meeting demands increases demands.	Consolidate and develop slowly or expand in all promising directions?	Moratorium to re-examine objectives and priorities. Publicize long-range plans.
4. *Maturity*	Success revives inter-organizational jealousies, even threatens sponsors. Attacks on autonomy and independence.	Forego identity and submit or revolt and break away?	Develop interdependent relationships focused on tasks.
5. *Development*	Self-satisfaction. Temptation to rest on laurels. Reluctance to work out new ideas.	Fossilize or break up into progressive and conservative, young and old?	Check objectives against changing situation, rejuvenate institution, build in indices of relevance.

The paper did make the agenda for the November meeting, but the meeting never reached it. At the time to close, the director thanked me and regretted there was now no time. I don't recall feeling surprised or more than a tinge of disappointment. That *was* the flow then, par for the course, and I had done what I could. My mind was on completing *Training for Development* and I felt quite buoyed at having the schema fit well into that.[2] And when, that book finished, I turned to my SIET Institute data, I used it for re-examining the building of the three interlocking institutions involved and the consultants' particular contribution to their development.

Walking the Talk: Consultants Model—For Good or Ill

…just individuals, however talented and experienced, are worthless, or worse than that, unless they are organised and managed and directed towards goals.

Lilienthal 1969, p. 287

"…the right goals" would be a better finish to the direction Lilienthal points. On my new schema for institution development, SIET was still stuck at stage two, even when I left early in its sixth year: it had not given up its mission involving significant innovation—that was fine—but it still shirked negotiating that mission with its funders and clients. And the more it acted according to this mission ahead of negotiating it with the key stakeholders, the more it sowed anger and risked loosing support altogether. SIET, like many institutions born with high hopes the world over, settled for continued but undistinguished existence. So hanging on to innovation was important—only not enough. The next chapter, on building innovative institutions in particular, will focus on the "more" that would have been necessary.

So much is clear—from the outside. At issue in this chapter is, first, how this scenario, so clear and compellingly seen from the outside, was invisible or at most marginal to us at SIET, and, second, how vastly difficult it was to redirect the attention and energies

---

2. P. 354 in the first (1967) edition, it stayed in the chapter of "Training Institutions" in the second (1978).

of others to it when I had at last made it to the new stepping stone myself, in poet Frost's graphic image, though I saw SIET very endangered by then. For this, the appreciation in the last chapter of how a decision-making moment comes swept along and goes swiftly by in a general flow, all heading in the same direction, was just the first step.

SIET was, I now realize, in an advanced stage of "self-closure", the disease political scientist Karl Deutsch (1964) has identified as threatening autonomous systems of all kinds: they become a world unto themselves. And SIET had so virulent a case of it that it had caused blindness all round from its very conception.[3] When it was then born with three limbs essential for healthy institutional growth malformed or gravely retarded, again no one noticed. Its declared mission, grand on paper to justify funding and also to reserve the largest possible field for all imaginable endeavors in the future, drew no clear boundaries to clients and peer institutions; without collaborative mechanisms in the design for working out the differences that would inevitably arise, this put continuing life support at risk. Then its internal organization, merely a simplified copy of the service organisation's, did not reflect SIET's particular and very different mission.

Third, the consulting component, which could have been designed to offset these quite predictable birth defects, made them worse instead. Each of us was found and recruited individually, and then set work with Indian specialists in just our field and advise SIET's principal director on how best to strengthen the department for that field in the Institute. All three defects tended to divisiveness and competition, with the result that the risks of self-closure for the Institute as a whole were doubled with its parts also all set to become little worlds unto themselves. The principal director was then the only one left to counter this divisiveness inside and this self-closure of the Institute as a whole from the outside, and this from the very beginning.

Underlying this unfortunate start was the fact that one and the same person had been the key mover at all stages, and that institution-building was not in his line of vision. That person was

---

3. Jay Lorsch and Paul Lawrence (1978) call this the stage of "the primary idea" and the "conceptual seed" and it would have made a useful preamble to my schema for developing new institutions.

Joe, but going exclusively with any one person would have run a similar risk. First a member of the expert international team to shape the idea, then the one to stay on and walk it through the Ministry and the Foundation, he then also designed the consulting component, recruited the consultants into it, and became team leader. The risk of this so-attractive continuity (that it would imprison the Institute in that one person's vision) could have been offset by policies and structures incorporating a broader range of perspectives, but this was not done. All went his way, for SIET's birth and its first year. Joe's way was individual enterprise, independent working, and quite pragmatic pushing ahead fast with whoever and whatever piece was ready. Program activities would determine institution-building, its shaping, pacing, and support.

At the end of that year, one more opportunity came to remove SIET's blinders: SIET's first principal director resigned. Quite in line with SIET's history this far, Joe made finding the next principal his particular business. In Pandi he found a kindred spirit. He battled for his recruitment, the battling necessary because Pandi came from the private sector, commanded pay and benefits beyond the government's scale for principal, and was most assuredly an outsider. Joe won. And with Pandi's selection the distancing we traced in the last chapter between SIET and its intended supporters became a declaration of independence from them. Self-closure was confirmed.

Blind to all else in this in-grown culture, initiative and enterprise rated high; when consultants showed either, they were seen as good models. My diary is full of instances less public than going public with the *New Look* but no less blatantly going it alone. Consultants changed session plans and made field visits on their own. One committed "his" faculty to a new research project that kept them from faculty meetings. They routinely assigned sessions to faculty colleagues to teach and so opened themselves to accusations of favoritism and taking sides; or, rather than risk a session not going well or even going differently than they preferred, they stepped in and did it themselves. This they did again and again, and often at principal Pandi's urging. Participants usually welcomed consultants "taking over" and consultants warmed to the commendation: a closed but disabling cycle. Building the Institute's own capacity was sidelined again and again.

Consultants made contacts outside the Institute with the same individual ease and eagerness. In fact, two undertook working elsewhere when things were not going to their liking at SIET. One day, staff members from a sister institution showed up at a small factory to carry out research of their own while SIET participants were there on a consulting assignment; a consultant had invited them. When challenged, Max claimed this as "his" site, i.e., to manage as he willed. Arnold published his ideas about India, SIET and all kinds of matters till principal Pandi told him to concentrate on writing course materials. Consultants, when in Delhi, discussed SIET's affairs at will with officials in the Ministry and in the Foundation.

Between consultants, this individual working led to competitive striving, not least for the attentions of the principal director whom all were individually set to "advise". This formal provision, well-meant to support his leadership and institutional cohesion, had more the opposite effect in practice. Pandi, already inclined to micro-manage, now had consultants colluding instead of challenging it. Often in the middle between principal and staff, consultants got drawn into the escalating rivalries and divisiveness among staff and between departments. In buying into the star-pattern of relations from and to the principal director, consultants unwittingly supported long Indian traditions while they also professed wanting to change them.

Once again it may be necessary here to pause and remind the outsider struck—perhaps even appalled—by the weirdness of this tale and the patently obvious resolution for it, that to us in the middle of it all it was quite ordinary, every-day stuff. How readily one dysfunctional step pre-figured the next and the next is well illustrated by how one recently arrived colleague set about his work. He had quickly assessed SIET's institutional weaknesses and was busy protecting "his" department against them, and most especially from the direction and consulting in the management department which Pandi seemed especially to favor. "Pandi wants me to take administrative charge, like Max does [in management]. I think this is wrong. There *are* disagreements [in the department] about the program design and also difficulties between people. But I am not willing to take it over." Clearly and consistently he helped his immediate faculty colleagues collaborate and take charge of all its affairs. But for pursuing this utterly desirable way of consulting, he was sure the department had to keep all others out. Of course.

Ordinariness was indeed the essence of our well-established direction, as it is of any other, and it stopped us noticing. The programs we were helping develop were always more noteworthy, exciting, and satisfying than the static. That they were mostly successful contributed importantly to holding our attention so fast, so long.

Those of us who had our eye on the next step, of augmenting SIET's own capacity to run programs, found further satisfaction in SIET's policies and practices for faculty development, and they are indeed impressive even now. Only more farsighted practitioners would have marked that, in the absence of more cohesion institution-wide, successes in this or that department put it at odds with the rest. The very ordinariness of each step and the sense of achievement along the way masked the larger hazards to the overall pattern by forging ahead so blindly.

To complete the stage and scene in which I intervened presently from my new angle, it only remains to exemplify the extreme dangers in which this unmitigated blindness could and did land all. Two situations will suffice for this. The first was my wake-up call. The second, a half year later, was of Pandi publicly undercutting my early efforts as newly appointed team leader to act on what I newly saw.

The wake-up call came at the end of the first year. Other notes of unease about SIET's overall development had followed the first in September, but it took a virtual walk-out by the service directors as a body to ram home the point that we and they were worlds apart. We had prepared and gone into the meeting with them sure that they would be impressed with SIET's remarkably good progress. When they showed instead how very angry they were, and this in front of the chairman and the board, we might have taken the hint, signaled our eagerness to look again and with their help change direction.

We could not get past being flabbergasted, as incensed with them as they were with us. Here were "we", mostly just the usual three—principal Pandi, team leader Joe and I—with our report of SIET's progress and ideas for the future all worked out. Its yellow cover denoted a new series just for these directors, its modern type, sparse lay-out and spiral binding already a hallmark of all SIET publications, and distributed well in advance, as was already the established norm. It set out the three programs to date that these very directors had filled to capacity, the additional program just started in area development for state officers, and also the several major new projects and lines of development we envisaged ahead. On most of its 32 pages, and then conveniently also listed at the end so directors would find them easy to use, were also points SIET had surfaced in working with the 90 officers to date for improving the service organization and its management. And now "they", instead of welcoming all this, were in revolt, and most of all at SIET's forging ahead so successfully and even beyond its mandate.

The rest of the meeting passed pretty uneventfully. After lunch, the chairman spread balm and encouragement: SIET should carry on—after all, it was still quite new. Calm and civility resumed. But enlightenment passed us by. If any clarities emerged about how SIET might carry on more acceptably, we were in no condition to hear them. What we learned was to be more cautious with information to the directors in future and certainly to call no more meetings of all. None of us saw that battening down the hatches and preparing to submerge was the very opposite of what building SIET into a permanent institution required, or even just for government funding of SIET to continue.

That startling confrontation woke me up to how severely divided the Institute was inside and how consultants' initiatives and ready stepping into faculty roles were debilitating instead of building institutional strengths. From then on, my urging consultant colleagues to extract themselves from acting as intermediaries between Pandi and the faculty became quite consistent: they had to learn to deal directly with each other. Many contacts over the next months dealt with this—with consultants individually and together, with Pandi, with sub-groups of faculty and consultants. I reached out, backstopped, and encouraged—my influence personal. When I became team leader six months on, I clarified roles more insistently and also became more explicit about it. To Pandi I alerted that "I will put more stress…on the consultant team's joint responsibility for its working", and immediately took on some disciplinary issues Pandi had with two consultants. This interfered with Pandi's usual way of working and he fought it. So arose the second exemplary situation. Here was Pandi, who

had warmly backed my selection as team leader, so unhappy
with my working for institutional cohesion that he disputed my
right to attempt it at the first opportunity and in public. At the
opening session of the next program for government officers he
himself introduced the consultants like this:

> Pandi: I want to say just a word about Mr. Lynton. We have con-
> sultants in all major fields [each waves as he mentions name
> and field]. The Foundation finds it convenient, solely for ad-
> ministrative purposes, to have a team leader. This is by ro-
> tation. Mr.Lynton happens to be the leader for this calendar
> year. The consultants are all consultants to the principal and
> responsible in their subject fields.
> Mr. Lynton will speak next, on extension education.
> Well, extension had to wait for another time [the diary re-
> cords]. "Mostly for Pandi's benefit" I spoke instead about
> the team and introduced its members again by charac-
> terising them. Any discomforts I must have controlled well
> enough, for I got "laughter several times".
> "About all of us [I went on], like other consultants we do
> nothing that someone else can do. Happily the Institute
> staff is now able to do most things. So you may not see too
> much of us...."
> I sit down. Pandi looks at me. I signal I have finished.
> Quite likely this dressing down of me by Pandi was un-
> planned [the diary continues], a controlled expression of
> immediate annoyance at a whispered exchange with me
> just minutes before and, more, of his underlying disquiet:
> Pandi: Rolf. [I lean over.] Will you take about 10 minutes?
> I: Oh no! Three.
> P: I thought area development 10, management 10, and you
>   10. What are you going to do for 1½ hours?
>   We laugh.
> I: What are *you* going to do for 1½ hours?
> P: OK.

January 5, 1963

Saddling the Present with the Future

Only drastic, even dramatic, intervention had any chance to set
Pandi and the faculty on a better course. Of that I was sure. My pre-
dilection for dealing with personal and interpersonal issues had

to yield to some institute-wide purpose—a different wavelength. SIET's future was that. Obvious in retrospect as the step most likely to move Pandi towards creating the necessary cohesion in the Institute, at that time it came intuitively: I had to do *something* big enough.

I made consultants meetings weekly, "maybe less frequent later". At the first, after briefly referring to Pandi's disciplinary concerns as just one of the many things "I will share, that's all", I force-marched the consultants into planning as a team. I set two weeks for coming up "with the main lines" of the whole consulting function at SIET, with the two final days off-site in which I would ask our Foundation liaison to join. The "outline" from that we would give to Pandi. Most likely he would feel challenged to better it. Best would be if he involved the faculty in reworking it. I would make the pending recruitment of the two new consultants depend on his putting forward a good enough plan for all of SIET for the next three years.

With its patent reasonableness and the involvement of all essential members, each with his proper part, this planning galvanized the consultants. Outside, disbelief greeted the attempt at first, in the departments and of course from Pandi. But that paled as we persisted and went off for the two-day meeting off-campus accompanied by our Foundation liaison as foreseen, and pretty well ended when I put a one-page "outline" on Pandi's desk which also invited him to set priorities for planning the details next.

With team meetings and the many more meetings with consultants individually and in subsets, my consultant contacts as team leader doubled. Many meetings were for undoing the small empires consultants had helped build their departments into. All focused on development issues in programs, plans, capacity-building and organization, and on making our approaches to these more alike. Conflicts between consultants surfaced as we worked on these, and some of the angers got expressed. But immediate purpose limited this.

With this way of working, consultants drew closer and felt safer quite quickly. Within a month we were able to agree to ways in which just one of us could go and speak for us all in most faculty meetings Pandi called, and so signal our new togetherness as well as save precious time for the rest of us. Broad sharing of

information quickly became the norm. Here is an extract from
the next meeting of the team:

> Morris again begins.... I speak on the way the meeting with Pandi
> got fixed and the need he expressed to be protected from addi-
> tional burdens; and hence my preference for focusing the meeting
> [with him] as much as possible on things for him to take up in the
> Ministry. Arnold presses for the larger plan...everybody agrees...
> also with Arnold's suggestion that, if possible, P should leave some
> draft with X for discussion at the next Board meeting. When he also
> proposed P leave the statement he [Arnold] has prepared of the
> consultants's role, Max and I talk him out of it, though I feel sure
> he would have preferred an explicit statement of this as well.
>
> Max has one of those satisfying opportunities of reporting on the
> high-level meetings he attended,...at length from notes, which
> were interesting and thorough. He was commended by Morris in
> particular! Certainly this and several other items that came up in the
> discussion leave us all feeling much better informed,...also about
> what is developing by way of policy in management training in the
> Foundation. On matters where I have something to say, I do so in
> the same atmosphere of sharing.... I refer to the matter of confi-
> dence: that what we speak to each other here ought not to be read-
> ily spoken about outside....
>
> I am again the one who calls attention to the clock and to my
> need to get back. It is fully ten minutes later that we break up, but
> not before several of us have expressed the need to continue to
> meet....
>
> June 5, 1963

At first Pandi found my denials and redirection very trying. My
contacts with him doubled that quarter, to explain, to stand tight,
to propose alternative ways, to listen to his anxieties, to counsel
patience, and overall to maintain and if possible strengthen our
relationship. Occasionally I let a point go by or settled for dis-
agreeing and seeing what would happen.

His big shift began when in a month the team produced its "position report on the Institute and a projection of an overall picture
of its development for the next twelve months in relation to
which the consultants' contribution could be more clearly defined". He continued to complain, also directly to the Foundation,
about "the enormous pressure" the consultants caused him with
this and the "additional burden" it put on him "and the faculty".

But he also recognized the goodness of it. He countenanced and presently even encouraged a spate of departmental planning our initiative set the stage for.

> ...a multitude of interactions with Pandi that day—12 to be exact...many short, around specific papers. Several times I go down...he comes up...on the telephone...general impression that he was happier and more outgoing...I wonder to what extent P gets reassurance from seeing Max in my office and the greater peace he may also sense among the consultants...with specific issues he raises, I continue very clear and definite.
>
> June 7, 1963

From about then the Institute "developed more cohesion and strength [and] the efforts of most consultants fed directly into this". Eight indicators for this stood out in subsequent analysis (Lynton 1970, pp 436–45). Consultants "proposed no plans or action steps without their faculty colleagues". Consultants'

> contacts outside the Institute, travel proposals and explorations of new work and service opportunities...came to be measured against agreed plans and priorities...that summer Pandi rejected several travel proposals from Marvin, Morris and Mel on this ground. Before long I could advise consultants in advance that a proposal would not be accepted.

The management faculty, which had been very exclusive, began to invite consultants from other fields to their meetings when discussing matters with which they could help. I used my hold as team leader:

> I would only move on recruiting a new consultant when the faculty who wished to use him had worked out a detailed task description. With Pandi I took the further step of holding up departmental requests for consulting help, even when properly documented, until the fit into the Institute-wide consultant picture had become clear [for 24 months ahead minimum].

This aroused Pandi's resistance once more.

> ...then one day...in a reflective mood, he first acknowledged that "there was nothing to do" about my firm stand on this, and then went right ahead with drafting the very comprehensive

proposal...which until then he had declared to be premature, impossible and unnecessary.

What I had not counted on was the truly bizarre lengths to which weak consultants would go to protect their privileged, well-paid positions as the new processes also clarified and tightened personal responsibilities and accountability and made them more public. Several consultants began feuds, two refusing to be in the same room with a third because of his living style which upset them, they said. One put forward as his own work a manual for publication which he had wholly copied from one used widely in the States. One, perhaps two, slept with another's wife, and/or sold in town liquor they had been privileged to import as members of the team. Though I tried hard, none of this was enough to get a consultant or two fired; now I would probably put my team leadership on the line for that. But when, towards the end of the year, personal antagonisms had reached such a pitch that continuing the meetings of the whole team seemed pointless, the Foundation urged their resumption. To them we had become a team to sound purpose. Also to Pandi. True to his old form, Pandi's first reaction was to meet with the quarreling consultants individually and in pairs, and find me remiss as team leader in not doing this. I disagreed and resented his intrusion and this implication, as well as the time which Pandi always asked for afterwards to tell me all about it. The silver lining appeared when Pandi himself then scheduled "regular weekly meetings with the whole consultant team from now on...quite rigorous [and] formal".

Pandi's toing and froing over those months, the analysis concluded, illustrated well "the strains" all of us experienced as we each moved our

> primary loyalty from a relationships with a self-chosen one or two to a work team or Department, and from working from face-to-face to Institute-wide operations and planning.... The needs of the Institute had to crowd in on him most severely before he would forego his reliance on one [or] other person at a time. The consultants' planning effort...was probably of strategic importance to magnify and speed up this crowding and so force Pandi to attend to the large system [for which he was responsible].

As the Institute cohered more and became an organized client system, it could also hold the consultants to respond as one, as a team. "Like a consulting firm" became the analogy the Foundation then also used in reappointing me as team leader and stressing newly "the context of *institutional* development" (their italics).

So the needed direction got established alright; institutional development was "in". But it lacked intellectual clarity and so also consistent pursuit. The continuing weaknesses would have held any new institution back, even one that merely replicated already existing institutions on which it could model its development. But SIET had been created quite explicitly to pioneer in a new field and, though no doubt with the usual qualms, its founders and supporters expected it to find news ways for its work and quite particularly make sure it did *not* become like the general run of institutions in India then. So SIET, set on innovation, had no model. And that meant extra hazards along with special opportunity.

Teamwork for Good

Under those conditions, effective contributions by consultants had to coalesce into institutional modeling until the time the new Institute had grown strong enough to take over the lead. From then on consultants were best on call for specific help with this or that part of the orchestration that needed some extra assistance. On analyzing the experiences with SIET Institute later, I came up with some general pointers for consultants modeling the development of a new institution:

- The team, i.e., "the modeling institution", must work with resources and methods that are within realistic range of the new institution, otherwise it will be resented for its arrogance or merely ignored as irrelevant. When modeling is supported by third parties, e.g., government or a foundation, as at SIET, this complicates it.
- It must work through inter-personal issues in the team early on, such as divisive relationships, insufficient openness, and failure to confront conflict and most especially dependencies

and leadership issues that directly effect ongoing consulting by individual members with the new institution as well. This early investment may be high and difficult to persist with in the face of pressing other work, but it soon falls to maintenance levels and will clearly have been worth making. For, if inconsistencies in the team's working with the new institution are left unrepaired, that makes its modeling untrustworthy and damages or even ruins the effort.

- The team is likely to thrive with making institutional modeling its immediate and clear purpose, but will also tire with being constantly on stage, as it were. That indirect cost needs to be reflected in time and financial provisions.
- At crucial stages the new institution may lose hope of keeping up with the team and its modeling and fear that further modeling by the team would threaten the institution's own integrity. Unlike deliberate preplanned demonstration, institutional modeling has its own momentum and looses credibility if turned on and off at will. At those moments of distress, the team serves its purpose better if it makes some extra investment in helping the institution over the humps, for instance, by offering to take key staff off-site to examine and if possible resolve the difficulties.
- Institutional modeling is furthered when the new institution participates in it at its initiative, pacing and with maximum flexibility altogether. Any writing up of it, for instance, is best done by it and for its own purpose or at least with the team collaborating.
- Modeling institution development requires consistent support from the team's own agency (the Foundation in SIET's case). In fact, *that* support sets limits to the team's ability to function as a model.

These generalizations confirmed the nagging suspicion all along that these particular consultants could never become team enough to do the institutional modeling that would have helped SIET most. They were the wrong crew for that. Institutions either did not figure in their experience or figured as work settings to stay away from. Not one of SIET's original consultants was anchored in an institution at home. They were individual entrepreneurs freelancing and would "do their thing" for the next two years at SIET. That made it easier for the Foundation to recruit them and also avoided paying overheads to home institutions. Soon afterwards international agencies found that this was false economy and increasingly contracted with home institutions for whole consultant teams.

As individual practitioners the consultants at SIET were then also all ready to buy into Pandi's similarly individual orientation, and as a result all the early key players at SIET operated out of individual perspectives as a matter of normal course, that is, blindly and for the most part without a second thought. How enormously difficult each found it to let go of that so familiar perspective and try an unknown other found most moving expression when Charles burst out in utter dismay at the first consultant meeting after the break late in the year. He had missed them, he said quietly; and then, much more in character, stormed: "I was *fine* as long as I was working away—no problems—and then I get myself drawn into an absolutely different world—a world that I cannot understand, that I didn't know existed till you pointed it out."

With this crew, and Pandi in command, support for institutional modeling at SIET could only come in small changes. That left the Foundation as a last possible source, and there it failed. It had gone along with Joe's design and lead in recruiting these consultants, and then in urging SIET's board to recruit Pandi. It used individual consultants—and Pandi too—as informal sources of information about happenings at SIET and as conduits for influencing developments there. But when paring the consultant team down by first one and then also a second ineffectual and interfering member would have cleared the air most effectively, it backed off every time, leaving Pandi and me together to invent writing tasks for the losers that would at least contain the further damage they might do if left to their own likings.

By the time I left, another year after the events recounted here, Pandi had in his laborious, meticulous, devoted way worked himself to a clearer understanding of what institution-building involved and, with his customary determination, had pushed SIET ahead of the stage the consultant team was stuck in—stage two in my schema. SIET had clarified what it wanted to be—its identity—and had begun to engage its main clients and partners in making it also acceptable and worth supporting. Five years from birth was not very far on the road to building the Institute. But it was far enough to present consultants, old and new, with the coherent Institute-determined development into which to fit their contributions from then on, and that made a new game.

This reversal of lead, from consultants to Institute, suggests interesting reflections about phases, times, and sequences that may guide consulting in new institutions generally. First, the state of institutional development of the consulting team probably matters most early in the life of a new institution. If this is so, the low state of this team at SIET then prevented it from helping the Institute at this crucial phase and may well have held it back.

Second, the state of the team may matter less, perhaps little, after the institute has worked out its identity enough for committing its staff and engaging its partners properly. In the course of identifying its long-range objectives and also using them, to quote the schema, as "a priority system for decision-making", the new institution may also have built the capacity to go on under its own steam. If this were so, then this team's effort of planning, and with that provoking SIET to decide on *its* priorities and carry out internal strengthening, amounted to essential help. Thank goodness the team held together long enough to touch off these apparently self-sustaining forces in this Institute. A different team might have made taking the lead for a time and then passing it on its deliberate consulting strategy in advance. That would have been a prototype strategy and especially promising for helping develop institutions with a heavily innovative mandate—on which the next chapter will focus anew.

More Inner Work

> If I were blind, I would be
> the first person to know it.
>
> Greg, 'Without frontal lobes'
> (quoted in Sachs 1995, p. 67)

> ...a tribute to man's mind to block out an
> inconvenient injunction—to interpret [it] away.
>
> James Fenton 1995, p. 35

Up to the utterly upsetting meeting with the service directors that first December, I too had put topmost attention on immediate colleagues and purposes, and left larger and longer-term concerns in the background: I knew they were there and that they mattered, and I certainly had experiences from earlier settings about how they could play out. But occasional glances in their direction and taking my hunches into account was the best I could do, I was sure; these far-reaching perspectives could not play a part in my practical, orderly, working day-by-day. The meeting shattered that illusion. The background was now front, right before me to assess directly and act on.

My progress in sorting it all out and getting hold of this new vision could only be stumbling and erratic, rather like a toddler's weaving first steps. The partial and halting explanations, which were all I could offer my colleagues for what I was newly after, must have confused them often and made the prevailing uncertainties and distrusts at SIET worse. But as I steadied direction and also stepped into the team leadership, Fall 1963 also became a good time for wider change. Both parts make logical good sense.

Looking back though, and making kind allowance for my lack of practice, what explains my taking long months after December to act more consistently in line with what I had come so forcefully now to understand? This is a quite practical question, for if an already experienced developer and director of institutions like me found it so very difficult to change, understanding that better might then make more sense of the often weird twists and turns colleagues took (Pandi as well as consultants) to avoid steps patently necessary to build the Institute into an institution, and the vehemence with which they suddenly flared up, as if out of the blue, and swerved back into bad-mouthing each other. Obviously, it was personal issues more than intellectual hurdles or situational hazards that made them so hesitant and erratic about striking this new direction, perhaps issues deep-rooted in life histories, clinging to the present obstinately like barnacles.

So, back to the record to learn what I can about my own part. Immediately clear is that a long-awaited change of circumstance at that very same time exercised enormous pull away: Udai arrived at long last, my first colleague in extension education. My year-long wait was over. Two more colleagues joined in quick succession, so we now had a department to build. With no effort at all I made this joyful state into a major distraction from the still larger task. I gave Udai and the department my foremost attention—and with that I was right back in my original position with blinders.

No thought was involved, certainly no overview. Otherwise, I would have known at once that that fresh attention on my department had better come from somewhere else; also, that the consultant team would be most in danger of losing it; and, with the team's better collaboration so recent and still fragile, yet also potentially strategic for the Institute's change of direction, this was a particularly bad time to transfer my attention away. Now that I had the opportunity, I explained to myself, developing one department properly would be the best contribution to make to developing the Institute, since that would make an inside model and so be even better than the team of outsiders. That possibility would have been well worth considering if we in the Extension Department had had as firm a grasp on the linkage issues with the rest of the Institute as we had on developing the internal components; but that was not so. What we haplessly modeled instead once again—and very well!—was that attention to good internal working and structuring could bring quick gains and so propel Extension to the front. So, back to competing, part against part, the very last thing I had meant to revert to. The result was that my consultant colleagues saw me desert them in favor of my extension colleagues, and some went on to conclude that I had actually talked up institution-wide perspectives as a clever ploy to advancing my part ahead of theirs—and succeeded. The record confirms the simpler explanation: at this first plausible opportunity I had reverted to my long-accustomed focus on the immediate. It was as simple as that and innocent of any scheming—or of thought of any kind.

My persisting with another habit that also ran clear counter to what I knew to be necessary had no tempting coincidence to explain it: I continued to keep difficulties to myself and my churning anger and other feelings about them most severely so. I recorded the events and my feelings in the diary, and acted on many, but I hardly ever shared what prompted an action, or where, in current parlance, I was coming from. One example will serve. The most I ever *said* to Pandi about his complaining to the Foundation about the more rigorous stand the team was taking in the Institute under my leadership was "that you might well have talked with us about it first". Yet, in the diary I wrote of my "great fearfulness [about] going this far" to confront him and that I was "very angry at being so undercut" by Pandi on whom I depended so utterly for all I was attempting to do at SIET and had thought I could by now rely on. None of this I said to Pandi, right then or another time. I did not even try to engage him in telling me how this—betrayal?—had come about. Instead I slid by it all and, without even a pause at "undercut", went right on to a possible action. I proposed he and I establish "some norms" for talking about the Institute with others outside, norms that our colleagues could then also follow. So, while in team, department, and everywhere I advocated more openness and many times helped others to be more open, I maintained my own personal distance. Or, more precisely, while I habitually and happily shared pleasures and approvals, when the going got rough I reverted to the clinician mode favored at the time: I kept my feelings to myself while prompting my colleagues to express theirs. The diary is full of "I did not press the point", "stayed quiet", "held back", "waited", and "let it pass". So I took into the supposedly new era the agreeable, considerate, well-mannered, often cheerfully outgoing person people already knew; the rest of me I continued to keep to myself.

Such smooth accommodation and avoidance of conflict are learned early in life. I think I can trace some of the roots almost to their origins, and with that recapture and marvel again at how childhood beginnings grew into the ever self-confirming sturdy points of view that served me well person-to-person and were now so limiting and also so very difficult to let go of for working with larger systems. The story of how my avoidance of conflict hemmed in what I saw and did further at SIET will resume on p. 200.

First a word about this early block, for it grew together with my disposition to fit in with people present. (My innovative, even radical streak, which actually characterizes much of my life and work, is less immediate and personal, so also freer.) Son in the middle, then also stranger in a new country and language, my positions encouraged circumspection from early on. Ingrained early and deeply, I think, was cowering at my mother's sudden furies: never, never would I risk reducing others to the hushed slinking about we all used to do after an outburst. Rare as they were, those scenes terrified me; I still shrink with the clear memory of several. I grew antennae that picked up mere whispers of anger, even possibilities of it to be sure to dispel, learned to calibrate my responses to fine precision, and got used to foregoing or postponing what I preferred for myself. My religion raised self-denial to a virtue; when "offered up", each would be rewarded later, and self-denial was a good habit to acquire for life anyway.

All signs confirmed that growing up that way was fine: I enjoyed many activities, made friends readily, appealed to grown-ups. By the time intellectual pursuits and career choices came in focus, they fell most readily into this same well-practiced pattern of quite subtle personal accommodation and also fortified it some more. By the time I scanned college courses to take (by correspondence, since it was war and we had no money any-way), my perceptive father foresaw me in a diplomatic career and economics good preparation for it.

War work in the factory followed, another strange setting in strange times in which personal likes and dislikes routinely came second. Over and over I confirmed my ease in the midst of just about any combination of people and circumstance. My onward outer story continued to flow between the same personal banks (detailed already in Chapter 2). "Human relations" became my field as this term was used in the forties and fifties: relations face-to-face with individuals and in small groups, insight and agreement the desired outcome, conflict to be prevented. Only late in the sixties, that is after this chapter in my story was well over and I too had discovered new positions to take, would my department at Harvard change its name to the much broader "organizational behavior".

So professionally too the emphasis on working with individuals and small groups in ways that fitted me so well personally was in the mainstream all along, even in the vanguard with my good connections with the Tavistock Institute in London and with Harvard and the NTL Institute in the United States. Professional alignment more than made up for my peripatetic history and catch-as-catch-can higher studies. From Asia too I maintained this fellowship. Then, in the late 1950s, several Tavistock colleagues started working in India and I learned to facilitate small group development on psychoanalytic lines. Soon after, the Harvard Business School started its long collaboration with the new Indian Institute of Management in Ahmedabad, and MIT's Sloan

School with the parallel institute in Calcutta. Both contracts were funded by the Ford Foundation, as SIET's was, so I met those colleagues regularly at Foundation meetings in Delhi. That was how I would team up with Warren Bennis to staff the "lab" for faculty members from six institutions.

At Erik Erikson's first seminar in India I had met Udai, my partner since then, and no one kept more up-to-date with developments in the profession than he, including formal research in which he also regularly engaged and published. He had completed his training with the NTL in the USA and pioneered small groups and experiential training in India, often with senior colleagues from the USA. Erikson returned for longer periods to work on his book on Gandhiji and I stayed in touch with him.

As far as I knew then—and know now—all these good colleagues looked at the world pretty much from the same position as I and worked from there on much the same lines I did, that is, from personal and inter-personal relations outward. That is where the roots were for all of us. This was true too for Maxwell Jones's work on therapeutic communities for which I had joined him in Oregon during my sabbatical following the Aloka experience. A major innovation there was the daily large meetings of all patients and staff on a hospital ward; but 70 or more though we were, the focus was still on individual improvement. Kurt Lewin's formulations of action research, on which the NTL was based, also focused on small groups face-to-face. This was what had so enthused Fritz Roethlisberger, George Lombard, and other colleagues at Harvard Business School just ahead of my year's fellowship in their department. Rogerian "non-directive counseling" was also in vogue there and then. Both the counseling and the small group work Ronnie and I had taken with us to Aloka and, made more rigorous on psychoanalytic lines, from there via Oregon to SIET.

So, in addition to my very personal roots in it, my focusing on inter-personal relations at SIET had that long intellectual grounding which I had honestly come by. Far from mere fad or passing enthusiasm, it was my anchor, the position I stood on and looked out from. When I included in my thinking the department I was in, the institution, or the wider community beyond—as I also did quite routinely—it was either abstractly, depersonalized and untested or, for practical purposes, from the same clinical perspective that I habitually used when working with people individually and in assorted handfuls. It was my immediate colleagues anyway, I was sure, who were my best and probably my only reliable informants about those larger settings, and the only avenues I had to getting any action taken there.

Looked at from this position, the generalizations I had learned about larger social systems projected outward in successive rings—the larger the system the further out the ring it was in and also the fainter. That they might be, instead, discrete stepping stones on any one of which to take position and look at the world from a fresh angle had no practical reality for me—till that December meeting in 1962. In fact, my own experience was quite against putting systemic issues in central focus. On the rare occasions that I had worked on quite explicitly organizational issues, I had ended up being disappointed, and those disappointments jarred still, even decades later. Nasty surprises from unexpected quarters left scars, and scars promote extra caution.

One took me back to early 1948. The British Institute of Management was new and still small enough for most juniors like me to sit in in the weekly staff meeting. I can hear my chief offer to "do a piece of field research" on the perennial complaint that papers didn't move and that deadlines for important decisions went by because of that. Field research was what we were specifically here for anyway, and where better to use it than right here, on our own problem. She could put me on studying how the files did move and where they piled up—a piece of Operational Research it would be. I can hear her pride. I don't recall feeling any anxiety, I was probably elated at being asked. Over the next couple of weeks I recorded signatures with dates on hundreds of files, then summarized and sent the results around, complete with executive summary. All that a competent study should be and done to schedule. Next, all hell broke loose. The files got stuck most and longest in the office of the assistant director, true, but she was far too well connected to be asked to change that and was furious at having her hold put on show so openly. Only then did I realize that her central part in all the trouble must have been known to all in advance of my efforts, all except me. I felt used, and suspected that organizational studies in general were probably a sham like this, a way of avoiding the *real* issues which arose in the relations between actual people.

With the organizational recommendations from our coalmining study soon after, we had fared no better: the board had locked them away. Yet, we had backed them with long quotes from Chester Barnard's classic, *The Functions of the Executive*, the CEO of one of America's largest telephone companies and currently of the Rockefeller Foundation. I don't recall feeling any great disappointment with that, or surprise—perhaps I had learned by then not to set much store on organizations actually learning from research. And no matter: I felt personally greatly enriched by my time with the miners and managers, also with having made overall sense of the myriad impresssions we had gathered and getting them on paper, even in occasionally elegant formulation. All that was satisfaction in plenty.

On the systemic side then there was much effort with little or no result. In the work directly with people, there was great satisfaction that also lasted—this had continued to be the balance sheet for the choices I had faced organizations with from time to time: for continuing the association of youth organizations with the European Youth Campaign in 1953, for instance, or for doubling Aloka's faculty, facilities—and funds—to make it a permanent institution. Boards would rather let institutions atrophy than go with recommendations for enlivening them. No surprise, only confirmation.

Now, three features about this earlier work on systemic issues may go far to explain the still-births. First, the early work was limited to *studying* the organization and coming up with recommendations—that classic pattern. Later, when organizational action was mine to take or be directly affected by (as watchdog to keep the European Campaign on track and as Aloka's director), I still viewed the issues "from the bottom up", that is, in terms of how well the organization served the people in it. Only if they were satisfied with the outcome would they stay and continue working, and work "effectively and efficiently", as the saying then went, otherwise they would leave at the earliest opportunity. That view—up—was true enough, but also not sufficient. It failed to take in even such a momentous, all-overriding issue as organizational survival in the larger world on which those people's jobs depended. So my recommendations even as a key actor had not encompassed the broader and longer view required for making sound systemic decisions and policies. In that larger world, both the London Docks and Britain's coal industry were headed for extinction even as we studied them and wrote about them, and Aloka's premature death had already been pronounced, we now know, by its funders.

Third, the explicitly organizational involvements had always been quite brief, as at the BIM study of files, or a subsidiary part, as at Aloka where I had merely scouted that larger territory. Each time I made a beeline back to the position I knew and liked best, and resumed the real work of improving personal and interpersonal relations. Nothing else could be more important or urgent, and views to the contrary were easy to "interpret...away". For one thing, I always had quite enough to do with whoever and whatever were right in front of me.

With this history, personal and professional intricately intertwined, I am trying to convey the tenacity of this sticking to the position I had made so thoroughly my own, the wondrous ways in which I chose and also funneled life events to suit and reinforce it and no other, and how in this process plus product it also acquired so powerful a logic that no other logic dislodged it. Having an opinion, idea, or view about a different perspective is a thing of a quite different order, a reed in the wind next to that solid tree. Opinions is what I and my prized colleagues had about systems, and often quite well informed ones. Opinions could be argued about and changed. Not so the position on which I stood (and in such good company!) and from which I habitually looked at the world, worked with, and was also known for by colleagues and friends. Such a position needs no explanation but is self-evident.

Seen from that position then, SIET too was small groups multiplied to institutional scale, that's all. How SIET developed and operated could be extrapolated from work with small groups writ large, and I and the other consultants could help it with that.

This suited me wonderfully well, as we have seen. I *liked* my position and standing *there*. The backbone of my professional practice, it was also a large part of me personally, of my maturing. What I saw from there was familiar. SIET, new as it obviously was and offering welcome opportunities for pioneering afresh, still had that thoroughly familiar feel I brought with me from years of experience and growing competence. I knew how to set about my work and that I could do it well, probably even better than earlier because of all the testing I had given it, many times and from all angles, and proving it to my satisfaction again and again had made it habitual. Further, by relentless recording, habitual reflection, and occasional periods of intensive study and summary writing, I had raised my awareness and foresight along with my competence. I felt good to have done all I could this far, and felt well prepared again for SIET. SIET in turn would add more experience and competence. The same good cycle.

To this long string of confirmation, selective like a genetic chain, SIET had then added three features which confirmed my position and view yet again. Or rather, without seeing this connection or intending its consequence, it was we consultants, with Joe and I as usual in the lead, who had succeeded with getting them installed early on.

Immediate programing and "output" was the first. Even though it meant hectic preparations and many makeshift arrangements, this would—and did—signal clearly that SIET was "in business". Within two months and from then on with only a few days' break between programs, it always had 30 mid-career officers in residential full-time training. Even in normal conditions continuous programs were bound to pre-empt faculty and staff energies, and starting conditions were well short of normal. Newly designed, with materials freshly assembled or still to come, and with only impromptu space, facilities, and support staff, crises were inevitable and make-do solutions were bound to add new problems as well.

Second was the quickly instituted rule that all newly recruited faculty would start with spending their first quarter as full-time participants. I proposed this, and that it took off and was never shot down still amazes me. For while it promised many benefits for their subsequent work, and rightly so, immediately it kept faculty size down. The systemic distortion that would engender I did not foresee, and neither did the others. With programs running full blast well short of local faculty, it was predictable that the consultants would "have to" step in and make up the deficits in staffing wherever they occurred. And, no surprise, they occurred most continuously in staffing training sessions. In this way, the expectation got established that consultants would do most of the training and Indian faculty would learn it from them. Only a short step then took consultants, also under severe pressure, to using session designs, training methods, and materials they were familiar with from home in America or England. Ostensibly all this would of course be "only for the start" but, with no let-up on the pressures, these expectations continued to dominate. And for longer still because most consultants warmly welcomed this reversal to active "doing" roles. Beset by pressures from all sides and feeling frequently in the midst of virtual chaos, session times and chalk in hand stood out as oases of quietly good familiar purpose and provided the most satisfaction—to the consultants.

Innovative purpose was the third feature that also, and predictably so, made it extraordinarily difficult for SIET to counter the understandably quite normal tendencies of new institutions to become preoccupied with immediate and nearby matters. It was the first institute of its kind. It was mandated to set about doing already known tasks in new ways and all foreseeable tasks it would review and pick up afresh. The opportunity to be creative attracted faculty to SIET. Consultants too had applied and been selected with innovation very much in mind. The most obvious start I made with innovating was to open training in extension with three weeks of experiential sessions focused on interpersonal relations and then also ending the 12-week program with participants in interdisciplinary teams working in small industrial units for another three weeks. These and other innovations took hold quickly and the Institute became known for forging ahead with its innovative mandate very creatively. Strings of other innovations followed, large and small. But this premium on innovation also charged the whole atmosphere even more. It signaled that absolutely *everything* may be challenged and changed. It immediately led to yet more meetings of faculty and staff, and those meetings took even longer although time and energies were already so tight.

In SIET's already overburdened condition, this premium on innovation had two other serious systemic consequences as well. Some faculty found the eclectic, electric atmosphere it engendered just too unsettling and recoiled from it. Some froze into permanent opposition to all new proposals, even on otherwise inconsequential details, and conflicts increased. And several faculty left, so raising still more the pressures on the rest and aggravating the distortions.

Perhaps most serious for institutional development was how the enthusiasm of the rest of us for innovation, which we also ratcheted up for one another, misled us to the disastrous notion that the most important function SIET had in its relations with its main sponsors, clients, and also funders in Delhi and around the country was to introduce them to the exciting innovations we were creating and our plans for more. We were taking the lead in the field, in short, country wide. And it was exactly for dealing with such implications of innovating that these relationships were quite unprepared by the meager and totally unbalanced attention that the SIET Institute had given them. This, above all, the Ministry and the directors let us know at the December meeting.

Against the multitude of demands that starting any new establishment makes, the faculty shortage those extra months made ignoring all larger contexts that much easier. Just six were on board that fall, nine in December, only just into two figures by the following summer, SIET's second. All professionals could easily assemble around the large table in principal Pandi's office, with the consultants exactly half the strength. And assembling all those so heavily involved made a nice reassuring sense of community while also allowing many practical questions to be decided quickly or shared out.

Of course, a quick start with the core task—intensive staff development—and striking out in innovative directions also had many benefits. It favored day-to-day practical action and learning, and SIET's population were practitioners. In line with Lewin's dictum that you need to see things move to understand them properly, the programs developed better out of the early experiences with them. Many participants joined in the enthusiasm for innovating and took this with them into their practices. And even without giving the larger setting the attention it would have received if viewed from a better position, in making a quick start with its core program and then keeping it up, the Institute quickly created a country-wide constituency of officers who backed its continuation when the impending storm broke. Early reader Don Klein writes:

> As devil's advocate, the entrepreneurial model proved to be very effective. Many needed programs were created almost overnight, the programs were a hit with their clients, key people

in the new institution showed considerable initiative and took great personal and professional risks in getting things underway, and a large stable of external consultants was engaged to infuse the new venture with their talents, skills and understanding. If it had gotten off to a slower start and spent a larger share of time developing a consensual vision and master plan, would it have succeeded as well or even survived? Clearly [SIET's governors] were outside the loop of decision making about the Institute's development. I wonder how much their concerns had to do with disagreements about programmatic direction and how much with their feeling/being disempowered (Personal communication, February 1997).

The main point here is that these good-looking features aggravated the blindness to larger system issues that most of us, if not absolutely all of us, brought with us, and that the successful launching of this or that part of the Institute, which gave such great satisfaction one after another, got in the way as often as not of the sound development of the institution for the long haul. Predicatably so, as we have seen and told. But that would have required looking at the world from a different position.

Long Way, Small Feet

For me, that December meeting was the watershed in this story of foregoing one position for another to get a new view of the big world. It brought my whole elaborate edifice crashing down and ended my innocence about it being the only one that mattered. Nothing less earsplitting could have done it. For so adept had I become over the years in that position that I had routinely pulled and stretched things to truly extraordinarily lengths and, looking back, often quite out of shape, at SIET just as elsewhere before. No need to change so fine-honed and well-proven a position that was also elastic like a rubber band but never broke. Anything beyond breaking point I either did not see, blind to those signals like Nelson at the Battle of Trafalgar, or when I did, could equally routinely "interpret away". Truly significant learning has to cut free of a root system like mine. Much work in training and organizational consulting seems to settle for far less.

And then the December meeting did dislodge me from that so precious a position—that is the other astonishment. Again the diary, following the note of vague disquiet entered in September, shows the forces building up like floodwaters behind a dam. Following the September entry, the diary shows two streams of growing consciousness. One took off from the pressures I felt to do more and more of what I was used to doing, always more; and, along with that, my mounting anxiety that demands would outrun even my ever-ready capacities, maybe quite soon and certainly down the road, since I could see no end to the escalation. Dismay came with the realization that this prospect, of multiplying my standard interventions, might be quite hopeless. That prospect became shrilly insistent by late November. I made nightmares with it, terrifying myself when least guarded and adding to my exhaustion.

Next came hesitant recognitions, glimmers at first, that continuing this way was pointless in any case, even were I somehow to hit a manageable pace, for with all my efforts I was still not achieving lasting effect. The same "problems" came up again and again, never settled. At long last, as if hit with a two-by-four, I *knew*, knew for sure, that I had to set about very differently my part in the consulting: my efforts needed redirection.

Interspersed in the diary for the same period are sightings of a second stream that also came more frequently and insistently in view. I noted more and more issues that urgently needed *somebody's* attention. I recorded only those that came to my attention unsought; even of those there were enough to convince me that problems and gaps were out there threatening to get in the way for all of us and no one was doing anything about them. Mentioned there were SIET's governance, the absence or near absence of contacts with clients and of any strategy for them, the dealings individual consultants had with the Foundation, policy gaps in recruiting and also in following up participants in their dispersed settings around the country, and more locally the lack of specifications, including fees, for consultancy services participants rendered entrepreneurs in the course of their training. Neither *ad hoc* meetings or ideas out of my standard kit could get even close to the foresight, intentional strategies, and continuing attention these broader issues obviously called for.

Several entries that fall also reported hints of dissatisfaction voiced to some colleague by senior officials in the Ministry and directors with the direction the Institute was taking and with things they missed. Nothing was done by anyone, and I merely noted them. And so I went into the meeting in December which took me over the top. The meeting did not cause the spill, nor did it show me the new position to take or name what I would see from there. It did, however, confirm the new direction.

I did not know what to do next, how to proceed better. I had no map for that unfamiliar new territory. Good maps for it were really still ahead, as the next chapter will tell. So for most of another year, I mixed occasional sallies in the direction of dealing with one system issue or another with telling myself that this wasn't really *my* business. That side-stepping was unconvincing though, because I picked up other things that were not "my business" either. *The New Look* and going public with it was an obvious instance that April. And when I took over as team leader soon after, improving the Institute's relations with its widespread constituencies and other system issues did become my business.

I started with doing my darndest to get Pandi to pay attention to them. I offered information and counsel, that was as far as I would regularly go even then. My own contacts with the Ministry and the Foundation in Delhi doubled from the next quarter on, but that still only made them on average four out of every 100 and hardly suggested a decisive shift to giving these external relationships their due importance, never mind making up for past neglects of them. What increased markedly first is the frequency with which system issues entered discussions with colleagues at SIET and then, most notably, the work the team did on Institute-wide planning that happily then touched off institution development with faculty participation.

It is difficult now—30 years further on, having had issues of institutional development in clear view for quite as long as I had then been used to, and being used to viewing and working with personal and inter-personal relationships—to look at my continuous toing and froing that year with much patience. Though my sallies into concerns with institutional dimensions in their own right became more frequent, for several months more they remained brief and made mostly diagnostic and intellectual points, and that too mostly on paper. When I ventured to mention what had for me become some organizational imperative to team leader Joe or later to principal Pandi, I found they did not engage me in discussing it, never mind getting to work on considering possible actions. Instead, they changed the subject or, when they considered what I had said, they quickly became theoretical about it. They were avoiding these topics, I surmised, and since I wanted to make sure they would not avoid *me* altogether, I dropped trying. So most of the observations and thoughts I had on institutional issues I learned to keep to myself, just as I did with my feelings about other difficulties. I recorded them in my diary, and left it at that. When Udai came, I shared them with him. When it came to action, even to action within my immediate realm of influence as in the Extension Department, I quickly resumed my familiar position even as I *also* reflected on institutional implications of what my colleague(s) and I had talked about only minutes before.

Within my constraints, as I tried this or that fresh position from which to see better what I now knew was "out there" and set to work on it quite systematically, three realizations struck quite quickly. One was that putting the focus on SIET as a whole and its development into an institution that would last made an enormous difference right away to the way things "came up", even those personal and inter-personal matters on which I had focused so exclusively earlier. Things were just never the same again after this shift. Ratchet-like, once shifted, the new perspective would not leave me again. From now on this institutional dimension and perspective was around me in all directions, like a ring.

Second, once on the move, my moving did not stop when I had reached the next position from which institutions as systems were in clear view. Just beyond that, when I stood *there*, appeared yet another view, and even cursory attention to it from a distance clarified my vision. So SIET Institute and its development—in direct view from stepstone two—appeared clearly and importantly related to a constellation of other organizations even before the makeup of this environment moved into immediate focus—from stepstone three. It is this succession of views, each wider than the last, yet also quite specific for its own realm, which makes Frost's picture of stepping stones and of leaps required to get from one to the next so very vivid. In time, I learned that the realities most worth acting on stood out clearest when

I took position not on the very next but on the next-but-one vantage point and looked back.

Thereafter, institutions-in-their-environments became the focus of my practice and writing. This unit I kept firmly in view; I even escalated it to make-or-break importance when I concentrated next on institutions set up specifically to innovate—my primary interest all along and the subject of the next chapter. Sound links with the system(s) they meant to influence were essential, otherwise they shriveled and died no matter how startling or profitable the innovations they produced. Helping build such institutions into networks—the natural next step—became my main focus of work with universities on four continents in the early 1970s and with two very large systems of public services from 1980 onwards (detailed in Chapter 8).

Of course, I also continued to meet individuals and work with groups, at SIET and since, and my competencies and ease also continued to improve. In fact, my third learning—this a happy realization that only grew on me as I tested it in practice—was that I could take one position or another at will, my original one included. This ease of movement between stepping stones became so smooth over the years that it now requires no deliberate attention. It took me some time to realize that this splendid versatility had its dangers too. Confusing others is one: they keep wondering "where I am" and "where, right *now*, I am coming from". In ambiguous and conflict-ridden situations colleagues have concluded that agreeable as I am in my soft spoken and considerate manner I might with that same gentleness lead them up some garden path. It was important for them to know whether I was listening to and working with them on some immediate concern to them personally or with systems concerns in the fore. I did get into trouble and, once at least, into much sadness, till I learned to signal clearly from which position I was seeing and doing things in the moments that mattered.

With acquiring this versatility and learning to handle its risks, Erikson's useful reminder that every new position required foregoing a present position remained true only in the same immediate sense that no two points can occupy the same space at the same time. I cannot take more than one position at a time—but I can choose to be in any one of several, and I let my choice be known.

References

Deutsch, Karl, *The Nerves of Government*, Free Press, New York, 1964.

Fenton, James, 'On Statues', *New York Review of Books*, Rea S. Hederman, New York, November 1995.

Frost, Robert, 'Introduction', *Complete Poems*, Holt, Rinehart and Winston, New York, 1964.

Lilienthal, David, *Journals*, Vol. 4, *The Road to Change*, Harper & Row, New York, 1969.

Lorsch, Jay W. and **Lawrence, Paul**, 'Environmental Factors and Organisational Integration', *American Sociological Association: Proceedings of Annual Meeting*, Boston, August 1978.

Lynton, Rolf P., 'Institution-building and Consulting: Complexities in Development Assistance', Ph.D. dissertation, State University of New York, Buffalo, 1970.

Sachs, Oliver, *An Anthropologist on Mars*, Alfred A. Knopf, New York, 1995.

7

INNOVATIVE INSTITUTIONS
IN PARTICULAR

> Seeing the System's Environment Makes All
>   the Difference
> A Prototype Strategy
> Engaging the "Relevant Environment"
> System Transformation
> What's in the Name?

To see a thing truly is to forget its name.

Paul Valery 1961

Developing a new institution to pioneer innovation is like pulling oneself up by one's bootstraps: logic and gravity are against it. The new-born has no experience of its own to build on, and it is to shun all others'. The European Youth Campaign, Aloka, the Small Industries Extension Training Institute, to reach no further back—obviously I had an incorrigible taste for working with just that kind of institution. My prize symbol became the spindly man in a Levine cartoon aiming a boomerang at an apple on his own head. Following SIET, the time had come to understand better what was involved, to see if there were more reliable maps to use in those ventures, and maybe to help fill some gaps.

Two streams of activities over the next years took me that last mile.

The first was heavy on theory. Ronnie and I had decided to stay on in Chapel Hill: a doctorate—*any* doctorate—would let me accept the tenured appointment in the School of Public Health that its dean had already promised me, and that spelled security for the family. For the minimum time the doctorate would take, I would sink my personal agenda. The full program at Duke on top of full-time work at UNC would occupy me totally anyway. "Sociology is what you need for studying institutions", counselled kind professors at Duke whom my department chair had gathered to advise on my proper doctorate, "not this psychology you talk." That sociology might also advance my professional interest was bonus.

In fact, a happy confluence brought developing innovative institutions to the forefront again less than two years later. When my committee detected traces of that same obstinate psychology in my qualifying "comprehensive" examination, they required that I take the one course (in the Business School) that would finally wipe it out: cutting-edge systems theory and method. I buckled down to the equations, got past being awed, and tuned into that thinking. What saved me, and more, was the final paper. I steeped myself in the literature on systems development, most of it quite recent, and came up with "Linking an Innovative Subsystem into the System". It amounted to an improved map, received an A+ and, with Professor Pondy's promotion and following repeated rewrites to satisfy the editor's red inked challenges, warranted publication in the august *Administrative Science Quarterly*.[1] Reprints, translations, and numerous references followed.

Seeing the System's Environment Makes All the Difference

The paper laid out two basic models for assessing challenges to innovate.

> One model treats [them] as a succession of discrete stimuli to which the system needs to respond with appropriate innovations. In this

1. Volume 14, No.3, pp 398–416, September 1969.

model differentiation and integration are functions of the frequency and force of the expected stimuli...[and] integrative devices...are linkages of minimal complexity and duration and will affect the system as a whole little or not at all. The other model treats the system and its environment as in continuous interaction in uncertainty and as aiming to achieve and maintain a steady state through this interaction.

A diagram (Figure 7.1) showed the difference:

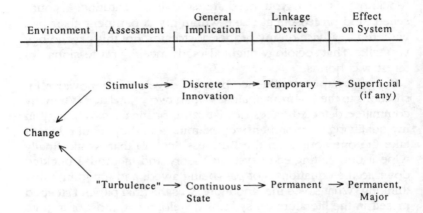

FIGURE 7.1   **Two Models of Assessing Environmental Uncertainties and Characteristic Linkages**

The paper went on to lay out both models, the first in three variations of ascending complexity. The extracts here are all about the second model, where the large system depends on continuing innovation for good functioning. There the overall issue is institutionalizing linkage mechanisms so that they function as permanent parts of a system that is continuously and flexibly engaged in change, that is, a system that is functioning effectively in a turbulent environment. Most of the data came from four major field studies published in the 1960s, three after 1965.

Analysis showed four dimensions to matter most: organizational differentiation, positioning of the linkage mechanisms in the system, their norms of operations, and their congruence with system structure. These were the characteristics of effective linkages for each:

> *Differentiation* was "clear both *vis a vis* the subsystems to be linked and *vis a vis* the decision makers for the whole system...and [it was] centered at the operating level, neither higher nor lower, where decisions could be effectively reached and implemented."
>
> *Position* was "equidistant between the subsystems they were to link...in terms of goals, time, interpersonal relations and structure.... The key linkers, [though] at different hierarchical levels within their various subsystems and in the system as a whole, [were seen] as having the most important voice in decisions." Effective linkage mechanisms abrogated "for the length of each meeting the distribution of authority, information and technical competence pictured in the hierarchical structure of the organization." The system "evaluated and rewarded according to the overall performance of the subsystems linked."
>
> *Operating norms* made most difference in two areas: conflict resolution and flexibility. "...openness with which conflicts were aired and hammered out in departmental meetings [mattered greatly]...[and also having] the kind and degree of flexibility determined by functional needs of the mechanisms and the particular situations with which [the system] is dealing at any time."
>
> *Structural congruence* worked both ways: effective linkage mechanisms had structures and norms that also characterized the large system, and that in turn had characteristics more like innovative subsystems than traditional operating organizations.

For systems in turbulent environments, the paper concluded, "problems of effective linkage are particularly difficult and particularly important...[and] the one issue that distinguished the most successful organisations from the least successful."

Across many differences of detail, successful organizations resembled each other in five aspects:

1. They differentiated the innovative subsystem sharply and formally.
2. ...they found a basis for establishing goals for improvement.
3. [They] focussed on problem-solving processes.
4. [The strategies they used] led to changes in the kind, distribution and amount of power.
5. [They] emphasized norms and skills that facilitated collaboration and problem solving rather than negotiation and bargaining.

...working out [the system's] distinctively appropriate pattern seems to be essential to effectiveness.... [The] shifting technological and informational needs of the system and the ways in which these can be met...and the emotions of the people actually involved in the changes which the linkage mechanisms are to mediate...have to be reflected in the openness of linkage mechanisms to further change, that is, their flexibility. The emotional uncertainties seem the more complex.

All this required the steady active support of the system's decision-makers—a "heavy cost [for which] the only justification...is strict functional interdependence.... Decision makers will seek to avoid this investment. Even if they assess the environmental needs correctly, they are inclined to underestimate the response that would be effective and the costs involved in the response."

Even as I was choosing these extracts to reproduce here, I was strongly tempted to underline phrases that pointed directly at difficulties and gaps still vivid in my mind from consulting with SIET. To see SIET as the Ministry's innovative sub-system for refocusing and reinvigorating its services to small industry was not difficult for me, and would not have been difficult for the partners at that time, just a stranger way of putting what everyone had in mind. The real difficulties would have started after that. On only one of the five essential characteristics had SIET scored a plus—the first. SIET *was* "differentiated...sharply and formally". Provided only weakly or not at all in the design, and so at best sporadic in practice, were all other four, with the destructive consequences described in the last chapter. All, I now understood, could have been foreseen.

About the systemic consequences, this theory-map would have predicted accurately how the consultants and SIET itself would react to the directors' resentment at the year-end meeting:

Discouraged and uncertain about whether they can perform their innovative task, they tend to withdraw and to create barriers rather than linkages.... They called attention to the limitations under which decision makers expected them to succeed, their "rigidity", "short-sightedness", "intolerance" and "conservatism", their unwillingness to collaborate, their wish to see the innovation fail...all concerned to illustrate those aspects of the total situation that are most favorable to their rationale at the moment.... The strains in the rest of the system and the ways people express them then tend in turn to isolate the new subsystem further.... Support for [it] withered, recruitment into it became more difficult, reports of innovative achievements lacked credibility. Soon the subsystem faced problems of sheer survival and, being...the less powerful, tended to develop substitute satisfactions, like fantasies that some day the others will learn to appreciate them.

A Prototype Strategy

So, along with the great satisfaction at getting the paper done, and actually and so prominently adding to the maps for building innovative institutions, having the map show up strategic errors in recent work was also decidedly sobering. True, the map was based on studies published only in the 1960s, that is well after SIET's start. But would I have really navigated so much better with it in my pocket? I doubt it, except, possibly, on two specific occasions.

The doubt comes with noting the numerous faults and inadequacies built into SIET's original design. If SIET's decision-makers had assessed the environment in the terms mapped in this paper, the design did not reflect it. The first place, then, for me to act differently would have been to draw attention to those deficiencies, and make readiness to repair them a condition for my accepting the invitation to work on SIET's development. In fact, given our hazardous family situation at the time, the Foundation's inquiry about my interest came as a God-send and counseled acceptance in any case. Add my steady interest in "seeing how things go" in up-hill circumstances and my usual optimism, I would have accepted the invitation eagerly still, even a decade later and with the map in hand. What the map *would* have done, I feel sure, is to point me to work early and systematically on "linking the innovative sub-system [the Institute set out to be] into the system" at large.

That would have created the other juncture for acting differently, and I explored it in my dissertation. A prototype strategy for developing SIET could have enabled all—the governing board as well as faculty and consultants—to "see how it goes" under actually prevailing conditions. Casting anchor at, say, the end of a year's operations to concentrate for a while on taking stock, and only *then* planning the intended expansion in the light of this review—that would have been better than forging ahead as we did, certainly safer. SIET's decision-makers might well have accepted this prototype strategy. Without delaying SIET's quick start with programs, which was welcome, next seeing to the continuing seaworthiness of the vessel for the long journey ahead made very good sense.

My dissertation closed with a list of specifications for this prototype strategy (Lynton 1970, pp 570–74). I have reordered it here to show its progress, first to that prototypical stage and then onwards to full operations:

1. Effective prototype development calls for high rates of interaction with the environment, both ways. The interactions need to be sufficient in amount and in openness to allow much checking and testing out...initial plans...and [establishing] trust....

2. It is important that this collaborative ground work...be plainly visible in the environment.

3. [It] calls for outputs beyond...its primary goals, in particular for services which the environment requests or opens itself to. [Innovative sub-system] outputs may therefore exceed inputs during this phase.

4. [The innovative sub-system] is therefore overloaded from the first, ...less on narrowly defined direct goal activities, ...much on building relations with the environment.

8. Preparation for developing the prototype into the operating institution is marked by heavy investment...in securing environmental sanctions [and] internally...in designing and starting off specific programs and establishing their implications....

10. Alternating scanning for promising new lines for developing the institution and securing early sanction for their exploration... can continue to set an effective rhythm for the relationship....

11. The internal processes involved in working on plans and specific programs are valuable too for delineating units...for effective work over time—subsystems—and tend to become habitual....

12. ...[they] also surface issues of relationships, [both] patterns and quality. These call for heavy investment next [which] can fall sharply as soon as relationships are congruent with activities, current and prospective. [The heaviest] costs come late in the strategy,

namely when the prototype is ready to grow to full-scale operations while also keeping up its efforts to relate sensitively to its environment as it expands.

5. [Then] the transition...will be more effective and efficient if new personnel are recruited who...share the norms already developed between the prototype and the environment....

6. Some imbalance between the new institution's outputs and its inputs is likely to become [permanent]...because [both parties] have accustomed themselves to [it], ...and [also as continuing] retribution for [its] separateness.

7. Dependencies [to be feared] from this imbalance and from other costs can be kept low if the institution's personnel derive satisfactions from producing these outputs...and if interactions between the institution and the environment continue at a high rate....

9. With this type of preparation—recruitment in line with norms, securing sanctions, specifying programs [and regular contact between all partners]—the development of the new institution [to full scale] is then fast.

Engaging the "Relevant Environment"

At the time I worked on the paper and the dissertation (1967–69), the "environment" was still an abstract notion: an undifferentiated "whatever was immediately around" the innovative institution. In that paper, the environment was the "system" which had set up a sub-system to come up with the innovations it needed and which it would consider adopting generally after they had also been tested on a small scale and in that protected setting. This simple parental formulation in those tumultous years showed up as laughably/tragically inadequate. It provided no guidance about who all should be involved from the larger environment: the actual neighborhood, for example, in municipal services, in national policy bodies, or, in immediate focus, to ensure that SIET figured in the union ministry's budget. For every issue the range of plausible people and organizations to involve was so vast and vague that it would boggle the unaided mind.

"Involve for what purpose" would become a useful way of sorting the mass of possible inclusions and cut a practical path to just the *relevant* environment—Eric Trist's term. Next comes clarifying what an interaction with the relevant individual and institutional players needed to be like, given its purpose, time frame, etc. These were initiatives for the *institution* to take on its own behalf, and that signaled a sea change in visualizing environmental relationships. John Thomas and I joined the work to recast them. As the 1960s turned into the 1970s, this became my second stream of activity for gaining more intellectual clarity about systems.

Once again a change in position was at stake, this time from viewing the environment from within the system outward to seeing it in its own right from standing *there*—the third (for me) of Frost's "stepping stones". Studies till then did "not distinguish between the real attributes of the environment and the perceptions of the environment of policy-makers and managers in the organisation…. 'task environment' and… 'task domain' epitomised [their] perspective…. Most studies discuss either the degree of uncertainty in the organisation's environment or 'exchanges' with other organizations" (Lynton and Thomas 1979, p. 84). Or they focused on internal structure and processes and how institutions adapted them to the environment, as if these internal matters were the dependent variable. "The literature is replete with discussions of organisational 'adjustment' to changes in the environment, in 'response to' and 'affected by stimuli' in the environment…[and] organisations tend to adopt the same reactive stance" (ibid., p. 84).

What this stance avoided was setting goals, policies and action strategies clearly and determinedly enough for an institution *to project into* its environment and, though properly open to modification, assert itself there. Looking outward to adapt to what was out there discounted the better idea of a more mutual relationship, one in which exchanging and negotiating benefits would be the aim. Even better would be being able to find common ground, as between partners. The specifications just listed earlier for prototype strategies for developing innovative institutions had interactions "both ways" for a start. Reaching out was doubly important for institutions which depended on collaboration with key players in the environment who were highly autonomous. Professional bodies, most public services, and political and voluntary organizations were of that kind, as also more and more consumers in the commercial world as they became better and better informed and more affluent.

Those years were rich for systems theory. Fred Emery and Eric Trist had published their work on 'The Causal Texture of Organisational Environments' in 1965; Paul Lawrence and Jay Lorsch theirs on Organisation and Environment in 1967—both were seminal. Of the 55 references in my paper on innovative sub-systems (1969), 45 were from the 1960s. A major sustained strategy for mapping institution-building overseas was well under way with funds from the Agency for International Development; Melvin Blaise and Milton Esman were especially prominent in building theory. Within 10 years there were enough studies to warrant publication of a 300–page "source book" for it (Blase 1973). By then I had taken part in an effort to distill guidelines for team leaders of institution-building projects (Rigney et al. 1971).

For incorporating the whole set of prerequisites, John and I found institution-building theory best with its emphasis on the diversity of environmental linkages, organizational doctrine or purpose, internal structure and processes, and the interaction of these factors. That it was being developed for improving international assistance was of course an additional attraction.

The basic diagnostic framework for institution–environment interactions in that theory is given in Figure 7.2 (also see Esman 1967; Eaton 1972).

John and I added colleagial linkages, hence the brackets. They filled a gap that stared me in the face when, in 1970, I took charge of a project to interconnect 20 major universities around the world which were all trying to develop centers for population studies and stood to profit much from sharing experiences about how best to do that.[2] This was a rare opportunity for action-research with 20 like institutions at pretty much the same early stage of developing an innovative sub-system for the same purpose under similar pressures "to produce", and also in widely diverse cultures. See, intervene, and see again: what happened and what can be done next? Ideal conditions, I felt, for maximal clarity and for gaining it quickly.

Of most interest to John and me was how environmental linkages affected the doctrine and leadership of innovative institutions.

2. About this first orderly attempt of mine to "go to scale" through developing this inter-universities network—itself a new institution—there is more in the next chapter (Chapter 8).

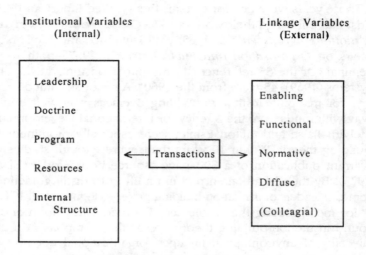

Institutional Variables   Linkage Variables
        (Internal)   (External)

        Leadership
                                                         Enabling
        Doctrine
                                                         Functional
        Program
                              Transactions   Normative
        Resources
                                                         Diffuse
        Internal
            Structure   (Colleagial)

FIGURE 7.2   Basic Diagnostic Framework for Institution–Environment Interactions

The Institution-Building Model distinguishes between linkages and between different purposes (Lynton and Thomas 1979, pp 89–96).

'Enabling' linkages provide the institution with legitimate authority...and give it access to the funds and other supports it needs. "Functional" linkages provide for substantive exchanges with the environment. "Normative" linkages deal with the establishment of standards in the institution and with its attempts to influence norms in the environment. "Diffuse" linkages are for building widespread understanding and support for the institution....

'Collegiate' linkages provide at institutional level what colleagueship does at the individual...one consortium of Catholic universities, for instance, [now] operates family planning clinics of a kind for which no one university wishes to take responsibility....

Beyond its use for overview and planning, the classification of linkages has practical values for the detailed designing, management and evaluation of linkages. It facilitates checking existing linkages for appropriateness to purpose and mutuality; both are required for effectiveness and stability of each linkage. Beyond that, if linkages are mapped and examined jointly, they reveal unattended or neglected relationships and other aspects of patterns important for institutional policy and planning. Such maps provide valuable data for decisions on institutional leadership, ...govern- ance, internal structure, resource allocation and operations....

In the Universities Population Project (UPP) of the University of North Carolina, comparisons of linkage networks typically revealed imbalances of three kinds, each likely to have serious consequences on institutional development if left unattended:

1. *Functional imbalances.* Irrespective of the overall density of linkage networks,

a. Functional linkages and enabling linkages for resources predominated;

b. Enabling linkages...were few and were used very unevenly over time. They were used most at the beginning...then atrophied within a year; in years 3–4 and 6–7, when crises characteristically occurred...they increased in number and strength and were used actively, usually under pressure of the university at large;

c. Normative and diffuse linkages were virtually absent. This... portends low legitimization and outside support.... Yet protection was especially important during the early critical period of new and highly experimental programmes..., before they were strong enough to deal with their environments on their own terms.

2. *Overload and conflict.* [There were] strong tendencies to make a few linkages serve many purposes.... [This] increased the tendencies of programmes to close themselves off from the rest of the university and from publics outside. For instance, enabling linkages with a government agency [for funding] imperilled...relationships with other units in the university...[and] extensive coverage in public media weakened legitimization within the university and the ability to mobilize faculty and departmental resources.

To the contrary, multiplicity and separability of linkages seemed to be an important principle.... [Where] a programme was linked to a single organization for enabling, functional, normative and diffuse purposes, problems and conflicts seemed continuous...and remained unresolved.

3. *Locational imbalance.* Asked which of nine linkage relationships they found most difficult, all programmes listed first either the university departments or national government agencies.... Programmes drew closer to either one and experienced difficulties with the other. This imbalance was touched off most frequently when programmes engaged in project work and project funding...

had become heavily dependent on one or two major clients [or] to escape this dependency, had multiplied their work contracts.... Either direction limited the programme's autonomy. [Some] basic university funds or programme development funds from elsewhere [greatly simplified this issue].

As the field-orientation of a programme made it attractive to public agencies and outside funds, this needed to be counter-balanced by strengthening programme linkages in the university. The second and third features which successful programmes had in common were a strong, explicit and well-publicised programme doctrine and a diversified leadership with notable strengths in designing and managing linkages.

Prominent in the doctrines of effective programmes...were specific statements about the disciplinary composition of the programme, its goals and priorities within and outside the university, joint decision mechanisms [notably for the allocation of funds] and frequent and full reporting of activities to established university bodies.... [Successful programmes involved] policy and implementing agencies in discussions and decisions concerning the development of programme activities [and these] were seen as "doctrine translated into action".

...Three leadership issues were prominent...

1. ...internal policy formation and structure and management of external linkages [were both essential yet] demanded different leadership styles:

2. A second issue arose from the need to manage simultaneously..."doctrine", specific programme activities, and the coordination of internal structure. Most programmes had difficulty developing leadership with competence in all three and in integrating them.

3. Providing separately for programme governance and for other aspects of institutional leadership.... in programmes with effective leadership, the structure of governance was derived specifically from the pattern of enabling and normative linkages.... [In] interdisciplinary programmes participating disciplines were included... while in field-oriented programmes agencies in the environment participated in the governance.... [The] first key decision taken by initiators of effective programmes was, in fact, who was to be included in governance.

System Transformation

Clearly, creating an innovative institution for pioneering system change came out of a very different frame of thinking from setting

out to do some particular thing differently because the environment "demanded" that adaptation. Policy-makers in India understood this strategic difference well as soon as the country headed
into world-wide trading and investing in the early 1990s: "changing the whole culture" of their organizations and gearing them
up to be ready to keep on changing.[3] To become learning organizations, in short.

To their anxious questioning I was by then able to bring pointers from two recent experiences of dealing with institutional environments. As founder-dean of a new graduate school of public
health in the American South, I had quickly instituted regular
"Thinktimes" for policy-makers in the state and the university.
Each "Thinktime" focused on an issue of pressing and well-aired
importance in the state. For a long weekend in a location directly
affected by state policies in the matter, it brought together 20 to
30 senior policy-makers with technical experts. A state legislator
or high official chaired it, e.g., the chair of the Senate Committee
on Aging. With him or her I had worked out composition and
location. The discussions were unhurried and off the record. University participants contributed recent data, and analytical and
technical expertise for quick assessments of policy options. Participants paid their direct costs (or their organizations did); not
one turned down the invitation.

For the new community-oriented school I was of course building both relationships and image with this in the university as
well as across the state. I was not surprised when some continuing mechanisms emerged for continuing the work on some policy options or some fresh emphases in teaching. What I had not
anticipated were quite startling shifts of direction on the issues
themselves. The sharpest took hold in the very first Thinktime,
on the public health consequences of off-shore drilling for oil.
The subject of hot and indeed fateful debate then was whether
the legislature should allow it or not. From the initial concerns
with air pollution and proper regulations to limit it, the focus
shifted to the much greater dangers that providing housing and
health services for the massive influx of out-of-state construction
crews would pose for the tourist resorts on the coast, which were

3. See the last section of Chapter 4 which dethroned "Lynton's crocodile"—or
   should have.

also important for votes and state revenue. I recall, these 20 years later, pictures screened at this Thinktime of storage sites in other states of unsightly mountains of long large-gauge pipes followed by anxious discussion, with maps of our own coastal area, about the nearest possible out-of-the-way sites and their transport and cost implications, given that the pipes were bound to be an eyesore. That second focus took policy-making in a very different direction to the first. Perhaps even more important, it deepened the discussion, paradoxically so at first glance, as the hard, concrete, detailed facts of the situation were taken into account.

That second shift was well illustrated when the sub-group considering health services specifically concluded that expanding the existing services in the affected areas on similar lines to expanding services in the state's growing cities would not serve the purpose here. The influx would bring in a quite particular population of young families with well-known special characteristics and needs, and they would come for only a year or two, till major construction was over. Expansion of services therefore had to be specialized, local, and large, but also temporary. With these important practical specifications, early contact with the contractors could help greatly; they planned the arrivals and departures of major batches of workers well in advance. Since contractors too would be mostly from out-of-state, the Health Department would do well to take the initative in contacting them.

In deliberately composing "Thinktimes" to represent major stakeholders and leaving direction and outcomes wide open, these meetings foreshadowed Future Search Conferences. Sharing the cost confirmed shared commitments to the outcomes. It was also in line with the mutuality of relationship the new School wanted to develop with its environments. Recruitment into its programs, field projects and their location, and time tables and advisory mechanisms for each program and for the whole School were other parts of the same fabric for collaboration.

In an international project in Colombia, also in the 1970s, I had set the stage for a more drastic intervention in the environment: to refigure the environment so that it would simulate the client's planned destination. The leading private university in Bogota was the client; a full-fledged graduate school the destination in view. The university's rector, an architect with a doctorate from

Cornell, personally conducted the negotiations in Chapel Hill over their several rounds. Any graduate school would have been the first in the country, but the graduate school he was after would also be singular in that its programs and degrees would directly address the country's major development thrusts. The University of North Carolina (UNC) at Chapel Hill, predominantly organized on the usual disciplinary lines, contracted through its Population Center to provide technical assistance.

Working first with the university in Bogota, it was possible to detail the combination of disciplines that would be included in the two programs which were to start the new graduate school— population and environmental planning. For population to become a leading field in Catholic Colombia called for the rector's particular backing, and all the more so since the medical school and its teaching hospital had to take part for the degrees to be comprehensive enough by international standards. Environmental planning was the reactor's professional interest and expertise. Pioneering with these two made the strongest possible prototype, with population the greatest test for commitment to transformative orders of change. This innovative plan for its highest degrees was bound to affect the university as a whole. The funding source for technical assistance propelled population to first place, but that may have been a good strategy anyway—to face possible opposition early when aiming for transformative change and so put system commitment to the test. Like marriage or the nation's presidency, institutional transformation too has a honeymoon for a start. Promoters' energies are still fresh then and any opposition has still to organize against unclear threats in the future.

In those circumstances, the mere mapping of disciplines to include in one or other program in Bogota masked much tougher and even more urgent tasks. Getting the backing of existing schools and departments, allocating funds and space, recruiting additional faculty, working out actual programs, teaching loads, appropriate compensation, and new or modified administrative arrangements on untested lines—all had to get under way. A colleague, native to Latin America, Spanish-speaking, and experienced in public health nutrition (and so close enough but not limited to population studies) moved to Bogota full-time to help get the first programs going. I managed the Chapel Hill end and directed the project overall. Three times a year I made week-long visits to Bogota and she as many to Chapel Hill.

For the first half-year, that is, till substantial clarities had emerged in Bogota about program composition and resources, and additional supports needed, I let matters in Chapel Hill rest on the formal commitments in principle that specific schools and departments as well as university administrators had contracted for. With clarities in hand from Bogota, we then created task groups from across schools and departments in Chapel Hill to match the program compositions and collaborations as planned *there*. Each group at UNC was made up of representatives selected by his or her dean or chair of department (and also occasionally changed over the years). She or he was the project's access to that unit as a whole for faculty consultations, teaching materials, advanced training for faculty coming from Bogota, and, most often, for help with program and faculty development there. While we greatly encouraged specially interested faculty in Chapel Hill to come forward to do this work (and especially those also proficient in Spanish and already familiar with Latin America), emphasizing *formal* links avoided confusing individual interests, however strong and justified, with the continuing systemic commitments of the schools and departments the work depended on. Payments for technical assistance rendered flowed in the same lines: they were negotiated with, made to, received by, and also accounted for by the school or department.

Arranging all this took many contacts and meetings. For the first two years, the project took a quarter of my time. The technical assistance part worked effectively and flexibly on this basis, also easily once started. Travels and exchanges started immediately once a component had become clear. With the organizational pattern established, parts of it could wait in the wings in the same way as an orchestra can be augmented or diminished according to the composition to be played. That this could be done in the oldest state university in the USA, cutting across its normal organization and operations, suggests that these unorthodox arrangements made good sense for the purpose and attracted the necessary goodwill. Permanent transformation would of course have been more difficult—even impossible?

What's in the Name?

Fragment to fragment clings; the things thus grow
Until we know and name them. By degrees
They melt, and are no more the things we know.

Lucretius, in Curtis 1945, p. 531

What's in a name that is so important that we have to clear it clean away before we can see something quite new? For UNC's part of the project with Colombia, it did not matter. Only tiny parts of the university were involved; the sub-system they constructed would disassemble when its specific purpose ended in three years, during which the contract paid all its costs and more. For UNC therefore this was a mere blip in normal operations, simply a brief episode on the classical change line, i.e., the upper line in Figure 7.1: stimulus from the environment → discrete innovation → temporary linkage mechanism → superficial (if any) effect on system. It is the totally new creation in the Colombian university that has no good name, because it exists only in the imagination at the start: turbulent environment → continuous innovation → permanent linkage mechanisms → major effect on system. The bottom line lacks even a named destination.

It would be "different" (from graduate schools elsewhere) because it focused on burning development issues. It would "transform" the university. What that would be like as it developed and what it and the university would shape into for good had to await the experience. "Look like" (or sound, smell, taste, over-all feel like) is right. The wordless image comes first, as freestyle lines on paper or motions in the air; odd shapes; blobs of color; jostling strange sounds. Only loosely grounded, images offer escape from names tied to past metaphors into meanings for what we try to grasp new, for visualizing what this transformation might be like that goes beyond mere everyday variations on well-worn themes. A switch, in short, to communicating in other than names to some different "language". A good rule of thumb is that whatever can be named already is off the route to transformation; the wrong wavelength.

Words will come, must come, but later: for sure we *will* name "the things (we) thus grow". Example: in recent professional literature I note "seam" taking the place of "boundary", as in "boundary management". The name change captures a change of image: "boundary", heavy with connotations of limit, wall, defence, and don't-you-dare-cross-it, is giving way to touching, putting together, linking up, aligning side-by-side or easy bridging, even of joining pieces that yet remain different. "Boundary" sets off attention exploring in a different direction than "seam" does. And from this transformation of vision different lines of action will flow as surely as fruit ripens in the sun. "The things thus grow...."

References

Blase, Melvin G., *Institution Building: A Source Book*, Agency for International Development, Washington, DC, 1973.

Curtis, Charles P., *The Practical Cogitator*, Houghton Mifflin Company, Boston, 1945.

Eaton, J.W., *Institution Building and Development*, Sage Publications, Thousand Oaks, 1972.

Emery, F. and **Trist, Eric**, 'The Causal Texture of Organisational Evironments', in *Human Relations*, Vol. 18, Tavistock Publications, London, 1965.

Esman, M.J., *The Institution-Building Concepts—An Interim Appraisal*, Research Program in Institution Building, Pittsburg, 1967.

Lawrence, Paul and **Lorsch, Jay**, *Organisation and Environment*, School of Business Administration, Harvard University, Boston, 1967.

Lynton, Rolf P., 'Institution-Building and Consulting: Complexities in Development Assistance', Ph.D. dissertation, State University of New York, Buffalo, 1970.

Lynton, Rolf P. and **Thomas, John M.**, 'The Utility of Institution-Building Theories for Strategies and Methodologies of Consultation', in Sinha, Dharni P., *Consultants and Consulting Styles*, Vision Books, New Delhi, 1979.

Rigney, J.A., Bumgardner, H.L., Ellis, Walter, Lynton, Rolf P. and **Jung, Christian W.**, *A Guide to Institution-Building for Teamleaders of Technical Assistance Projects*, Office of International Programs, NC State University, Raleigh, NC, 1971.

Valery, Paul, *The Art of Poetry*, Translated from French by Denise Folliot, Vintage Books, New York, 1961.

8

GOING TO SIZE

Images for Long-shot Strategies
Numbers Matter Too: Minimum Concentrations
  at Each Juncture
A Work Agenda

a mustard seed…the smallest of them all
…becomes a tree,
and the birds come and nest in its branches.

Gospel of Matthew, 13.31

a large part of man can never find its expression in the mere
language of words. It must therefore seek for its other lan-
guages—lines and colors, sounds and movements.

Rabindranath Tagore 1922, p. 196

Innovative institutions aim to make a difference beyond themselves. *What* difference precisely and how, and how much it mattered in the light of history many forces will influence, as also the deliberate moves that took it there. A governing idea encompassing it all though is essential for sound working from the very start. And that idea must break through the pull of words from the past, just as a satellite needs to escape earth's gravity to orbit.

Images for Long-shot Strategies

A Tree Grows in Indonesia

In the systems development work I did for five years in the 1980s with Indonesia's Ministry of Health and its services in the provinces, the image for making that difference was a tree. Purpose determined that the tree be large and strong, for it was to help the Ministry counter the prevailing powerful tendencies to concentrate policy- and decision-making at the center and help provincial governments take on more and more of that for.themselves. Since the same centralizing tendencies beset the whole government at that time, countering them would be extra tough, but decentralization had also been declared an overall policy. Hence, how health got on with it and learned in the process could also serve as a pilot for others. And the policy was backed solidly by facts on the ground: the tens of islands—counting only the larger ones—that made up Indonesia, stretching over 3,000 miles, were simply too different for the same service structures, processes, and priorities to serve all well or more or less equally well—ever. So, with national unity sufficiently affirmed, decentralization was the new direction.

My charge was to help develop the manpower for this in the provinces so that they could take over these functions, at the Ministry so that they could let them go, and with both so that they could rework their relationship to support this shift of responsibilities and control. Other consultants worked on policy and organizational issues, and on strengthening the statistical and monitoring components for the shift; rather separately, the project also had other consultants working on reorganizing the research arm of the Ministry. I went initially for one year, extended that by another and eventually stayed for five, the last three as team leader (Lynton 1986).

The image started simple, of course, as all really telling images do: just three parts—roots, branches, and treetop, with the trunk to connect them.

The roots were the inputs. Starting with the policy to decentralize, and time and funds allocated locally,, inputs also included the foreign consultants and some material aid. Imaging inputs as roots was not to keep their cost out of sight; on the contrary, I make a point of drawing clients' attention to cost. Roots convey two much more important notions. One is that the growth of the tree largely depends on them, for height, strength, and also speed of growing. The other, an important reminder in all third-party assistance, is that inputs become important in the *taking*, not in the giving: they matter to the growth above ground only as and when the tree draws on them.

The *crown* of the tree and its highest fruit, nearest to the sun, were "changes in norms and structures" in the Ministry and in the provinces and new capacities to sustain them, that is, the changes that would last and be most pervasive systemically. From the ground these crowning fruit would be least visible, even though they would be the most strategic outcomes of the project.

Visible fruit on branches at mid-level were program outputs along the way, such as management training, training materials, and local faculty. These fruits, growing in plenty from quite early on and immediately nourishing, were also welcome confirmation that the tree was growing well. But, like the apple in Adam and Eve's reach in Eden, it also tempted to end efforts right there. Nothing was better than this visible fruit for convincing decision-makers, in Indonesia no less than in foreign agencies, to praise the project and see it as successfully over. Keeping attention focused on the systemic developments the project aimed at became more difficult past the fruit ready for picking, especially when settling for them would avoid the struggling undoubtedly involved in working out the transformations of center–province relationships and structures at the top. The tree image showed very simply what was close to hand and what distant, what was visible and what underground (but no less essential), and how all had to work together.

Most importantly, the tree underscored the organic nature of the task—essentially of *all* innovative tasks. Conceptually, its component parts—inputs, program outputs, systemic change—and also how they fit together could be fixed. But then they had to make their way in the real world, with speed of growth, shape, eventual size, and strength all subject to all manner of changing conditions. Figure 8.1 shows the tree as it ended up.

The intricate root system shows 16 kinds of inputs (a box for each) and has grown from the two levels envisaged in the prospectus

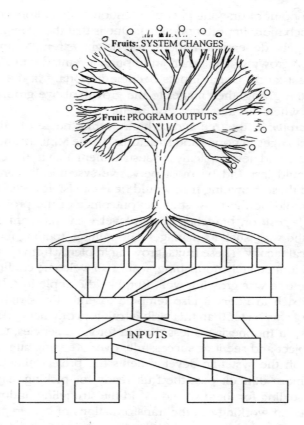

FIGURE 8.1   Decentralizing Indonesia's Health Services

to four and greater depths. Most deeply and securely rooted were the original technical inputs for health services staffs: task analysis, case research and writing, impact evaluation, and occasional later additions. Training and consulting skills were the next level up, and advanced programs above that. "Consultant interns" were the fourth and newest input, and the most complex, sensitive and spread out in any case, needing the steadiest support at the end.

Above ground, the tree branched out into eight major kinds of program, project, and consultancy outputs. They included inter-sectoral and inter-provincial training and consulting. The crown, to top it all off, identified six areas in which the national and provincial systems, and their work together operated with "improved norms and structures", e.g., personnel selections based on job criteria, national staff sent as participants in provincial programs, national networking of training and consulting resources, and their recognition as a professional association.

The work in Indonesia is the tree for this chapter, so we will return to its actual unfolding, numbers, and other practical aspects in later sections. Here, staying with images and imaging some more, I note how very different this tree image is from images that, looking back, catch how earlier projects of mine to build and direct innovative institutions actually worked in the wider worlds they were meant to affect. Better imaging at the beginning could have alerted me to major shortfalls in their design, certainly for Aloka and the SIET Institute.

Aloka: Star to Jester's Cap

For Aloka's design for influencing newly independent countries in Asia and Africa, the underlying image had been a simple star: Aloka was at the center and program participants the rays to their countries. What followed *there* from their 12-week experience at the centre, sponsor WAY and then Aloka too left unplanned and without further support. It would be what participants made it, with whatever support they mobilized locally.

In the event, we did a little better. The star image can show this with the little circle stuck on the end of each ray, like pompoms on the long ears of a jester's cap, as in Figure 8.2.

The small packages at the country end of the rays were first-aid kits for system change that Aloka put together over the years to quieten our nagging questions about the onward difference the training was meant to make. In addition to the selection of participants in pairs and some payment by their organization for their participation, which were in the original resolution to set up Aloka and had organizations sit up and examine their commitments and priorities, we added items as they occurred to us over the years. We located some Aloka programs in countries from which participants came (six in as many years); gave preference in admissions to candidates put forward by past participants and

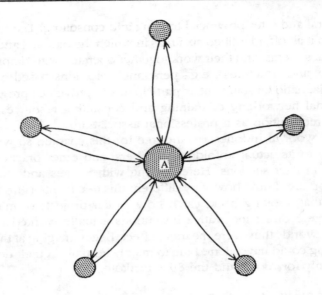

FIGURE 8.2   Aloka in its World

their organizations; created 10-day programs for senior officers from the organizations that showed the most promise; recruited past participants with the capacities and inclinations to join again as faculty (17 over the years); and in my touring, I did what I could to encourage, cajole, and help organizations and alumni along. The oddly assorted kit itself betrayed the absence of planning for onward developments in the participants' organizations and countries. Though more of a kit in the end than most training programs provide for ensuring that training gets actually used, it was still only tiny for influencing Aloka's world of newly independent countries, scattered over two continents, vastly populated and beset with no end of pressing tasks and crises—unlikely to matter more than the proverbial crumbs cast upon the seas.

SIET Institute: The Bells in a Ring
Though it had even less of a kit for system change than Aloka, SIET's promise for significant impact was much greater just because its world was very much smaller, and also more cohesive

and accessible. The participants it was meant for came from a particular office of a ministry and its branches in the states, and to those they also returned after training. Since that ministry also paid all training costs, it had a live interest in seeing the training used.

So SIET's image was the same star but set in a definite ring (Figure 8.3), not opening like Aloka to a world with virtually no horizon.

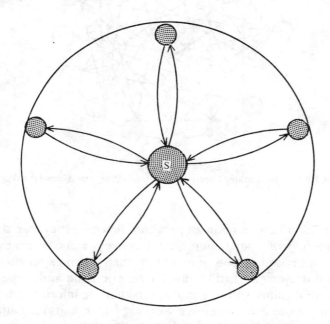

FIGURE 8.3   The SIET Institute in India

The UPP: Nets and Networking

For connecting population programs in universities around the world so that they could build on one another's experiences, the image starts with a necklace of 20 pearls, with each pearl also connected to all other pearls as in Figure 8.4.

The pearls were the 20 universities in the Universities Population Project. The project linked them, and the secretariat (in one member university at a time) stimulated and channeled

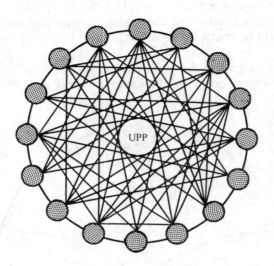

FIGURE 8.4   Networking University Population Programs Around the World

information flows among all program directors. It prepared and issued periodic newsletters and summary working notes on questions raised by one or more directors. When experiences in several universities had clarified a generic issue and some options for dealing with it, it pulled together the information, produced a more comprehensive working paper, and distributed it to all program directors (for them to distribute further as each wished). Each population center paid for recording, documenting, and providing information about its own operations and for questions it put into the pool. The directors together constituted the International Task Group. The heads of nine universities that had population centers and also high influence in their regions constituted the International Study Group and the project's governance. The project funded biannual meetings of them and their program directors. They took turns hosting the meetings. To those meetings were also invited additional program directors in the region.

Though initiated at UNC's Center and the secretariat being located there for the three years of American funding, this design made the universities equal partners, with UNC first among them for just that time. Towards the end, directors and the Study Group considered other funding sources and moving the secretariat to a second region, even relocating it by regular rotation. By that time, centers in two regions had started necklaces of their own and the university in Bogota had begun to parley its center into the broader graduate school I have already described.[1] Indirect evidence confirmed that several directors were also routinely in touch with others without going through the secretariat.

That the project in fact ended after three years is less significant than the broadly successful experience it provided in linking widely scattered and different universities for a specific purpose as peers helping each other, with none in the position of being expert or leader. The book-length review of the project (Lynton 1974) showed significant progress towards its original, quite limited objective of helping new population centers around the world start on the best possible footing.

Project Test Pattern: Tight Core, Outreach in Waves

This project set out to create a network of consultants who would be available to local congregations anywhere in North America. In three years it became a permanent institution—the Alban Institute—and continues innovating still. I was consultant first to its originator, Loren Mead, and then to the dozen Associates he pulled together to think through the project, develop its policies, and take an active part in pioneering the work in their parts of the country.

To help me retrace the ways in which this seed grew large, Loren recalled how the issue of using successful local experiences in similar situations elsewhere was first joined—the issue of multiplication. Continuing this multiplication with system support came next—amplification. Finally, whole church systems, plural by then, institutionalized particular innovations and in that process also incorporated important norms about focusing,

---

1. See the previous chapter, pp 224–26.

researching, organizing for, and managing system changes in general. An anecdote he called it.[2]

> About January 1972, with you acting as consultant, the project Associates met for assessment of what we'd been doing and to plan the future. At that time PTP had completed an abortive first-step in congregational change [an attempt to initiate change on a self-based planning effort by adding a bit of planning assistance], had restructured itself to try to use consulting skills to induce change [because of the tentative learning that whatever changes had occurred in the early experiment had been generated by the relationship to me—the outside agent in a low-grade, semi-consultant role—rather than by the training we had given in planning]. We had planned and organized 13 teams of consultants and designed a plausible consulting pattern; had deployed those consultants with a research feedback system to client congregations; and had had a couple of research analysis meetings.
>
> What was clear at that point was that we had a technology [consulting] that did have change impact on the congregations within certain limits, that we did have a research process that helped us figure out what we'd done, but also that we had a technology that was too expensive and uncertain for mass use [and] to do much about thousands of congregations.
>
> Bill Yon, I think, made the "a-ha" statement. He said we had a tool like psychoanalysis—where there was a perfect fit between patient and doctor, there were limitless possibilities, and...promise of developing incredibly helpful information about the operations of the human mind; but psychoanalysis clearly was no adequate answer for the mental health problems of society. The question, he put it, was to find how to use the tool we had in a way that it could have bigger bang for the buck. And he made a proposal: to use the consulting skills and research [the tools we'd developed] at a particular "crisis" in the life of a congregation. The "crisis" he proposed [we] concentrate this special effort on was a change of pastors. The hypothesis was that that would make considerable system change deliverable to a far wider constituency. It was no accident, his analysis also noted, that it was during periods of pastoral vacancy that congregations generally had a little surplus money they could use to pay for the tools.
>
> When the assembled Associates cheered, it was obvious that Bill's homespun wisdom had carried the day. That's what we decided to do.

2. Private communication, July 1996.

The next question was—what did we really want to have happen as a result of this. I'm not sure who said it—I think it was George Reynolds: "Well, we think we can make a real difference and that research can document it, but I'm really more interested in longer-term change—I want to change a norm in the church system." As we worked with what he meant, it settled into something like this: we identified the fact that almost no congregations had access to consultative help during pastoral changes as things were then; but when we had finished the research, we hoped to have made it routine, across the church, that when a pastor left, the congregation would be offered consultative help.

The plan of implementation directly addressed that need. We selected ten bishops to invite into the research with us. We chose them for their smarts but also for political clout—we wanted people other bishops listened to. We wanted people who, if they found this worked pretty well, would tell others and would be listened to. We further decided that we would not try to "control" the process entirely—we would let the bishop choose the consultants he trusted and use the process he was comfortable with—but that for nine months he would offer consultative help to every congregation whose pastor left.

Project Associate teams went to each of the ten bishops to develop the research contract; other teams went to selected sites after the nine months' effort and did on-site data retrieval. The material was edited and published some time later as *The Minister is Leaving* [Seabury Press, San Francisco, 1974].

Two things happened in the period after the research. First, the bishops who had been asked to do the research continued to offer consultative assistance to congregations whose pastor [had] left, also after the project was over. It became standard operating procedure in their dioceses. The second thing was that other dioceses rapidly began their own version of what was then called "vacancy consultation".

Today almost every Episcopal diocese does provide consultative assistance for any congregation that loses its pastor. The quality of the consultative work varies enormously, as does the way the bishops understand consultation. [We have discovered two generic misunderstandings many of them have: 1. Many bishops think of the consultant as their own "staff" person and use the consultant to maintain "control" over the congregation; and 2. under the pressure of clergy needs for jobs, many bishops understand the "vacancy" crisis as an issue of job placement, whereas our understanding is that it is primarily an issue of congregational development.]

Several other things happened after the research that would not have happened otherwise:

1. In my new permanent role [as director], as the Alban Institute emerged out of PTP I developed several contracts in other denominations to teach executives what we had learned in the PTP research. Each of those systems too incorporated ideas from the research into their set of procedures for the change of pastors.

2. A second, short piece of research used the PTP research as a starting-off point too. That is how the role of "interim pastor" got established. Again, in the years since, the role of interim pastor has become standard in many denominations.

3. We collaborated with peers elsewhere to develop independent training programs for "interim consultants" and "interim pastors", notably with the Mid-Atlantic Association for Training and Consulting.

4. With a small grant we helped the interim pastors themselves develop "The Interim Pastor Network", which now has an independent organizational structure and is self-supporting. That network has now taken over the training of consultants and pastors. Several denominations have also developed networks of interim pastors of their own.

So, Rolf, there in a nutshell is part of what that small beginning led to.

This luxuriant growth, from Project Test Pattern twenty years ago to Alban Institute now, can be summarized in four phases, each adding a fresh image to overlay the old as if they were transparencies on an overhead projector. For clarity I present them here separately:

A. "Associates"/peers field test and perfect innovation (Figure 8.5A).
B. They pinpoint a rare but regular life event in which this innovation is especially promising, and invite systems to use it for *those* and pay the costs (Figure 8.5B).
C. Innovation and guiding norms spread through the system. Institute continues research and publicises it, also adds capacity-building in client system (Figure 8.5C).
D. Institute invites and responds to peer systems to join in; self-sustaining programs spin off (Figure 8.5D).

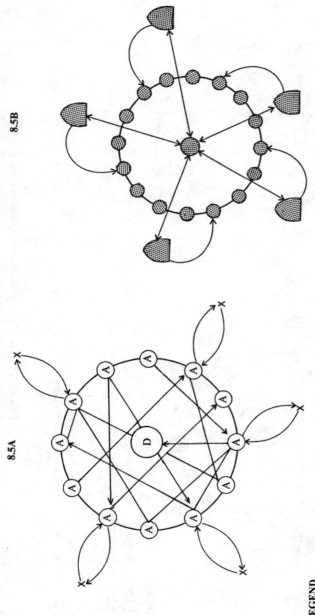

8.5A

8.5B

LEGEND

Ⓓ = Director

Ⓐ = Project Associate

✕ = Local Congregations

◖ = Diocesan, Religious Head, e.g., Bishop

◕ = Other Religious Congregations, e.g., Synagogues

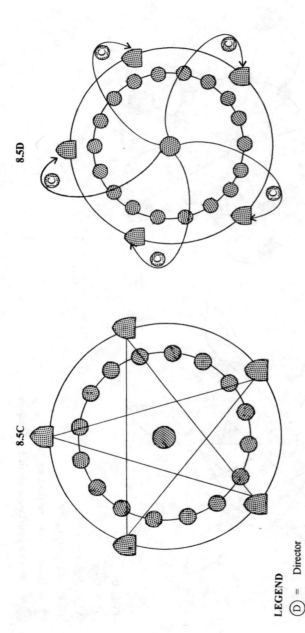

8.5D

8.5C

LEGEND

Ⓓ = Director

Ⓐ = Project Associate

✕ = Local Congregations

◖ = Diocesan, Religious Head, e.g., Bishop

● = Other Religious Congregations, e.g., Synagogues

FIGURE 8.5 From Project Test Pattern to Alban Institute

The tree image located going to scale firmly in the organic realm: even though the growing encompassed technical components that operated to predictable precision, the process as a whole, its pacing and even its eventual outcome, i.e., the size and shape of the tree were worked out only as it made its way into its particular multi-layered environment. In a new direction, certainly, but height and contours only broadly determined. The necklace image made peers of all participants: individuals, groups or formal institutions, like university centers or churches, all became learners and sharers together. Without teacher for the unknown ahead, all were colleagues who brought diverse strengths and needs. So, successful ventures to scale had dense collegial linkages. They also created strong programs of education and publicity for building goodwill and well-informed publics—the "diffuse" linkages that innovative institutions commonly neglect.

Building these features into designs, some from the start, others as changing conditions demanded them, also made markers of these features points for public reference. Public markers were important, lest attainments along the way were mistaken for merely personal preferences of enthusiastic innovators and so invited doubt and opposition.

Fixing markers of progress and making them public was doubly important where the finder/founder/planter of the innovative idea had then teamed up with a bunch of folk rather like himself who lacked credibility (and often competence as well) for getting the innovation into the large system and to spread widely. While perhaps best for that creative, daring first phase, they were not and never meant to be also best for going to scale. For that second phase, of involving the system, Loren had added high office bearers in the system itself. Even these were not mechanically selected, as if counted off the organization chart or region by region or by seniority, but by taking such diversities also into account they were chosen precisely for their likely influence in their church country wide. That was *their* part in ensuring the next growing phase. The selection of universities to be represented by their heads on the International Study Group, the unit of governance for the UPP project, reflected the same distinction. For each phase from seed to tree, function governed the design, composition, and the mode of working of the mechanism(s) for it.

Numbers Matter Too: Minimum Concentrations at Each Juncture

The worlds Aloka and SIET aimed to affect differed vastly in scale. Over its six years, Aloka drew 364 participants into its 19 regular programs, 27 of their senior officers into special supportive programs, and 17 past participants who looked promising as second-level multipliers in their countries again into faculty internships at Aloka: the altogether 26 countries from which they came had over a third of the world's population. That made Aloka a drop in a bucket. A drop has to be very potent to make a difference in a bucket-full.

At the opposite end of the scale, in equally vast India, SIET Institute was created quite specifically to upgrade the consultant services the Union Government provided to small industries. Six hundred consultant officers staffed those services then. For training them in batches of 30 at the planned rate of three programs a year, seven years would suffice for training all. After that, if turnover and new intakes continued at the then normal 10 percent, just two regular programs a year would suffice to train the newly recruited 60.[3] So, unlike Aloka in its vast sea, SIET would have capacity to spare in the not-so-distant future.

The opportunity to help plant a tree in middle ground—between Aloka's oceans and SIET's pond—came with the five years of work in Indonesia in the 1980s. Vast as Indonesia was, with its then 150 million people on 3,000 islands stretched along as many miles and grouped into as many provinces as India had states, its health services too were very large and widely varied—but still limited.

---

3. That calculation, incidentally, with the prospect that SIET would have "capacity to spare", provided Joe and me with logical backing for persuading SIET to add a second line of regular programs when it was barely a half-year into its first. The new programs were for area development officers in the states, a much larger pool of potential participants. The larger numbers, and also that they really made not one pool but several—one for each state, each at very different stages of industrial and administrative development—all this promised opportunities for many kinds of interventions. It also matched our vaulting ambitions better than working just with the established central services!

We set out with clear three notions and they were strategic:

1. We would persist with developing innovative and competent people till there were enough of them in strategic places in the national-cum-provincial system to continue working innovatively, i.e., a minimum concentration in each place.
2. We would link these innovative nodules into networks to nourish and support each other, to keep innovation growing and to branch out further.
3. We would get this network recognized as formally as possible and made permanent as an innovative sub-system in the Ministry.

These three together would constitute the manpower development component in the larger program to help the government decentralize its services.

Strategic decisions were immediately to be made—and unmade. Basing the work in the Ministry's division for training—Pusdiklat—could not be challenged, low though the training unit was on the totem pole of that system (as it is in most systems around the world). Happily, Pusdiklat had a strong man at the head when we started; just as happily, when he moved on soon after to head the much weightier division of hospitals, he appreciated my continuing to stay in touch with him and also with heads of other operating divisions. But the advance selection of provinces I disputed and succeeded in changing on overall system grounds: yes, we would work first in "the outer islands" where health and health services needed improving most, but only in one to start with, and right from the beginning we would also work with an advanced province—both at the same time. Maybe the more advanced could show the way. More likely, we thought, in the more advanced province issues of innovating in this system would show up soonest and along with them also the indigenous capacities—and gaps—for dealing with those issues. And Java itself, with the three most populous provinces, and still dominant in national affairs and also in the Ministry, *had* to take part, no question. Otherwise, we were sure, any hope of affecting the Ministry would disappear. In the event, we started the provincial part of the project in one of the stronger provinces in

"outer" Sumatra, and in West Java soon after. By the end, all three
Java provinces participated fully.

Changing the center–province relationship required that the
work be done with both at the same time. Developing capacities
in the province(s) so that it could take more responsibilities for
planning, decision-making, implementing programs, and monitoring could only progress as the central Ministry in Jakarta let
go of those responsibilities and let provinces assume them, and
that too in their own ways. Similarly, vice-versa: the two were directly inter-dependent.

Officials at the center were bound to find this divestiture difficult even to tolerate, never mind encourage and help it along.
That all were physicians would make extra difficulties, unprepared as they were by training and professional practice and high
standing to exercise authority indirectly. And for the officials in
the provinces (also all doctors then), the signals from their colleagues in Jakarta had to be extra clear and repeated many times
before they would believe their incredulous eyes and bother to
develop the new competencies and habits they needed for actually exercising the responsibilities their colleagues at the center
had held heretofore. These predictable complications were topped
by one more here: this drastic change, even reversal, of center–
province relationships would be attempted through the time-
honored felicities, meticulous manners, deference to social
status, and delicate circumlocutions of Java, and with a Javanese
born and bred into them at one end at least of the transaction
and usually at both.

The consulting design reflected these anticipations. I insisted
on two very experienced consultants joining me full-time, each
to live and work in one of the paired provinces for the six to nine
months we estimated it would take to start the process off there,
while I worked the Jakarta end.[4] Their task was as sharply focused on system change in each province as mine was at the center. To maintain this focus, we had other consultants come to Indonesia from time to time to make the needed technical inputs.

4. Udai was one of these. To make sure the second would also be "very experienced", I advertised for a "grey-haired" consultant. Michael Merrill applied,
   qualified in every way but color of hair—his was red! He joined together with
   Alexandra—the beginnings of wonderful colleagueships and friendships.

We maintained an international panel of short-term technical consultants and used altogether seven most repeatedly.

In two respects particularly is the work in Indonesia worth further attention here: its considerably greater growth and strength beyond any foreseen, and its progress with ensuring minimum concentrations of system capacities in many key places and the monitoring of this.

About the projected growth, the "End of Assignment Report" tells this:

- After June 1985, Indonesian "consultant interns" replaced foreign consultants in most and, by September 1986, in all technical assignments....
- Intensive trainer and training system development has reached all eight Provinces planned in the second, up-scaled phase of the project.
- In the five most advanced Provinces, *minimum concentrations* of trainers have been developed...capable of running independently programs for health services staff at all levels in Task Analysis, Case Teaching and Consulting Skills and in training additional trainers.... In one province the network now has three levels: 30 at provincial, 120 at [area] and 170 at [local levels and] has become a guide to later Provinces....

  [Figure 8.6 reproduces the pyramid in the Report that showed the concentrations of trained staff and of trainers at provincial and national levels of the system at the end of the project.]
- [The Ministry's training department] has strengthened its capacity to service and coordinate these developments in the Provinces.

  Beyond the outcomes projected in the 1983 Project Paper, two higher levels of competence have also been developed and put on a regular basis.... [This has] led to the identification and system recognition of continuing professional leadership for them, and now make the outlook for continuing development and expansion promising. These are:

  At level 3, the 7-week advanced programs for management trainers—three so far, for a total of 88 participants selected for their outstanding work in earlier technical and trainer programs.

  At level 4, the program for now 41 consultant interns and developing a permanent consulting service in the Ministry.

  The *depth of this capacity building* deserves attention.... Only since the first groups of trainers returned to their Provinces and to Pusdiklat [the national Department] from an Advanced Program

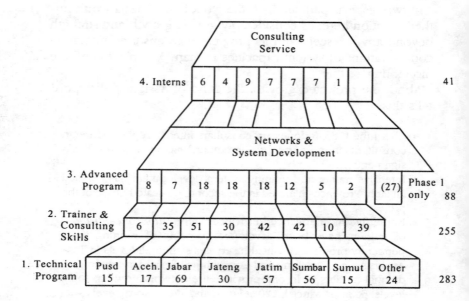

FIGURE 8.6   New Training System Capacity in Provinces and Nationally

have major network and system developments become evident
and influential.

Improved work norms and structures are particularly notable because they promise continued development. *Nationally* four may
be particularly important:

— advancement of trainers by performance based criteria and
processes;

— integration of significant sets of field-oriented training materials
and methods into career programs;

— regular use of consultant interns between Provinces and in the
Department; and

— the Department's recognition and support for the formal Association interns have formed.

At provincial level, the readiness to release from among their most competent staff consultant interns for assignments elsewhere shows that they value the program highly. Inter-sectoral working has become frequent. Among trainers, team working and careful planning and reviews have become norms.

At its second national meeting, *the Association* detailed rigorous criteria for advancement in four further steps to independent consultant status [a recognized official classification which would also carry financial benefits], selected officers and took steps to formal registration. Pusdiklat welcomed this and offered the Association office space and other continuing support.

Four *current issues and recommendations* stand out:

1. *Further increasing numbers* ...disaggregated to Provinces and into the seven specializations, it becomes quickly clear how very small system capacities still are when compared to needs...in many places [they are] still short even of minimum concentrations to assure survival....

R[ecommendation] 1: Probably most important is to recognize such discrepancies as normal and to carry on the step-by-step multiplier model, i.e., at provincial level [the minimum concentration is] 1 leader + 3 advanced trainers + 3 trainers + 4 area trainers + 4–6 local trainers [a total complement of 15–17].

R 2: Quickly arrange technical assistance and fellowship programs for next year.

2. *Quality maintenance* is at high risk under prevailing...pressures to expand fast, cut budgets, save inputs....

3. *Preoccupation with crises and overuse of few trainers*

R 3: Continue to chose programs and projects which serve both development and immediate services and locate them for best system development outcomes.

R 4: Enable trainers and interns to work in pairs and small teams and secure funds accordingly.

R 5: Press ahead steps towards full consultant status and pay [for when local consultants qualify for it].

R 6: Actively foster regional linkages in order to create quickly minimum concentrations of dispersed but key resources [while individual provinces are still short of minimum concentrations of trainers for themselves].

R 7: Press ahead with giving local training centers assured access to these new resources.

4. *Planning and management capacity.* Still new and unpracticed, needs further support, especially at national level.

R 8: Press ahead with recruiting a senior OD consultant with special competence in network management.

[The Report ended with a "Review of Project Strategy". Ten "preliminary pointers" made the list of plusses:]

- willingness to push ahead in a few Provinces ahead of others;
- identification, from the very beginning, of technical inputs acceptable for shifting attention to the field of actual management situations and practical actions; with others added where and when useful...this approach created spin-off projects and, more important, collaborations [with other practitioners, system units at various levels and communities];
- insistence from the first on selecting and advancing participants on performance and organizational support criteria;
- responding to unplanned requests from senior staff for related inputs [they needed in connection with these developments];
- flexible funding for quick allocation and reallocation of resources;
- locating a senior consultant in Provinces in turn. [This] signified special importance, [and] kept efforts moving and focused...long enough to establish new norms;
- raising Pusdiklat's interest in and respect for developments in Provinces. HQ staff went there for their training and returned refreshed by contact with the field and with important new relationships;
- Advanced Programs becoming an important reference and increasingly sought after;
- making intensive work on personal, team and organizational development a normal part of most programs;
- [advancing] particularly promising participants to faculty [interns] in the very next programs [of that sort].

Among the steadily growing streams of internships [the Report concluded], the one involving system development interns from Provinces in working with the [central Department] may turn out to be especially significant.... [They are uniquely well qualified to help the Department] review its role and functions in the light of strong developments in the Provinces, revise policies and priorities, and also develop new mechanisms for guiding and supporting regional networks of trainers and consultants.

A Work Agenda

"Going to scale" is already a better image for the transformations involved than "expansion", with its overtone of one unit growing larger and larger like a balloon, and far, far better than the till-recent concentration on "diffusing" innovations, which hides the essential transformations altogether. Better names will surely come in the course of doing more, and also more orderly, work on taking off from successful local experiences to transform large systems.

What holds this work to snail's pace will come into better focus in the next two chapters. Both inner and outer limits are the matter, and the fainthearted among us try to look wise while merely immobilized in the middle, hesitating to make up our minds and act. It is a losing position. From many corners the state of the world echoes the "what do we do *now*" level of questioning I faced in the recent meetings with corporate executives in India mentioned earlier: "how can we change the whole culture, how can we best approach what we have to do and then also do it". So present positions cannot hold. In the face of that prospect it makes no sense to go on understanding less about scaling up than about any other major area of our professional work, and do so little to catch up.

In a lecture to inaugurate a new center for applied studies in Delhi University in 1992, I roughed out a seven-point agenda for this work (Lynton 1992, pp 55–63).

Two directions of promise are immediately clear:

1. Retracing how any of the major attention-getting changes in the last two or three decades did in fact amplify world-wide, e.g., the concern for environmental safeguards, the actual decline in family size, and the emergence of influential consumer movements.

2. Instituting concurrent recording, action research and, where useful, policy making and field operations for large scale work.... [It] looks more and more like a complex and sustained process, with diverse beginnings in many places and all manner of people taking part, [and will] need support in many novel ways and [come to] encompass larger and larger areas....

These two directions already seem to me more promising than pursuing into more detail the negative question of why this or that patently successful local effort has failed to get larger or amplify. Research studies...have already substantiated a set of conclusions about this....

3. Action research is needed and also possible to establish which aspects of the large system to be influenced are strategic to include in the design, operations and culture of the innovative unit, and also what limits and opportunities their inclusion creates for innovation. How different can the innovative unit become and still expect to influence the large system? Also, how different must it be in order to innovate?

...incorporating those features at every intermediate level to the whole system involves designing and developing linkages between the unit and several layers of the large system, and also the processes for identifying and managing the essential differences between them and for negotiating across these boundaries.

4. Strategic work is to be done on designing and operating these intermediate linking mechanisms....

Preliminary indications are that significant initiatives, committed effort and supportive arrangement that work are mostly local, that the "centre" of action is *there*, in the places that people in public affairs, professionals included, often see as the "periphery".

The processes that matter are highly *interactive* between people and parties at the same level or between adjoining levels in the structure. These people and parties prize their autonomies, and the processes of development and interaction take very varied forms.

5. Opportunities for important work are also offered by action research and consultation with local bodies which are willing to assume increased responsibilities for development in their area and [are also] open to linking up with like-minded others.... Experience suggests that [they] already have more opportunities for assuming developmental responsibilities than they tend to use and that higher level officers are often quite willing to support local initiatives. Only testing the limits may effectively show where the [limits] are, and action researchers can help local bodies [and higher officers] design and do the testing....

6. [Follow through and research] cases in which development responsibilities have already been reallocated by structural interventions, some on a very large scale....

7. Work [is needed] on interlinking these units of initiative and action into associations and networks...and interlinking networks across levels [of larger systems, e.g., a city, a state or province]. Work shows wide varieties of ways in which social pioneers and creative bodies organize support and link up.... The patterns [are] highly diverse. They are also very changeable: organizations start, links are formed, many disappear, new ones emerge.

...directors and university heads [in the UPP project] found "link-age issues in connection with collaboration [one of the two that were] most important, most difficult and the most common root of distortion and failure. ...associations and networks tended to have a star-shaped pattern of relationships: one institution mounts the energy to collect and send out information...and [does] all the usual activities, and little attention is given to developing contacts at the periphery, between the member institutions themselves. Pro-gram directors consistently stress their need for the opposite model: a loose association of organizational equals, shared lead-ership, and flexible information and other resource flows" [Lynton 1986, p. 13].

"Think globally, act locally" is an admonition that has gained common currency, with a truer and more widespread apprecia-tion for how very large and interconnected the world's problems are and the often major transformations they call for. It poses nicely what is at stake for working effectively: to have accessible, as if on revolving radar, the whole range of requirements for go-ing to scale while focusing on particular moments for decision and action, one after another. Both the particular and the overall have to be in play and inform each other. With that attention on both, many habitual dichotomies and the simplifications they promise turn out to be no help at all; worse, they mislead. For work on transforming large systems, the center–periphery and the leader–follower dichotomies need discarding, among others, for change in either half limits change in the pair. Not either/or but and...and is the proper mode for this work. Both have to be present.

No less is this true for us who profess to understand and work on going to scale. We can take in only as much scale and com-plexity as we can personally stand inside of the wide world out-side. To all the rest we simply go blind, or we domesticate it to our measure. So, good outer work on going to scale has to go hand-in-hand with good inner work on readying the person who sets out to do it—the practitioner. And to have what it takes—clear eye, clear head, stout heart, and openness to share the work with many kinds of others—as well as to use the inevitable short-falls and failures along the way for learning keeps this work going.

References

Lynton, Rolf P., *Institution-Building for University Population Programs: A Short Guide for Policy Makers*, Carolina Population Center, UNC at Chapel Hill, Chapel Hill, 1974.

————., 'The Training Component, September 1983–1986: End of Assignment Report', Unpublished, Ministry of Health, Indonesia and US Agency for International Development, 1986.

————., *The Sound of Sense: What's So Hard About Being Practical*, Centre for Applied Behavioural Science Studies and Action Research, Monograph Series No. 5, University of Delhi, Delhi, 1992.

Tagore, Rabindranath, *Creative Unity*, Macmillan, London, 1922.

9

THE PERSONAL DIMENSION: MORE INNER WORK

Three Scenes, Same Actor
"Presence", "Personal Authority": Finding
  Some Pathways into What That Could Mean
Authority of Person, Position and Situation
Fresh Soundings for Presence

...to be receptive to intimations of transcendence we must turn the mind from a storehouse into a finely tuned instrument...free to perceive....

Upanishad, quoted in Sondhe 1996, p. 13

*...it is too little to be ready,
one must also be really there.*

Martin Buber 1961, p. 3 (emphasis in original)

One's measure of the world and the position taken in it cannot be truer than the instrument: the practitioner, myself. Person and direction of life's efforts crystallize together—or dull together.

Here, for two reasons, I will first hold each still and separate a while—the person in this chapter and a life's direction in the next. As with a diamond and its 56 facets, precision determines brilliance and value. Hence, to highlight one facet, I want to be sure to place adjoining facets to throw new light on it and also not let some attribute which is really crucial slip by unnoticed. The second step is to examine the words for the inner meanings that major work calls for, so that they get washed of past meanings and emerge fresh, or we may even replace them with new images more telling for these times. More refined formulations are not our aim here, never mind new theory; grappling for fresh (or refreshed) meanings is. And for that our start must be with noticing more, with fresh attention, and so also with prizing more highly what we see. This chapter will thus hold the focus on the personal dimension—that which determines the scope and depth of what we can each see: the instrument. And the next chapter will hold the focus on what there is to see in the world "out there" that needs us to be fully present.

Three Scenes, Same Actor

I open this personal dimension to observation and sharing with three scenes. The two briefer scenes—one regular, the other singular and quite recent, and both with this chapter in mind—show me at different times and plays. The third has an important other person on center stage, with me watching: I wonder and seek to understand how she can be so totally present and what her strong presence can tell the rest of us about what makes for personal presence, what it is, and how it affects others. The three will throw light on each other as the adjoining facets of a diamond do on turning.

Scene One: at squash. I play three or four times a week, have kept it up for many years. At 72 I have no concern left about technique, only about stamina, strategy, and divining my partner's patterns well enough at high speed and in that small space to make this morning's game "a good one". Really no concern about winning either. What matters is that I play well at my standard and for my age; that at the end I have played "my kind of game"; that it is indeed I who have been on the court. (With the three clauses in the sentence just past I must be unravelling more personal ways to clarify my intent—rather like peeling an onion.

I will in this chapter also share my occasional awarenesses of inward meanings connected in some way to my observations. Those will be in parantheses.)

For me to be so present at squash, to do myself justice there, as the wise saying goes, I have attention only for the ball in *current* play between those walls with that day's partner in particular. I have no thought for his or her doing her best to get out of my way (the culture of squash and very occasional exclusions have taken care of that in advance); none for the rally just past or even the next, or for my growing exhaustion, or for strategy for the game as a whole. Those make thoughts for between serves and between games, and, of course, for reflections and resolutions after the game is over. No thought about breakfast and what's for the day. If, despite my knowing that they do not belong here, some festering crisis at home or at work intrudes even in passing, the next serve or return will reflect the distraction: it will be too "this" or too "that". At other times I astonish myself (and partner) with a shot or a position in anticipation of his or hers that was "impossible", outside my range: I couldn't explain or even describe what I did and would not know how to do it again. At that brief moment, I had it "all together". I played with utter abandon, that is, with all of me present: my best.

Scene Two: the past that is present and the future that is present. I am in our joint family home in Hyderabad, India. It is Monday, the last in October, first light. Book in hand I am on my way with a cup of tea to my favorite reading place on the balcony over the undulating sea of green leaves in front of the house, the green doubly appealing for having been planted not yet a decade ago into this rocky dry landscape of Hyderabad and being so lush. I idly pick up a daily paper lying open-folded. If I had anything on my mind, it is this chapter, the next to write. I am "through" with the previous chapter in the sense that the day or two it will still take me to finish it do not occupy my mind. I can let it unwind; I see its ending. So this next is preparing to come out. But at the back of my mind at best. This first hour or two of the day is my quiet time, kept free for ruminating, reflecting, reading. Unfocused in any deliberate way that is. Any planned thing follows this loose opening to my day.

But in as much as my mind is on anything, it is on this chapter and in particular how best to get into it. How to write about this quite essential inner work and not, especially in this book of a life's particulars, have it appear "metaphysical". (The word touches off a distant memory. Back in Aloka days, I once responded to a newspaper interviewer that community development officers might do well to listen more to villagers. "Oh, Lynton, he's metaphysical", then India's Minister for Community Development, S.K.Dey, was quoted as commenting on that interview.) I must stay firmly planted on the ground in this chapter, immediate and solid, and have readers join me there. Only after I have written about personal things will I take off in far-reaching directions. I know that these two dimensions, the most inward and the furthest out, are really paired. Only with eyes clear can I see far and also scan widely with blinders gone (or at least known and allowed for). And with little or no fear of what I might see. Any one scared stiff in apprehension exhausts all energy inward, bending what s/he sees to his/her own comforting. "I am ever busy building this wall all around", Tagore sings, "...I plaster it with dust and sand lest a least hole should be left in this name" (Tagore 1956, p. 23). To let no light in. To appear strong and finished smooth like a billiard ball, to be moved only by force, if at all, or only the least distance, and be quite the same in the new position: as if untouched and untouchable. (I scare very rarely, and then not much.)

In my awareness now are leaves before and just below me—the sea of them that will shade the romping, chatty children who will presently troop through the creaky gate into the little school ground below. Leaves on trees. Trees, as in the tree image in the chapter just over: so the present reaches for the past. And into the future: from small seeds—children into adults grow.

My eyes light on the quarter page open on my lap, one-eighth of the middle sheet. "The Speaking Tree" labels the column. There I light on the first quote for this chapter, from the *Upanishads*, about becoming fine instruments, for seeing clearly. Metaphysical?

I seem very ready to play this morning, as the take-offs from leaves and trees show. Can there also be a more ranging readiness to take in pretty much *anything*? At *any* time? Does it need long habit to acquire it (if that is how it can be done, and how long is "long"?) And can this readiness then be marshaled to a fine point for action with abandon—my best—as on the squash court?

Writing this morning episode off as chance, a happy coincidence that immediately yielded a quotation, would surely tell nothing. My readiness had a forward direction too: getting on with the next chapter. It had both disposition *and* direction. And the world to feed on. Not all the world, but "my world", the world I touch and which touches me and which in that sense I make up. It is all I have.

Scene Three: September 1995. Mallika Sarabhai has two days of dance and dance-demonstration engagements in Washington, DC and Ronnie and I will spend those with her. We have known the family for all Mallika's life and stay with them when we are in Ahmedabad. The second Aloka program was housed in her great-aunt's compound, her father wrote the preface to the Aloka book, and Ronnie has written *Born to Dance* (Lynton 1995) about Mrinalini and Mallika and the Darpana Academy with which they play so prominent a role on the Indian dance and art scene. Now, driving to Washington, I was all joyful anticipation.

Those wonderful, relentlessly full days then also set me to ruminating about personal presence. As Mallika, entering Baird Hall at the Smithsonian, rain-soaked, talking animatedly with people milling around her, lit up on seeing us and rushed over, I was struck again with how wholly present she is. I feasted on it and marveled: how *does* she do it?! When, after Mallika's solo performance, others remarked on that very same quality, using the same word for it—"presence"—I began to pay special attention. What is it anyway that I name "being present" and what goes into it; what is my part in what I "see" in her or rather *find*; and what in this subtle compound suggests more general pointers perhaps worth wider sharing.

Extra awareness is all I achieved during those brief full days themselves. Back home, I wrote my way into making sense of these questions for myself out of this so-live experience.

Days, then weeks, passed with this. Other tasks often interrupted, but many times I also halted to leave my thoughts alone a while. This was not out of frustration but, as the extracts will show, with the awareness that I had taken a line of thought as far as it would go. I wanted to get out of the way of the Mallika–Rolf story, spiked by those two days, and leave "itself to tell how it can", the way Frost writes a poem: "It begins in delight, it inclines to the impulse, it assumes direction with the first line laid down,...and [it] ends in a clarification of life—not necessarily a great clarification, such as sects and cults are founded on, but in a momentary stay against confusion" (Frost 1964, p. ii). So I also kept aside all thought about what kind of writing this piece would turn out to be or of what use to others; not even the idea of this book was then on the horizon. But I did "live with" the story as it unfolded; even during fallow times in the writing of it, as I was reading or walking or dreaming, some line, some phrase would intrude at "odd moments" and touch off a new thought or some further refining.

Eight weeks and 15 single-spaced pages later I was done. A "working done" for now. After the mandatory reading by Ronnie and the usual reduction of long unbroken sentences, I sent it to eight close friend–colleagues for comments. The freshest image that came back likened the story to a "symphony, with its several themes weaving in and out at greater and greater depths". The excerpts here incorporate many comments.

"Presence", "Personal Authority": Finding Some Pathways into What That Could Mean

> ...as in yonder valley the myrtle
> breathes its fragrance into space....

The image is Gibran's Prophet telling about "giving" that is indistinguishable from "being". It is lovely—and utterly simple. Perhaps it appeals even more because it is lovely by nature (not crafting), unbounded (not choosy), and quiet (oblivious of all attention).

My mind surfaced this verse as I tried to get my arms around the sense of "being", as in "being present"—fully, truly present. That is presence of a different order from reporting attendance, as in a class or courtroom, or on parade. And this presence opens to all, "as in yonder valley", not just to some people or for some of the time. Humanly speaking, of course. That I let "being" jostle "giving" aside, even overpower it (in the basic sense of being the greater of the two) feels right: maybe being truly, fully present *is* the greatest gift any of us has to give.

Mallika is the best person for me to explore this with, for I don't think I know of any other person quite as vividly "present" in my reckoning as she is. I can only start with me: I want to recollect Mallika's "presence", those days and earlier, when exploring the experience with presence and trying to strike direction(s) and find paths to give "presence" denser and deeper meaning.

This will come, I anticipate, with a kind of attentive walking over this ground—unhurried, without determined destination—to learn what I can, to discard foggy patches in my understanding, and make fresh clarities last. I ask your company in this walk, a kindred spirit. What I *see* and what *you* see (or don't see, or see differently, as we walk)—to clarify—that is the quest. That, and what to make of what I—we—see. This second level will often be only barely different from where we already are in our appreciation.

I hope for some deepening too as we cycle back again and refine a recollection, or as we see the same thing afresh from a different angle or in different company. Through sharing what we each see, and what we make of it, you can also help me separate out what I bring personally to these understandings of mine and clarify what is "out there", what is Mallika's (or, by implication, any other's) part, and what is mine. In the perspective language that John and Joyce Weir urge for keeping crystal clear our own responsibility for what we see, the "presence-in-me" of all out there and the "Mallika-in-me" in this particular instance are all I ever have to work with in my life. So, in our walk, I will also halt from time to time to insert an image or whatever else is going on inside me that strikes me as relevant at this point, and how I intend to proceed from here onward taking that too into account. I may not like the fragrance the myrtle gives off so freely; I may even find it quite nauseating! And yet I can still resonate with its freedom—to be itself—and to be as fully present myself.

Enormous Energy—And It Shows

"After 40 we get the face we deserve." What strikes me first, and again and again, during these 18-hour days, is Mallika's enormous energy. My marveling at it is no doubt backed by my acquaintance with the many kinds of things she does and the responsibilities she carries in her life any time and anywhere: she *ought* to be exhausted, preoccupied, etc., etc., but she isn't! What I meet instead, at any hour (*all* hours?) are clear looks and a resonant voice speaking complete sentences, even whole paragraphs; her

looking quite lovely, even fresh, animated when moving—usually briskly—but very much alive too when quiet. (Or is it I—
we—who carries this sense of M's aliveness [= "presence"?] over
into her quiet moments?) Energy, amazingly continuous energy,
yes, and that energy is all ready to engage at once and with great
spontaneity.

Mallika goes quiet quite often, is not at all frenetic in gesture
or action, and is not always active. Nor does she hug attention
(though she certainly has and holds mine!). Very directly engaged she surely is, listening and conversing with one or with a
handful of people, as when sitting around a table. And that engagement seems to me very precise: finely matched and meshing. This is no less so in the auditorium full of students in the
morning and again in the darkened hall full of sophisticated
adults who have each paid $16 to see Mallika in "Sita's Daugh-
ters" at the Smithsonian that same night.

She must be physically well, to be so vibrant. She eats and
drinks with relish—but food chosen with care. (At home the
menu is well-known: vegetarian, much of it fresh, preferably
home-grown.) Regularity of eating seems to matter less—till she
is "famished", then she "wants to eat" and looks for nourishment.
M doesn't assume other members of the troupe to be as flexible.
Their hosts "*must* know that people on stage must eat *after* the
performance", but, incredibly, they seem surprised and unprepared.

This high energy is surely part of Mallika's "presence" (just as
low energy may account for much of the inattention and mind-
lessness with which folk step into the maelstrom of city traffic in
India: fuzzy, uncoordinated, vague, not even caring perhaps, already close to lifeless, certainly low on energy). M refreshes her
energy too, I note. She naps in the car in between places, or at
least her eyes are shut.

Pruning and Paring: Energy Focused

Without something more, though, energy and the ability to mobilize it merely indicate capacity, potential, the resources M (or
any of us) has available to call on. What converts the energy into
personal "presence"?

Paring is evident, a *not attending* to some things in order to attend
to others. (This points in the direction of coherence, of integrity;

even at this point I feel sure we will return to that.) What and how M shuts things out has lots to do with her presence, I think. She *husbands* her energy, minds what she applies it to, uses the immense energy she has available with fine economy. She tunes out whole episodes. Here is an instance. At some point quite early on, Mallika tunes out of the efforts by the rest of us in the car to try and find our way through pelting rain to the theater that first night. M rests.

She spends no energy on disappointments, at least on voicing them. (Also on feeling them? Some, maybe. We know of some very personal ones that hurt deeply. Day-to-day ones at least, then.) We finally find the theater and arrive, wet and bedraggled, only to learn that the play had started 20 minutes before. It was about Ganesh and had had good reviews. The showing that night was specially for the Indian community, headed by the ambassador, and for the DC press: an invited audience. The organizer of it, the same Indian lady on the Smithsonian staff who had charge of Mallika's performance, had made a special point that afternoon to extend an invitation for it as soon as M arrived, expressing the hope that her attendance there would publicize and promote Mallika's own performance the next day. "It was not to be", concludes Mallika now simply, "let's go home". The matter is closed. I hear no mention of it again.

On another occasion, when I ask Mallika about her rule-of-thumb figure for the daily cost of the troupe while traveling in the US, she says she doesn't know, that that is the business of the sponsors. She *does* know expenditures from Darpana (her Academy) funds, is indignant at the waste of Rs. 6,000 when all the troupe were asked to come to Bombay prior to departure to get their US visas personally, and it then turned out that Mallika could have collected all. Again, any member of the troupe does anything required to be done: no hierarchy, age or sex difference, just muck in. It *must* be so, she says: automatic, neither requiring nor deserving attention, certainly not Mallika's. She has excluded a leading dancer from foreign touring for not falling in with this.

Multi-layered Awareness, From a Quiet Center
The description so far of M's "presence" is still awfully crude. It is flat, as if M (or anyone) attends merely to topmost things—the

series of things in the foreground. Competently, to be sure, in some sense fully. But is presence (and its recognition by others) a total and exclusive all or nothing, crescendo or silence? Or is it like the few symbols on a radar screen that go beep and so attract *all* attention? Perhaps the radar image helps. For many things show up on the radar screen that do not go beep just then, and so do not call for attention at this moment, now. Bigger and smaller things, closer and more distant things. In terms of "presence" then, its universe at any moment comprises many things at different levels of awareness, some held where they are, others pushed back or pulled forward, and just one or two surfaced for immediate attention. There is depth in awareness, in short: a third dimension.

The experience with Mallika confirms this picture. When we first met her this time, she was straight off the train at Union Station. After giving us enthusiastic bear hugs and introducing people with her whom we did not know, she reports that the troupe's luggage had not arrived, specially checked though it had been in New York. It had been left behind, presumably, standing on the platform there: all stage sets, costumes, personal belongings. "Just like India!", she laughs, "good for the newcomers (in the troupe) to experience" in high-technology and high-reputation America. Then nothing more about that, even though M would have liked to change clothes which are also wet from the rain "pouring through the roof" at Union Station: arrangements for retrieving the luggage had been made on the spot, with people detailed to look after it all. At several points in the lively and ranging conversations in the next hours, M wonders aloud about the missing luggage and its retrieval, for only a moment or two and for no response, then goes right on with something else. A blip—and the item gets relegated again into some depth. Clearly, M has the luggage concern in her awareness, somewhere not far down, while she continues, so fully "present", attending to others. A repeat of this combination comes at lunch the next day, an invitational affair for the whole troupe. The rest of the troupe has got "lost", inexplicably, and are still "lost" when luncheon ends and the room closes. M hopes they get lunch "somewhere"—of course Washington hosts are with them. Nothing to do. She repeats the hope several times during the afternoon busy with other things.

That Mallika has this multi-level awareness is not special—we all have that and manage it, unless specifically disabled—but there is something specially adept and limpid about the range and depth of M's management of hers, the high spontaneity with which she gets things up front and also phases them out. And about the clarity she has for each right away as she brings it up and mentions it in rapidly ranging conversation. Nothing woolly or unsorted, despite the speed.

Rootedness

So, "presence" conveys depths: layers upon layers of awareness; things to the fore, then receding; things bubbling away; things in the wings waiting for signals; and also energetic and adept management of these awarenesses.

This surfacing of things to give attention to does not bestow importance, only importance *now*, urgency; or if not urgency then at least readiness, timeliness. M's presence, as I experience it, signals unseen depths, that at any moment she "comes from" way down.

That order of grounding and rootedness, the steadiness, and then also the readiness and speed to surface things for attention, I associate generally with a long and rich personal history that has been worked into a whole tapestry: a coherent fabric of a lifetime. Perhaps Mallika's youth and youthful ways make this presence of hers, and the completeness, all roundedness, depths, and personal stillness from which it springs extra striking because I expect those qualities to come much later in life. (Like *my* presence, say?!) And M has clearly worked even some of her weightier learnings into smooth habits—here comes the economy: they need little awareness by now. Of bewildering complexity as they must be, she has them already "make a piece", make sense as a whole, patent sense. Presence.

"Here I am, and Also Looking to Learn"

But even if much depth and complexity are involved, the construct that Mallika has fashioned and displays does not strike me as a take-it-or-leave-it construct, a brittle assertion outward of who and what she is, a proclamation from a high tower as it were. On the contrary, she engages, turns toward the other with the facet(s) best suited for that encounter. Which is also two-way, as if to say, here I stand and I also look to learn; I give and also hope to take. No, I do not depend on you in the sense of all agog to change my tune, or to double or harmonize with yours. I do that quite readily when it is "for real"—a good saying if for sparse use! I have seen M for real with a wide variety of people, also in open mix, as in crowds, engaging and unfazed, utterly herself: present. I fancy she is present anywhere and under all circumstances (within reason). I mentioned to Mallika my this sense of hers, that she is "more present than anyone else I know". She was pleased, I think. "It took many years", she said. Nothing more.

(20 October now, nearly a month since those Washington days and the fourth time to turn to this piece of writing. Other tasks and occupations have inserted themselves in between. I don't really mind that, for if what I am here working out, in my head and heart and now also on paper, makes any sense at all, that will clarify further and show through as I turn it over and over, and also as I give it space to become itself, that is, leave it alone. The dross falls away, more pure essence remains—so I hope!

On the earlier three occasions of returning to this writing, I read from the beginning each time. As I read, I edited, e.g., substituted better words. More voluminously and time consuming, I also took off on tangents that intrigued me, adding examples and fresh thoughts, also drew more connections. One time I never made it through to the then end.

This morning, right after getting up and getting the usual tasks done before sitting down in the sunroom with my cup of coffee, I was all ready to jot down notes about additions or expansions to make when I would get to it, the third item of today's writing agenda. I ended with a small page full of notes. They are about living with consequences, whatever they are; about range and ranging [and how very wide these are when they go with great personal presence]. That recognition then connected me with "positional authority", which is one of the kinds of authority that I have promised myself to distinguish personal presence from. And here, now, the available time is gone again. Till tomorrow then.)

Density: Assemblies of Experience Ready to Use
(Tomorrow now: Words, phrases, images stick to "presence" as I continue my routine reading. This time, "intensity", as in "intensity

in gesture and feeling", is such a word. A piece in the *New Yorker* uses it to characterize a quietly inveterate reformer/supervisor in the Chicago post office. I do not know what this writer means by that of course, but intensity is not a quality I would associate with personal presence. A sense of "density" is closer, of having things *close* together, tightly and surely connected, and thereby accessible in useful units of many parts.)

Connectedness, having things together, may reflect an actually closer proximity of things—not merely together but *closer* together—and explain the rare speed with which Mallika makes useful connections. (Distance and speed may be misleading images here but the practical effect is the same.)

No doubt, Mallika has her high energy at the service of high intelligence, but much practice too is surely at the back of this picture. I imagine long strings of times when she has connected things in a particular way and, finding it useful, again and again now makes those connections speedily by habit. That is, wherever she now is, M "has been there before"; has thought about this and that part of it many times; and is now past having to think about it, in the present moment at least. Presence appears fine-honed and from the depths (whereas intensity suggests something frenetic, some explosive matter only just controlled). Presence is intensity tamed, and now channeled. No wanting to be anywhere else, or in a different shape/another skin.

(Two days later. The four headings under which I have some jottings since I wrote last are: readiness; variety of experience—committed, responsible; spiritual; and discipline. Then comes "ingathering". That is my word for what may be the movement that characterizes M for me most of all: arms thrown wide open, and then, in an immediate and all encompassing sweep, she scoops all up and brings all close to her self, tight, ever so close.

I'll say more about each item below, but need first to reflect a little more on what I am doing here, at this stage. Am I merely finding fresh words, metaphors, images for the same things? Or am I really spiralling down into the right terrain, and the same features reappear in a fresh light. The way, for instance, that the green leaves on the tree across our little pond "become" greener in autumn when they are next to the bright yellows and reds, or a Cezanne portrait has shadows in green that "make it" quite right? Do I look at the same facet of presence differently after seeing some others? Even *one* other? *Any* other?

And one more step: are my attempts to describe and understand personal presence not merely deepening but also converging, coming closer together, like going down a funnel? Is what emerges *denser*? This recalls the comment my father sent me in India after reading my newly published *The Tide of Learning*—over three decades ago as I write! It was doubly telling because I had sent my parents new books as a matter of course, not expecting any specific response, and father wrote very rarely anyway. This time he wrote that he liked it. "You have to churn milk over and over again to make butter", he explained. Is my understanding of "presence" really solidifying as I go on? And what about *my* wishes, about my presence and how to understand and assess it and the part that and those have in the solidifying mix? Wishes for me but also for M and for her actually to be as I understand her. And ditto for me and my presence, and others'.)

Readiness: Informed Spontaneity

The "readiness" in my notes includes the notion of fine anticipation, of being "at the ready, on the mark...", as a fine sprinter is totally ready at the starting line when the gun is about to go off: M seems to have the precise energies required just then marshaled at the ready for propelling her forward. Just those, not others, and those energies already aligned in a particular combination of sets or patterns. This consummate patterning again reflects lots of experience and practice, varied enough and examined, and with *personal* meanings already derived for her own feelings and responses and for consequences internal and outward. All these together make experience. And, updated as events offer, all-round experience becomes ingrained and ready for the next event. Maybe clusters of well-practiced experiences get developed, a pool from which to draw whatever suits the new event best. The way a musician or storyteller draws on a ready repertoire (Don Schoen's metaphor [Schoen 1983].)

Certainly, M has been party to a quite extraordinarily broad range of events to make experience of. Many far out ones have come routinely for her with belonging to one of India's leading families, with contacts in the absolutely top ranks of science, the arts, business, politics, and education. More of that below. In as much as those events and the opportunities for experience they offered were not of M's own making but of her family's, they came with her position, and so yield *positional* presence/authority. Here I want to recognize the mere fact of this enormous range of events from which to make that high order of experience which may go with such striking personal presence.

From her many-splendored base of early encounters, M then fanned out on her own account. While she continues lively contact with numerous people in similar class/station/position to hers in Gujarat, in Indian society in general, and in the international world of science, art, education and politics, I note with special interest her widely ranging encounters with people and situations quite different from her own, and among those especially the many relationships that endure. Some are with families in the little houses and very ordinary streets just outside the home compound, others with people in all corners of the globe. In several places she has lived and worked for months, even a year or more (e.g., in Paris for her part in the internationally acclaimed *Mahabarata*). She keeps up close collaborations (Africa, Japan, England, Australia), and there is much visiting to and fro. She learns the new language, new idioms and ways; so much so that she is at home there also, familiar and comfortable in those situations. And also known there, of course.

The experiences are distinct for her, not jumbled or flattened as if uniform. M's tales are of particular places and people, and full of particulars. She speaks of the diversity joyfully, ranging all over for her stories and examples, just as she does for her actual arrangements for publishing or dancing, or for visiting or receiving friends. It is as if frontiers and external differences did not exist, only people of all sorts in diverse circumstances, and those all in her field of vivid attention.

Being in Charge: Deep-etched Experience

Fashioning experience, in my books, is always an active enterprise; experience does not just happen. It comes with personal and responsible reflection on events, with wrestling for what events mean, for personal learnings that matter, that is, for pointers to making a difference next time. Even extracting experience from an event, which is only the first step to behaving differently, cannot be had by passive waiting. Experience comes with actually mining it.

But life events that affect others as well hold extra lodes of experience to mine, particularly those in which I am in charge and so shape events for others, as is the case with long-lasting enterprises like parenting or running a dance academy. Leading demands an extra order of commitment and concern, a constantly heightened awareness, and an often searing need to learn from experience. Mallika is four-square in all of these relationships, and mostly at the very top "where the buck stops". So these experiences of hers in charge etch extra deep. Do *these* then make up a large part of the deep down from which she is so present?

First, the day-to-day management of several top responsibilities: M keeps them separate in space and time and moves deliberately between them. When in Ahmedabad, the mornings are for rehearsing with her troupe of professional musicians and dancers at the dance academy, which she also runs. The afternoons she spends at Mapin, the publishing house she started with her husband—they are the senior editors; that office is enough blocks away to require driving. Back to Darpana in the late afternoon, but now for dance classes. (Darpana has 700 pupils.) Upstairs is her flat for private time, also for breakfast and lunch and the children; dinner is at the main house, on time and social. "Taking hold and letting go"—M turns *her* diamond. Here is the fine ability, again, of shedding and being fully present at each occasion in turn.

There are two exceptions to this (determined?) separation of times and settings: the children and the telephone. Anahita, then four, sometimes dances along during rehearsal, and when she gets in the way—which in the complexities of Indian dance and the generosity of Mallika's movements is quite inevitable—M either skirts her or swoops her up in passing with peals of laughter. The family dachshund often runs in and out at the same time, creating quite a commotion, but tires soon when he attracts no special attention. M's then 10-year old son, Revanta, already an eager and able dancer and performer, also dances along many times and with abandon—but at the side; the dancing is now more important to him than his mother's attention.

The telephone is no minder of Mallika's separation either, and not all calls can wait, international ones for instance. So, a cordless phone. No, it is not regularly at rehearsals but it does get brought in at need by a member of staff (alerted to this special call? or him/herself assessing this need?). And M immediately takes the call, present here too, focused and personal to the caller. If she steps out of a group dance, the others usually go on without her and she rejoins them as soon as she can, fully present again.

Inner Discipline: True to the Core

Discipline comes to mind here—the internal kind. If it began with external necessity, as, for instance, with the precise movements that classical Indian dancing and becoming a star performer certainly require, M has made it her own long since. In that dance M has eyes, neck and head, hands and fingers, and feet at separate command, each to "tell her presence" in its special language. (Presumably the same multiplicity of body languages then also makes M highly vulnerable to showing *in*attention—being personally absent while physically present—and would quickly communicate personal slight to those in the know.)

(November 5 today, over a month since I started this! Though I want to get round to playing personal presence out against authority derived from other sources, I decide to read first all I have so far.

It reads as if with each sitting I have dabbed additional patches of colour onto the evolving canvas. Makes sense just as the fall landscape outside "makes sense": sunny, varied, patchy, and between seasons, certainly still changing. An unfinished symphony particularly lacking a core, a place for the eye—the I—to rest. I have no problem with that: that core will come into view if and when it will.)

On then with the notion of discipline—personal discipline—and its possible part in the astonishing readiness I see associated with presence, the immediacy with which M seems to have appropriate *sets* of coherent responses and initiatives at the ready. Indian classical dance, with its multiple languages for the different limbs, all for telling the same "tale" with overall coherence, exacts discipline beyond any other dancing. If anyone could know in advance that that order of discipline would be involved, M must have known, if only from being around her relentlessly practicing, coaching, demanding, internationally famous mother.

Did she have a choice in that ambience? Yes, for dancing. For discipline? I don't know. Kartikeya, M's brother, seems highly disciplined too in his life and his endeavors in other fields. And most other members of the wider family we know also score high for discipline, three generations of them. All work steadily at enterprises that demand high discipline and all stand out in theirs. I see Mallika's children and how *they* make headway into dancing—they played with it first and then danced their way into the discipline it takes, all seemingly at their own pace and grounded in their own wish to do this.

This *inner* location of discipline seems quite clear. I see Mallika assume it when she deals with her children. It pervades the way that whole household runs. Its members, of any age and any station, are continuously in positions of having to choose how to approach an issue and what to do, and—this is the point in my mind here—quite accustomed to then living with the consequences.

Certainly it is second nature with M. And she knows something else which is important: that the choices she makes so briskly, and more pervasively her presence altogether, are good enough to go on with. At least for right now; any refining can wait. Right now, moving with it—presence—is primary. And (I will need to cycle back to this) this presentation of self is not self-righteous but engagingly open, not stand-offish or a brittle take-it-or-leave-it. It flows on, as if to say: this step, this I-with-you-now, may not be perfect, not *quite* right or fitting, not even the best I could do if I took more time and thought, but it is (plenty) good enough to get on with—and *that's* important, keeping the flow moving, immediacy. I will deal with the left-overs, the fine-tuning, the completions, the plausible explanations later (if still warranted and promising). Certainly I live with the consequences—the immediate and also the later ones. I have come to terms with imperfection long since—mine and all around me, over the ages, everywhere. So I need not pretend; so I am fully present as I am today, now, with you. My presence, my life as a whole as I have composed it and others acclaim it, is OK—I can even say better, lots better, than merely OK.

Spiritual Dimensions

Spiritual dimensions intrude here. For M they are deep and encompassing, and she includes them as explicitly and readily as she embraces all else, and in similar manner. They are present in the basic fabric of the universe; not as touchstone rules of conduct by which to feel constrained, but woven in, inseparable, and obviously all-encompassing and ageless. With its deep roots in temple worship, Indian dance leads readily to that live appreciation. Perhaps it is in that consciousness of the ageless link with the sacred that Mallika creates and performs her dances of social judgment and condemnation: "Mean Steets" about "the ordinariness" of violence, "Sita's Daughters" about the oppression of women and the triumph of pioneering womanhood, and several dance dramas to protest man's wanton destruction of trees, rivers, whole nature. She speaks matter-of-factly of the simple people of India (of the East? not elsewhere?) as still firmly grounded in religious traditions and of how all-embracing that is, especially in the villages, even now, and much more than they themselves know. I don't know to what extent M has studied and examined all this, but it seems omnipresent, suffusing all I have tried to indicate here to make sense of her presence.

Most telling for me of Mallika explicitly in the spiritual realm is seeing her practice pranic healing. We are in the spacious living room in Chidambaram, the parental house. At lunch, which included as usual 10 or so of us of various ages, a long-time writer colleague of about her age speaks of a harrowing recent experience with his eyes, leading almost to permanent blindness. That was avoided—just—but has left varying weakness of sight and virtually constant headaches which crest periodically in ghastly, totally immobilizing migraines. He senses one in the offing this noon, and the premonition of it is already terrifying. Mallika offers healing. Immediately after the meal she invites him simply to sit on the floor, facing her. Ronnie and I ask about staying, go and sit by them; the children and others as matter-of-factly go off about *their* business. Mallika—or Mrinalini—setting about healing is just another part of what quite normally goes on here.

M is already very quiet, inward. Others sort themselves out without her. Presently those lovely movements! She extends and opens her left hand for receiving the energy of the universe and guides it with her right in gently rounded motions toward the hurting neck and head. Holds them there. No more gesture. No more movement. Silence. Minutes pass. Presence. One to another.

In the universe. At the end, the man speaks wonderingly of the "tornado" at the back of his head as the healing progressed, then realizes with surprise that there is no longer any sign of migraine.

Towards the Larger Self

I don't know how, where or when Mallika and Mrinalini came across pranic healing, but their adding it to what they do is a nice example of the enlargement and personal growth that is also in the air around strong personal presence. They do it; family, friends, and asssociates also expect it. Mention a fresh idea, a knack for doing something, a new phrase, a different way of looking—and M is already trying it for herself, for fit.

About pranic healing I do know that mother and daughter together made a point of starting to learn it with the help of the best practitioner and teacher of it in India, a Catholic sister, in habit, from Kerala in the South (where Mrinalini comes from). They stay in touch with her and look forward to continuing their study of it and to further practice. Can she try pranic healing to reduce her cholesterol, asks Ronnie. No—here comes the realistic fit—M does not think she is far enough along for that, so Ronnie better get in touch with (M provides the contact). But for an area of pain Ronnie has had from time to time (following recent surgery) yes, certainly. And they fix a time the next day.

Authority of Person, Position and Situation

The "presence" I have been trying to identify, describe and understand here is *personal* presence. Perhaps "authority"—*personal* authority—would carry analogous meaning. And while I truly delight in the so important fact that M's is a woman's presence and so, in my view, of extra importance at this time, it is the *personal* nature of her presence, more broadly, that holds my interest.

For there are at least two other sources of "presence" (or "authority"). One other source is *positional*, i.e., authority that goes with age and/or status in the society, the place of one's family in the community, professional attainment and functioning, and of course with being in a particular level in an organizational hierarchy. Certainly, birth into a family at the very top of Indian society also feeds M's presence. Independent, modernizing India .has greatly reduced the positions, properties, and incomes of hereditary princes and traditional landowners. Established business families like hers, with large properties and incomes already for several generations, moved into social and political prominence with Independence. With that, many new possibilities opened up.

Possible and impossible are the words to use with positional authority: it creates a range of possibilities but does not determine how or how far they may be explored and used. Others use similar positions to M's for lives of ease. In other families that is: a life of ease Mallika's particular family—*her* position—all but closed off. Like all members of it, she was expected—and also expected herself—to find absorbing interests of her own and develop at least one of these to distinction. The drive and effort had to be hers; all other resources she needed were either readily to hand or she could start off. Generation after generation, a truly astonishing number and variety of enterprises bear public witness to this fine meshing of high and creative energies with wealth and position: a textile museum of world standing, the start of Montessori schools in India with Mme. Montessori herself; the first interactive science museum in India; a large innovative school; a physical research laboratory; and a variety of leading institutes for architecture and design, psychological services, management and environmental education, and industrial and social research, each then also the base for uncounted programs and projects and public positions. The family members who head them continue, severally or jointly, in various arrangements to run and develop the family's industrial and business enterprises as well. The Darpana Academy for Performing Arts that Mallika has taken over from her mother to run and develop further and the international publishing house for India's arts and crafts which is her own creation with Bipin are her particular contributions of high distinction to what is also a wide and fast-flowing stream of public efforts of the family as a whole.

Two further aspects of position also find telling expression in Mallika's presence. One is her position as woman. Contrary to norms prevailing in much of India and indeed the globe even now, her particular family held daughters to be the equals of sons and expected them to be quite as resourceful, enterprising, competent, and remarkable as their brothers, and it had done so over at least two generations already when Mallika arrived. So her characteristic familiarity with meeting and mixing with top rank scientists, prime ministers, internationally renowned artists of all kinds, labor leaders, and pundits that I had remarked on much earlier as part of the rich experience that informs her presence now, came too with her position in this particular family with its steady contrariness in what women should and could be like and do. At least she had compelling models all around her for absolutely intrepid opposition, glaringly and even embarrassingly public opposition included. That last one landed an aunt in jail as a political prisoner several times and for years altogether, and landed *her* parents, Mallika's grandparents, in Ahmedabad with making the 2,000 mile rail journey to Delhi and back every two weeks without fail to visit her; because support is what parents give their children, no matter what they take a stand on and do. That the stand would be thought through and morally-based was assumed. And meanwhile, just as matter-of-factly, Prime Minister Nehru, who put that aunt in jail and kept her there across all appeals, came to stay from time to time at the parents' magnificent house, for he was also their friend.

The property and income sources of her family's position fell sharply when M's father suddenly died in mid-life, so what we see now is the adult presence M actually developed after her close, resourceful, and famous father died and in much reduced and often threatening circumstances. This is the other aspect of position worth a moment's further examination. At that point, M might have given up striking out on her own, now that she had to earn the resources for it, and could have settled for a humbler position. Instead, she renewed her resolve, and her mother and brother backed her up in this, though liberal financing was now out of the question. Generally, that sequence—first a position that makes a wide range of things possible, then a sudden disaster and lasting deprivation, such as the partition of the continent forcing migration with only bare lives to save, or a bitter family feud that blocks access to possessions and to accustomed sources of income—is just the sequence that propels survivors who are also stouthearted into recouping their losses through starting afresh with new enterprise and the extra determination born of that very adversity.[1] So, while M's birth into that unusual family of hers opened so many doors in God's large mansion, she must have developed the presence I write about here in quite determined and probably sometimes contested independence.

In locating the source of authority outside the person exercising it, positional authority differs essentially from personal presence which has its roots and constant nourishment from within. "Authority of the situation"—the third source (for which Erik Erikson prefers "factuality")—is likewise outside the person. Whereas position creates possibilities for people to use (or not use), any real-life situation sets technical, economic, and social limits for *anyone* in it, quite irrespective of personal likes and capacities. Socio-technical systems theory speaks of this kind of authority.[2]

M's sharp and ready recognition of what the realistic possibilities are in a concrete situation and her not wasting time churning over and around unpromising moves and wild shots; her recognition and, yes, acceptance of stark realities—all these are very much part of the presence I explore here. Divine impatience, yes; push the limits, yes; try a long, even crazy wild shot, yes. But be under no illusion about what each is and make no investment beyond what it deserves. So all that's then left is—presence. Personal presence. "...fragrance into space". In many valleys.

Fresh Soundings for Presence

Seven weeks later we were again in India. Mallika, only just back from a six-week tour in Nigeria and other West African countries, and about to be off with the troupe to dance in Australia, was

1. This is the same up–down sequence which guided our selection of "future entrepreneurs" for the special programs at SIET Institute (see Chapter 5). We also selected the *second* sons (since first sons were usually "meant for" carrying on the traditional work of their families), and not daughters (who were "meant to" stay at home and would otherwise run into extra difficulties outside, for instance with bank managers in attempting to borrow money for a business or government officers for getting a license).
2. I use it in my consulting practice to quickly delineate with organizational clients the areas of freedom that actually exist or that can be realistically created in the system and so make room for change; and I then endeavor to keep attention and action steadily focused on those areas. See also Chapter 1.

extra busy meantime getting Darpana's new theater finished for
the opening of that year's especially grand commemorative festival, which she then led. In a private moment I alerted her to this
attempt to write about her presence and to my hope of showing
it to her quite soon. "Of course! Anything. I'll love it." She assumes it will be published.

Meanwhile, I have responses to the draft from Ronnie and three
dear friends and colleagues. They are most encouraging. Two
readers urge going another step or two, towards integrating some
parts further and mining more meanings of the whole. All readers
dwell, most kindly, on the high value of mixing here what I see
and recall with what is M out there; on the fellow feeling, loving,
the likenesses *they* see in the two of us; and also on the wishes
I imply, e.g., I wish I could be that present, even under pressures
as great as Mallika's. "Is it my perception", Lynne Kohn muses,
"or your description? Where does the impact of the person begin
because of who she is [a genetic heritage? a fortuitous fit with
parents for nurture? a movement towards friends who reflect
back the light and love of life?] or is it my interpretation of your
description which defines or suggests what I see and feel? [I read
about a myrtle once, and it spoke to me of you...]".

Those first readers, I knew, would approach this writing already "on my side"—and so also on "M's side". Now readers of
the book—*you*—make up a third and more independent strand
in this intricate fabric.

That others, quite independent of me, have also attested to M's
special, extraordinary presence already affirms *some* independence from whatever I resonate with, in her presence or as
I write. For Lynne, the story as a whole was

> the reality of the contact between boundaries of self to self,
> presence to presence. For a strong presence these boundaries
> are clear and well maintained; and these boundaries are also
> permeable, open to others, to new impressions, selectively,
> yes, but also by disposition. If we stay open, we receive the
> details of one person's presence and mix it with our own—a
> fragrance appreciated.

She went on to wonder about

> the ground, the rich nurturing soil in which Mallika is rooted....
> Although she asserts her independence in her flowering, there

is no uprooting, no hybridizing, and no grafting which precedes her presence today...a lovely expression of the depth of
her culture, her family, her commitment to self.

The many uprootings and other sharp discontinuities in my own
life-experiences suggest that staying in one place may not matter
much. Our children speak of "good taste" as the one continuity
they have carried with them across all our many moves. For me,
what they describe as "good taste"—in personal get-up and manners, surroundings and relationships—is certainly rooted way
back, at least three generations back or more, if some inherited
jewelry is a good guide to taste in things.

The single aspect of Mallika's presence that stays most prominently in my own mind is how absolutely habitual it is for her
to link decision and consequence and to be responsible for both.
Most striking is this matter-of-factness with her children. No
shielding from experience, and so much experience is gained
over the years. The person—M or another—is left to manage the
rate at which to advance into more taxing arenas of experiencing. So also, presumably, to assess her or his strength for taking
risks and for coping with consequences and living with the rest.
And, in this process, over the years, making those assessments
well for feeling good about oneself. Not perfect (there's no need
for that), but good enough to go right on. So fears get small and
rare, and there is every reason to be present. She had learnt fairly
early to overcome all her fears, Mallika replied to a question of
wonder and admiration about her composure, presence, lucid
descriptions, and ease in interacting with the large audience at
a meeting. There were too many things she had to do, wanted
to do, and fears would only have held her back. "I felt she spoke
directly to me!", adds Kay Jamison, Australian producer and col-
laborator, who reports this from their recent tour in East Asia.[3]
"She has fears and vulnerabilities, like all of us, but doesn't allow
them to control her.... She acknowledges them and puts them
aside. [With her present] I feel emotionally part of what's happen-
ing and can risk as well."

Another early reader, colleague, and friend since the late 1960s,
Don Klein, prefers

3. Private communication, March 1997.

the word "appreciation" [to "presence"][4] because it combines two related aspects: 1) a positive, appreciative feeling; with 2) an appreciative connection with the subtleties, essences, and nuances of a phenomenon. So it is this inner feeling of appreciation that enables M to be so fully, fluidly, and flexibly available to whatever is going on.... In sports there is the experience of effortlessness that happens when a well-trained athlete is, so-to-speak, "in the groove" of his or her performance. It is that effortlessness that M manifests apparently in everything she does.... I doubt that this is an intellectually based or consciously choice-driven phenomenon...probably far more intuitive and unconscious a process. She is too busy being to decide what to be or how to be at any particular moment. Presence is...relaxed concentration, without tension...able to easily move across, perhaps even transcend, mind-induced barriers or boundaries....

Fortunately, that gift of being fully present is also given to the [other] who is present. It is self-enhancing—in the sense of what Jung referred to as the big S Self, which is the spiritual essence with which each of us comes equipped—as well as enhancing of others. By being fully present one brings the gift of connection to one's own and the other's spiritual Self. It's an invitation that can hardly be refused; or an offer that the other person can hardly fail to accept.

I think presence has something to do with what Carl Rogers referred to as "unconditional positive regard", which for him was the essence of a healing relationship. To connect with others in such an unconditional way only within the therapeutic relationship is to be conditional about when one allows oneself to be unconditional.... In so doing [lots of therapists] miss an opportunity to be fully present for their loved ones, colleagues, and others in their lives—including, I suspect, very often themselves.

...most very small children have presence [Don reminded me]. Their energy is unrestrained; they are fully themselves... their gaze is clear, compelling, and complete; they are not embarrassed; they do not need to look away.

4. Private communication, Fall 1995.

At issue for us, then, is how to maintain this self- and other-enhancing healing presence (or regain it), look straight at the adult world and "strike a line of purpose across it for somewhere" (Frost 1964). These are the one or two concerns to which a healing practitioner devotes most energies and focuses her or his life's work on—to make a difference and make it count, and feel good with. Lest Mallika's dancing and publishing should line her up with poets, pastors, and pianists as too distant to matter centrally to social scientists, her doctorate—in business administration and psychology—severely narrows that escape route. More basically important is not to confuse the means with the ends. For her, dancing and publishing, even managing and funding institutions, are the means and modes for her life's directions, just as clearly as training, organizational development or counseling, and social administration are means and modes for social science practitioners for theirs. Ends—to which to use these means and modes—have this distinctly different sound to them: women's empowerment, prizing India's rich culture, and also the environment of this earth are three challenges on which M focuses her life's energies as she choreographs, dances, publishes, administers; or, as also neighbor and prominent citizen, she goes to battle a state or union minister to remedy a wrong poor folk on the streets just outside her home compound have urged her to help with. It is all of one piece—Mallika present. M is counted on, in the past, now, and in people's expectations.

Identifying attributes of someone's presence is of course not "being present"; present is when the attributes come together. Attributes, those I observed in Mallika and recorded here, and perhaps more, make a useful checklist though for identifying those situations in which one is not fully present (yet?), and so not oneself, from those in which one has it "all together" and lives and works at his/her best in abandon. Only the latter are situations to choose for work in which clients and others are to benefit. The former are situations for learning and deliberate coaching, and for many of us some may remain "beyond us", simply out of realistic range. Situations of violent conflict immediately come to mind as possibly beyond me—early terrors may make my assessments of high conflict untrustworthy—and also work with enterprises, though legal, which offend personal values so they repel.

In addition to the glory and joy of personal presence actually present, it is then also a measure for the order of social issue a practitioner can responsibly engage with—the greater the issue, the more personal presence it calls for, the more openness to oneself, to colleagues and to others involved. The next chapter will display issues to calibrate personal presence and openness against. The top ones, those crying for most urgent sustained work, require

> a quantum jump in openness: no openness, no sharing; no sharing no amplification; no amplification, no significant impact.... Without ready openness and sharing, [also] of personal and professional limitations and occasional failures, competencies...atrophy and narrow down, with the further result, which amounts to a disaster, that openness and sharing become more and more frightening (Lynton 1992, p. 69).

Personal presence could well have started this dire chain of nos: no appreciation of self, no presence; no presence, no openness.

Small children have no problem running this chain in the opposite direction, nor have more earthy adults than ourselves later. This is the significance I attach to the greeting people native to the Kalahari Desert call to each other: "I see you, yes, I see you". The ability to "see" oneself and each other truly, and to take true measure of the great issues in our world comes with being present, first, to oneself.

References

Buber, Martin, *Between Man and Man*, Beacon Paperbacks, London, 1961.
Frost, Robert, 'Introduction', in *Complete Poems*, Holt, Rinehart and Winston, New York, 1964.
Lynton, Harriet Ronken, *Born to Dance*, Orient Longman, New Delhi, 1995.
Lynton, Rolf P., *The Sound of Sense: What's So Hard About Being Practical*, Center for Applied Behavioural Science Studies and Action Research, Monograph Series No. 5, University of Delhi, Delhi, 1992.
Schoen, Donald, *The Reflective Practitioner*, Basic Books, New York, 1983.
Sondhe, Nagesh D., in *The Times of India*, October 26, 1996.
Tagore, Rabindranath, *Gitanjali*, No. 29, Macmillan & Co., London, 1956.

10

TRANSCENDENT CHALLENGE/:
THE /OUND OF /EN/E

Focusing on a Transcendent Challenge
Positioning: Realistic Roles and Expectations

*...at every step these days in Africa I am assailed by the over-
whelming question... "What am I to him, and he to me? And
what am I to do about it".*

Van der Post 1962, p. 90

*The ultimate question for a responsible person to ask is not
how he is to extricate himself heroically from the affair, but
how the next generation is to live.*

Boenhoeffer 1972, p. 7

Challenges galore for healing and prevention face practitioners in the social sciences, yet most of us—who, *me?*—avert
our faces and like Lord High Executioner Koko in *The Mikado*,
whimper that we weren't there. The vast and growing predicaments in the world, near, far, and ahead, engage practitioners
and professionals very, very little. On this sharp—even obscene—
contrast, I focused my session in the series to inaugurate Delhi

University's Center for Applied Social Science early in 1992 (Lynton 1992).[1] As again now with this book, I set out to challenge such abject sidelining of good energies and by telling episodes out of my own half-century of practice tried to raise courage and sights for wrestling anew with predicaments that truly matter. The alternative is professional irrelevance and personal tearing.

"What's so difficult about being practical?" was the subtitle for the session and, within minutes of starting, I had participants mine their own experience for direct evidence of how hard they found it. For range of meaning I used economist Robert Heilbronner's focus on "transcendent challenge", namely, one "that faces [humanity] within a thinkable lifespan". His leading example was "making our economic peace with the demands of the environment" (Heilbronner 1990, pp 99–100). The cutting edge was this, he explains:

> The closing window of environmental tolerance will impose an utterly new condition of caution and constraint on a civilization whose historical thrust has been in just the opposite direction. Added to this [and directly relevant to India and the South generally] is the much larger and more intractable issue of persuading poor nations that are seeking to raise their standards of living to cut back on their industrial emissions because they are warming up the air of rich nations on the other side of the globe.

Individually, in private first then publicly, participants in my Delhi session next identified challenges they attached transcendent importance to. They were, in order of frequency: realizing human potential (as against mere survival) and bringing lasting peace; living in harmony with nature; economic "justice" in the face of the poverty–population–employment equation; women's empowerment; and inclusion of all—blind, lesbian, Kurdish refugee, Harijan and Brahmin, wealthy, the singular—so "there be no stranger". This quite familiar litany of the world's predicaments could then be the agenda for social scientists to be practical about.

Next question, same procedure: What were they, the social scientists in the room, working on in fact? That list was very different

---

1. The excerpts in this chapter are all from that monograph.

from the first, even under these alerting circumstances. Only four (out of 60) worked with people central to their challenge, e.g., with poor women to "empower" them. Twenty sought to "model" their values in their teaching and research, so that they would at least not be party to the challenge but demonstrate to the contrary that it was quite feasible, for instance, to include "everyone" in their circle of relationships. Five dissociated this question from the first: they worked to earn their livelihood, further their career, become recognized in their field. None mentioned working at institutional and larger system levels to make significant impact on the chosen challenges more promising.

This was actually a bridge-building, attention-raising device, for gross discrepancy between what social scientists see as transcendent challenges and what they actually work on is virtually universal. No point therefore in dwelling on supposed shortcomings in this or that culture, educational preparation or current situation.[2] Everywhere, it seems, other considerations determine these choices—professional status, grants, promotions, no doubt, and also the awsome complexity and scale any one of these challenges present. On both grounds it is easy to turn away disheartened. And meanwhile, the challenges pile up and grow more intricate and threatening.

A practical alternative may be to start with putting issues of quality and scale together, instead of juxtaposing them as if these were practical alternatives. Good sense and research tell us that high quality and dogged persistence are both essential for effective work under just the conditions that transcendent challenges pose: radical innovation, sometimes reversal (rather than incremental adjustments along familiar lines); heading into unfamiliar

2. The dissociation is not limited to social scientists. The Institute of Scientific Information in Philadelphia, USA, analyzes journals around the world and publishes a biweekly. Of papers published in a recent five-year period, less than half received any citation at all in another journal within those five years, meaning that more than half were not deemed worth building on. In a related study of reading habits, engineering fared worse than the social sciences; only about one-quarter of all papers in the handful of leading journals receiving any further mention at all, and architecture much worse (fewer than 1 percent). Clearly, most of the researches on which even these published papers were based had no transcendent challenge in focus, or at least none that interested colleagues enough, or was clearly enough connected with one to get read at all (Balasubramanian 1991).

ground (which makes the work and the prospects doubly difficult to publicize); and running straight into opposition for sure,
some of it desperate because of dethroning. We also know that
the intensity and persistence demanded by this work will conjure
up illusions and perversities (the way parched travelers in the
dessert see water where there is only more sand), foolhardy
shortcuts, premature assertions, and heroic posturings.

These conditions are best met where people know each other
well and realize they have to work together. That suggests the
strong possibility that work on a large scale will come with multiplying and interlinking well-functioning small (often local?)
groupings, not by expanding into ever larger units. Masterful
craftsmanship is involved in designing and managing the necessary connections. If this picture of going to large scale is even ap-
proximately correct, then quality work is not the alternative to
quantity but its very means.

My overriding concern is therefore with raising the quality of
work, including the much needed work on amplifying locally
successful efforts. I see five phases of the work deserving special
attention at this time. They form a cycle.

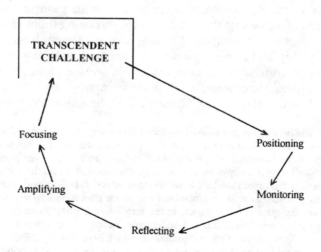

FIGURE 10.1   Five Action Phases for Special Attention

In this litle schema, focusing followed immediately by carefully positioning oneself sets the stage for the other three which earlier chapters have already examined in my own practice.

Focusing on a Transcendent Challenge

Good focusing brings three features of a challenge together: (1) A unit of work in which the essential elements of the challenge are importantly in play, that (2) has promise for doing something creative with them, and (3) is—or can be—well enough connected with other units to form the larger system for making a significant, lasting difference. Social scientists have to identify these places of convergence and then act like a magnifying glass used for setting paper alight with rays from the sun. Without the glass, the rays remain diffused.

Only "utter familiarity" with people and situations will lead surefootedly to this identification, or as the father of allopathic medicine Hippocrates put it long ago, "hard, persistent, responsible, unremitting labour in the sickroom, not in the library" (Henderson, quoted in Curtis 1945, pp 253–54). This presence—at the right place and time, and length of time—has three aspects particularly worth paying attention to. One is how to get close enough to the situation to see the current interplay of people with tasks, technologies, time, and territory; and also to understand how precipitating events come about, how they are normally handled, and with what expectations. The second is openness to what is or can be unique about it that promises opportunities for radical change. And the third is the ability to build an overall picture from which to draw good enough understanding for guiding action. Familiarity also means being no longer seen as a stranger in that place for pioneering.

Closeness to the Field

Life's compulsions or deliberate choices are really the only two ways to get "into the field". American social reformer Dorothy Day reports this interchange about it with Harvard's legendary sociology professor Pitirim Sorokin (Day 1952, p. 242):

> "How close are you to the workers?" Pitirim Sorokin asked me.... He himself was the son of a peasant woman and migrant worker and was imprisoned three times under the Czars

and three times under the Soviets. He too had suffered exile in the forests, hunger and imprisonment; he had lived under the sentence of death and was, through some miracle,...allowed to go abroad. He had the right to ask such a question and it was a pertinent one. Going around and seeing such sights is not enough.

Unchosen, highly influential, even if not utterly determining, life circumstances and events are in all our lots: place and status at birth, family, caste, religion; talent; sickness, disaster, migration, lucky breaks; wealth and palatial living (for a few), prison (e.g., Boenhoeffer), concentration camp (for Jews in 1940s Europe), war; routinized lives for most. The first issue is what we do with this forced familiarity with the unchosen circumstances and events of our lives—whether we can use them to get close to others in similar circumstances and victims of like events, thereby seeing the opportunities in them for new direction and strengths. A second issue is what compulsions we create for others by what we do and do not do. These actions of ours then, whether inadvertently or by design, bring our children, colleagues, neighbors, and others into close contact with certain circumstances and events with which *they* thereby become familiar. Those consequences may be agreeable or disagreeable at the time, but they are broadening in either case.

The other way to closeness is self-chosen. Dorothy Day chose to make a life of radical poverty, living with the abjectly poor, giving up "one's privacy, and mental and spiritual comforts as well as physical". She opened houses of hospitality for migrant workers, 26 at one time, which were usually so crowded that "the colored take care of the white children, and the white the colored, while the parents hunt for homes and jobs. Such an extreme destitution makes all men brothers" (Day 1952, p. 242). With this she certainly grappled with a transcendent challenge, and effectively so for immediate relief and general example. But, without good enough recording for systematic study and sharing, social science and action research it was not.

More relevant here is going to live with people and situations for some time, such as Harvard psychiatrist Robert Coles did with his family and then wrote his books about racial integration in the American South in the 1960s[3] or the young French philosopher Simone Weil did by becoming a vineyard laborer, then a factory worker, each till she understood them and their situation to her satisfaction. These are much lesser engagements than Dorothy Day's or other workers' for life: Weil, Coles, we ourselves, can always leave and can also call on other resources out of reach of people fixed in their situation. And the research interest itself puts a different construct on the experiences. But the difference can be minimized. During the months in the field, Weil "strove to avoid anything which could make her lot different in the slightest degree from that of her companions in the workplace" (Springstead 1984, p. 25). She carried out the same tasks as they, worked the same long hours, ate the same food, lived in the same housing, participated actively in neighborhood and union events.

Whatever the personal motivations, valuing and putting to use *all* one's experience of closeness is the starting point. When in doubt whether past experience still fits, it is probably well to update it in the field, even briefly, for confirmation. Then, once in the field, it is essential to take enough time for the situation to unfold at its own pace and for subjecting data to circumspect examination for context, attribution, likely meanings, etc.; this is an important precaution against too early and too elaborate analyses and technological enthusiasms. All this means giving more importance again to clinical competence, albeit with whole neighborhoods, organizations or still larger systems as client. It also makes institutional planning and budgeting of applied work extra difficult, though not necessarily the funding of it. Significant work on recognized challenges seems to attract more and more funds and other support because of its plausible promise and potential importance.

Openness to All in the Field

Into this chosen setting the action researcher brings no specific agenda. He will "let it tell as it will" (Frost 1964, p. ii). This resolve is very different from going to the field to collect responses to prepared questions, in mind or on paper, or even in an unvarying

3. Beginning with *Children of Crisis: A Study of Courage and Fear* (Dell, New York, 1964).

role. Going as a participant observer, resourceful helper, and counselor is more like it. Analyses for larger meanings come later.

Artists tell of capturing the moments so, fully. "To do that we must put all else out of our minds...become that moment, make ourselves a sensitive recording plate...give the image of what we actually see, forgetting everything that has been seen before our time" (Cezanne quoted in Gutterman 1989). In his book *Listening with the Third Ear*, psychoanalyst Theodor Reik (1948) has a splendid chapter (Chapter 16, pp 157–72) on what he calls free-floating attention, and it is extra valuable here because he includes listening to himself and his reactions as the situation unfolds. Predetermined, willful attention, he finds, prevents "surprise. People who practice it always find confirmation of what they already know [and that is] a hindrance to the progress of scientific knowledge...[It] often leads to a fixation of our minds...on the immediate object or on the one relation that happens to be in the forefront of our thoughts.... Energy must be differently distributed [so that] important parts...reveal themselves..., usually in an unforced idea. It is the condition that helps the oppressed minorities in the kingdom of the mind to win their rights"—a particularly apposite metaphor for working on a transcendent challenge.

Penetration is the word Simone Weil used for what has to happen: "above all, our thought should be empty, waiting, not seeking anything, but ready to receive in its naked truth the object that is to penetrate it. What that truth may be we have no way of knowing ahead of time, nor should we project any of our own personal hopes on it" (Weil 1951, p. 56). In the spiritual traditions around the world, this "orientating" attention, as Weil calls it, is prayer: a waiting for God. "...all faulty connections of ideas...are due to the fact that thought has seized upon some idea too hastily and, being thus prematurely blocked, is not open to the truth...we have wanted to be too active: we have wanted to carry out a search..." (Springstead 1984, pp 68–69).

What then is the use of all our prior learning and professional qualifications, even of the first-hand experience I recommended so strongly earlier, and specifically of preparing for this new work in particular? For Reik, experience in practical real life and thoughtful preparation are not at all

useless or superfluous...but an important psychological pre-
requisite for the idea that occurred to him unforced. In a sense
it gave sanction to it inwardly,...clearing a particular path, disposing of particular possibilities, which must then make way
for the consideration of others.... We cannot produce valuable
unforced ideas by an effort of thought, but thought is often
their preliminary condition (Reik 1948, pp 171–72).

This clearing of paths and readying for fresh possibilities I include in "mapping" a chosen direction. Don Schoen writes of the
practitioner's accumulated "repertoire" of relevant experiences as
the essential capital with which to approach new events (Schoen
1983). Stonecarver Eric Gill did not regret even the long years of
architectural training he had then left for good:

Having had it, I was laid open to influences which would otherwise have been less potent and salutary. So when I went to
Chartres...it was not merely with an eye to the outward appearance of a good building but with some power of appre-
ciating its structural substance...probing its very guts (Gill
1941, p. 277).

Third there is the personal, emotional element in preparation
and the sense of readiness that comes with it. Some workers
need this reassurance more than others, of having done all they
could before they went into the field. My early American colleague, Jerry Scott, anxiously anticipated "standing around with
his teeth in his mouth": very self-conscious, he meant, uncomfortable, and that too for unpredictably long minutes, hours, even
days. Whatever it takes to keep energies free for "the penetration
of fresh truth" is important to do, that is the general point (Simone Weil, quoted in Springstead 1984, p. 69).

Underlying the preparation for specific work and the day ahead
is, of course, the range of resonance that continuing inner work
refines and broadens. Many writers record their depression, sadness, even despair with what they see: "inward darkness"(Weil);
"the long loneliness" (with which Dorothy Day entitles her autobiography); grief, heartache (with which, for Frost, all significant
creative work begins). "Truth cannot be divorced from suffering"
(Weil), at least the dismay professionals often feel at "foregoing
a present position" (Erikson) in order to open themselves to a

more useful one. And then also the corresponding swing in the cheering direction. Foregoing and waiting become easier with practice.

More basically important are two other observations. The joys of discovery and contribution seem to reflect in the highs, depths of depression being counterpoint to it. Committed practitioners resonate over an altogether greater range of emotions. And this stretching with experience seems permanent, like immunity from a disease that comes from having it once, some from even a small dose of it.

Building the Overall Picture

Free-floating attention touches off playful combinations of current observations, impressions, and past experiences—part of the repertoire that includes memories of past situations and people. Even on second look, some may still be quite telling in this fresh encounter. Reik finds his insights just preceded by "a momentary slackening of attention and diversion of interest in another direction,…then the surprise!" (Reik 1948, p. 171). Immediate impressions and feelings at the moment of encounter are well worth noting. Schoen recounts a banker's inexplicable discomfort in a top-level meeting to decide on whether or not to make a large investment: all the figures favored investing but "something didn't feel right" (Schoen 1983, pp 63–64). Only in reviewing it later, when the hunch on which he had acted had proved correct, did the banker put his finger on the flaw: the deference with which the white haired directors were treating him, half their age, though the local culture prized age. Many times pieces fall into place at odd moments away from the site, like first thing on waking in the morning. A dream may suggest an important combination.

Playful improvisation alternating with letting it all rest when the picture refuses to come together seems the best prescription. "Improvisation is a gathering together of all the evidence you have of how to resolve going from here to here to here. It's similar to painting." This is trumpeter Dizzy Gillespie talking. Improvising is "the hardest part of music and it gets harder the older you are". Less playful, less energetic? Heads too full already for fresh combinations? Young program designers excel in fresh thinking, older ones in shaping the thoughts to the realities of the day (Delbecq and Van de Venn 1967).

Above all, building a useful picture takes time—its own time; it cannot be forced. Valid understanding emerges, sometimes all at once, sometimes laboriously, layer upon layer. When Simone Weil became a factory worker,

> she had hoped to find there the camaraderie she assumed to exist among equals. She did not find it. With that disappointment she discovered the still more abject state of such utter unending hopelessness that it shut out human contact; also that all doors shut to changing one's hated condition can cause this disaster as often as destitution...realistic hope goes [first, then] a sense of being included in the mainstream goes, and a sense of bitterness comes in, and then a subculture of anger grows and takes on a life of its own (Springstead 1984, p. 56).

This description fits places in America now where medical tests show poor children virtually from birth to "sense the hopelessness in their parents and learn to fail" and are best called "lost children"—lost, that is, unless some (existing) successful early-intervention programs with the parents retrieve them (Olesker 1991, p. 43). "'Community' is misleading [in the inner cities] masking...the breakdown of social order, and the confinement, often compared to imprisonment, experienced by many residents" (Vergara 1996, p. 112).

On similar lines historian C. Van Woodward reports "unexpected illumination" only well after he had responded affirmatively to a request to run a seminar at the University of Tokyo and his proposal for it had met "with an extremely polite but quite firm request that the subject matter be confined to the Reconstruction period.... [Only] after some weeks of the seminar had passed did I discover what lay behind the insistence upon concentration on Reconstruction.... The Japanese, of course, were currently being reconstructed by the Yanks, and they identified with the defeated Confederates. They wanted to know what reconstruction was like from the South's experience" (Van Woodward 1986, p. 104).

By the time Woodward wrote about it, the unorganized playful putting together of initial impressions had of course been sifted, sorted, and refined through further reflection offsite. Following just one person's progression can show the layering through which realistic understanding comes about, or is confirmed if it came in sudden insight. Putting this experience in Japan in the Summer of 1953 together with others later, awoke Woodward to his parochial understanding of "peculiar": Southerners often described themselves as "'peculiar people' [but] looking back over the visitations of misery, invasion, defeat, suffering and humiliation that most nations have endured,...the South was probably more typical than peculiar among the peoples of the world" (Van Woodward 1986, p. 108). It was rather the other Americans who were "peculiar people". And, as a next layer of reflection, was it not these very immunities of the great majority of Americans from the common experience of others "that helped breed the illusions, naivetes, impetuosities and innocence of American nationalism that now frighten both our friends and foes abroad?" (ibid., p. 132). Then, 24 pages later, the next layer: instead of using experiences in the American South to build bridges to understanding developments on other continents, why not reverse the process? And he tops this with wondering whether the critical point in all ethnic relations may be "the shift from the paternalistic to the competitive type" (ibid., p. 92). Such grand bridging is anchored in that same open, free-floating attention way back that allowed an initial fresh look.

In no phase of my cycle is this sequence of playful creativity and orderly reflection for building a picture more needed than for addressing the so-far neglected fifth component in my cycle—what I call amplification. Over our four decades in India, I have learned that just about anything in the world currently exists in the country somewhere: the most elaborate technology and sophisticated social arrangements as also the most abject poverty; and programs of strikingly clear successes and also miserable failures and neglects. But each exists unconnected, isolated, without major connections required for work to scale on some transcendent challenge. So demonstration plots by the thousands since Independence have reverted unnoticed to their previous undistinguished condition or survive as virtual museums for occasional visitors to see, or were set up under such artificial conditions that they held no practical promise even from the first. Sheer goodness of results is to bring or breed copiers and advocates of system change even though studies consistently show that there is nothing automatic about making innovative sub-systems visible where policies and widespread public action are involved. The neglected dimension of amplification must be included in any delineation of significant units for action research and consulting.

To the responsible practitioner, better focusing then shows on three dimensions:

- the work is envisaged on a large enough scale to affect a transcendent challenge and commitments to action match it: a "vital engagement" (Erikson) has been truly staked out. To work on one, or at most two, would husband any one practitioner's energies wisely and also project the right purposive identity;
- the work is located where the challenge is actually encountered and the options are faced, and those situations will "speak" as they develop. Fresh understandings will emerge; and
- connections have been built to the larger arenas of action so that local action will matter to the whole large system.

Positioning: Realistic Roles and Expectations

The roles commonly mentioned in self-descriptions range from unobtrusive observer ("what I would really like to be is a fly on the wall") to change agent (in the organization or community one works in) or social reformer (in society at large); from motivator, trainer, counselor, and/or evaluator in working with individuals and groups to social engineer, organizer, and developer in large systems. We set out to initiate, influence, facilitate, help, support, understand, advise, demonstrate, and reform. Perhaps some of this ranging can become more deliberate, responsible choosing if we pay attention here to only major roles—say the two or three which are of basic, lifetime importance: the backbone of a professional career.

The track record suggests that some favorite aspirations drop out at that stage—out of my role as a professional that is, not as citizen. Change agent is one, except in a quite limited sense, and initiator and developer may be others. This is not because we have done particularly badly in those roles but because major recent changes in society at large have just not come about through agency or initiation of this sort. Examples include the marked shifts to smaller and planned families, the much higher awareness of environmental threats, the quickly spreading habits of self-care in matters of nutrition, exercise and maintaining one's health, and the drives to enhance the position of women, disadvantaged minorities, and the handicapped. Nor have we had, as professionals, notable influence on containing the spread of fundamentalism and ethnic strife, the increase in violence along with the growing international trade in arms, or the ready recourse to war for managing conflicts. All of these shifts have come about as citizens in many places, including us, became more aware of an issue, informed themselves, experimented, learned, persisted, protested, organized themselves into groups (first locally, then more widely, and eventually on a large enough scale) to provoke political attention—all this with media support and stimulation.

The reformer's role fits no better. In the role of "missionaries", as they termed it, Yale University history professor Woodward traveled to America's Deep South in the 1960s with student activists from top-drawer colleges in the North (Van Woodward 1986). They took part in the famous Selma march and

> listened to Martin King's eloquent speech in front of the Alabama state capitol.... With the passing of the Civil Rights Act of 1964 and the Voting Rights Acts of 1965, it seemed as if the end was in sight. Once more, just a century after the first instance, Northern intervention had put down Southern rebellion and brought freedom to oppressed blacks. In a mood of self-congratulation, Northern crusaders were about ready to lay down their arms—when suddenly, without apparent warning, black rebellion exploded in their own backyards with more violence than they had seen in the South. For four summers, from 1965 through 1968, the black slums in city after city were set aflame by looting and embattled mobs that left smoking ruins. More than 150 major riots and hundreds of minor disturbances occurred in those years. The worst, in Detroit, required 15,000 federal troops to restore order, left 43 dead, more than 1,000 injured, and 2,700 businesses sacked, half of them demolished (ibid., p. 92).

Analogous situations and reminders are everywhere. All tell that reforming and developing is a people's own business. Outsiders can be on call at best as "resource persons".

As citizen then, to involve myself closely and deeply with others in a transcendent challenge, I can

- identify the different postures required of all who are serious about working on it;
- act in that position and persist; and
- mobilize support for my stand and actions among friends in the immediate circle and community beyond.

In short, I need to be what I talk about.

As social scientist, I then have additional things to do as well. I have grown to value especially four:

1. What I call mapmaking: laying out—using information, concepts, and theories from anywhere—what all a promising approach to the challenge is likely to require, from technical understandings to locations and processes of political action, and the budgets for them. This map I will use first to demarcate the unit of work, test it out, and modify it.
2. Modeling what all this better informed and wider professional understanding indicates as necessary, and monitoring this modeling.
3. Identifying—if necessary creating—relevant settings in which I and also others can explore and practice participating effectively in this work.
4. Designing and possibly managing, at least for a time, systems for amplifying the effort to the scale required for meeting the challenge.

Each of these additional functions and roles has personal, professional, and institutional dimensions.

Mapping the Requirements

Current maps for working on a challenge, mostly mental maps that emerge only in discussion but also those embodied in program designs, characteristically fall seriously short of even minimum standards. For a start, they do not separate rigorously what the work requires to get accomplished (no matter who carries it out) from the views, interests, and wishes of the mapmakers—or the clients. They are also too small and drawn with too light a stroke, too hesitantly.

The strong—apparently universal—preference social scientists show for drawing pigmy maps for approaching large challenges is doubly intriguing when ever-larger systems are so much in the news. All Europe is becoming a Community and bodies for regional co-operation are becoming stronger and more inclusive. Whole river beds and mountain ranges are mapped across even national frontiers for stemming environmental disasters, and "global action" husbands what ozone layer remains. Evidence from within the social sciences themselves makes larger maps imperative, to include not only the obvious immediate actors but also those to act later, much later; also, the people who will be affected by changes but had little or nothing to do with bringing them about; and, very importantly, opponents to the changes. Instead, social scientists go on projecting work a bare one or two years ahead, then end it sharply, as if what would happen after that mattered little. The discrepancies are so blatant that only personal limitations can make any sense of them, such as fears of getting overtaxed and perhaps overwhelmed, and so losing control. Elaborate rationalizations then give profession-wide credence to these personal fears.

Rigorous mapping would also make for more vigorous mapping: larger numbers, also in budgets. Fewer units, then? Perhaps, with more intensive work in them. On several grounds this can be the better option. One is to guarantee the minimum concentration of effort and other resources at every point of action required for achieving and then maintaining strategic change, since less will not do. This requirement throws doubt on programs and projects that depend on individual participants first unlearning established ways and then managing change back home without planned support.

To give minimum concentrations their strategic importance, it may help to recall that all existing arrangements are held in place by actors colluding to do just that; changing too, if it is to be more than momentary or maintained by force, requires people to collude in *that*. Colluding for such a positive purpose we call collaborating. The California School studies of the 1960s come to mind. They showed, with meticulous statistics and other detailed data, that white teachers who went to class expecting colored and black children to be poor learners and difficult, saw and behaved toward them accordingly, and that those children, expecting their teachers to regard them so, neither asked for nor received the help they needed, with the result that they did indeed perform poorly and were sometimes "difficult", and—horror!—that *all* in this perverse way also set up the very same destructive cycle for the class to come. Teachers also graded the work of disadvantaged children lower than others', so fortifying their expectations one more round. Changing things significantly is indeed difficult. Many actors need to come together to heave and pull things in drastically different directions, and also have to keep heaving and pulling till the new, just as self-reinforcing cycle is as established and ingrained as the old.

Good enough mapping will also show the linkages by which the immediate unit is to affect the larger system(s). In fact, it is the *large*, eventual system(s) to be affected that good mapmaking focuses on, and the lead unit is located on it with its connections.

Modeling the Different Position

The modeling meant here is not an imaginative construct, as on a computer or on an architect's or hatmaker's table, but quite concrete behavior to match what the work requires. It starts with choosing the unit to work in for its realistic promise and goes on to joining up with actors there. Modeling comes with what I and others then actually do. The next step, of sharing the experiences, increases the learning, and reviewing it systematically from time-to-time helps modify the plans ahead.

Everyday detail must not blot out the overall map to which modeling is geared. It was precisely for lack of a larger institution-building map that the consulting team at SIET Institute got lost in building departments and planning programs (described in Chapter 6). That experience also showed clearly that there is no neutrality in modeling. Instead of institutional modeling, the consultants modeled institutional scattering. And the institution they had come to build suffered a series of crises and lasting distortions.

Three other aspects of modeling also deserve attention. Acting in line with a realistic assessment of oneself is one: strengths and weaknesses, blindspots or unsureness under stress, and the like. The work must not exceed people's capacities—the practitioner's or others'. Support-building is the second, keeping very much in mind the difficulties in the change process that a competent practitioner should anticipate. Having a colleague along, for the extra pair of eyes and checking afterwards, and also, as in the classic Tavistock designs, for the consultant who has become the particular target of hostilities then to leave, are examples for good starting of the work and for ensuring that normative and diffuse linkages get built soon after. Eschewing the limelight is the third: it is for the actors to own the changes. Recognition for professionals has to come in other ways and off-site.

Creating Settings for Practice
Designing and creating protected settings in which immediate and future actors can experience in advance the kinds of predicaments they will encounter full-scale and full-blast in the far-reaching developments ahead, and first rehearsing effective behavior in those safe settings holds more practical promise than elaborating plans to intellectual limits. In those settings, the facilitators become modelers directly, and all-round learning is more likely. Self-understanding, team-building, linkage development, mapping, and most other key components of change efforts can be enhanced best by practice, and then reviewing and modifying them.

For professionals too, developing and maintaining professional standards and discipline are best sustained by regular practice in settings that demand them, irrespective of our likes and dislikes. Keeping good records of work is an example. Monitoring progress in implementing decisions of professional bodies about quality maintenance and ethics is an example for the profession as a whole. Settings of escalating difficulty can be identified in which practitioners at all levels of experience are likely to encounter predicaments they need to practice handling.

This is, of course, how we encourage children at home and colleagues at work to enhance their competencies and capacities in good time. If children are to grow into adults who live effectively and happily at close quarters with a wide diversity of others, schools can be composed for that experience in advance. To make environmental protection habitual, children can be put to keeping the school and its grounds clean. If we live hoping they will in time take fresh positions on important issues and act on them with considerable independence, this also regular programs can provide. Limits to such preparation will more likely be set by current practitioners and our own readiness to model strategic developments than by hesitations in the generations of the future.

Support Building and Amplification

For effective work on a transcendent challenge, support-building has to transcend the personal contacts to which it is still habitually confined. The designing requirements of large and sophisticated networks of institutions—of different kinds and across cultures and probably countries—along with the requirements of information and other technologies for new operations and management are way beyond colleagueship in the prevaling sense. Effective amplification depends on radical upscaling of support.

For a start, practitioners ready to pioneer can involve themselves in large-scale support-building, familiarize themselves with what all that goes into it by way of resources and processes, record the experiences, and share them with us all. Developing the network of some 20 universities around the globe engaged in building population institutes served this purpose for me; at least we surfaced common problems and shared learnings from experiences here and there in trying to cope with problems.

Aiming at radical innovation on a large scale adds issues of a taller order. Even with involvements pared down to key stakeholders, involving *all* from the very beginning raises anxieties high, risks takeover by power-hungry politicians or getting torpedoed by known opponents right at the start or at least being held up. Maximum involvement as a principle grew in the era of *incremental* change efforts and proceeding only on agreement. British stonecarver Eric Gill describes the dilemma and how he himself side-stepped it when he changed his career.

> To ask permission would be to ask for prohibition; to explain would be to flout their whole world.... I did not even consult them [but] just, so to say, walked out on them—took on an entirely different kind of work and one which they could not, with their conventions and traditions, regard otherwise than as a betrayal of my family, my education (i.e., the education I was

supposed to have had) and my friends.... What a downfall of all their hope and pride!... I did the only thing possible: tell the kind friends afterwards and if possible live the disgrace down (Gill 1941, pp 275–76).

That the people he had worried about then "didn't make half as much fuss [as] I thought they might have done" surprised Gill. In my career that delightful surprise came usually at the very beginning of my more far-out departures. Ahead of my naming the challenge for fear of facing its full and daunting implications, key stakeholders in it and/or in my future turned out to have long been aware of both the need and the opportunity. At first mention some offered to join actively or at least with continued support and good wishes. Experience with Future Search conferences lines up with this. Patently honest engagement from the beginning brings with it a honeymoon period for testing possible moves and for undergirding future moves with onward goodwill. That Aloka's board, way back, met only twice a year and 5,000 miles away from the training center may well have been less of a blessing than I then thought; when, after six successful years that did not include them, they decided against upscaling, they may have felt too little engaged to appreciate the further opportunity enough to champion it with the funders. Twenty years later, as dean of the new school, I again started its core activities very quickly, but then changed to building mechanisms for ongoing consultation and joint planning with state agencies and with schools and departments in the university. In addition to building goodwill and commitment, the institutions then also protected the school in the state at large and championed its continuation when budgets became suddenly tight. We worked on plans three years ahead. Longer-term implications surfaced manageably and concretely.

Realistic Dispositions

In tune with my generally sunny disposition, I have learned to go ahead with a stout heart—but not starry-eyed. Trusting the process to work out well is realistic if the mapping is even reasonably accurate, the time for action ripe, and I and other key persons fit the task well enough. Many forces need to work together, but they need not work without error. If something was missed the first time, it will, as in psychotherapy, come up again if it was important. Relationships built realistically will become robust quite quickly. The many faulty actions, omissions, and delays that occur are best regarded as opportunities for learning: a joint task, too, that strengthens all parties. The doubts galore, about next steps to take, are best taken to the field, for observing, listening, and working things out there concretely, and letting those developments guide pacing. The art of the possible is *there*. So waiting is good—but in readiness, attention poised. And kudos goes to the actors.

With all this, reflects Frost, prepare

> to be all charming and even bearable, the way is almost rigidly prescribed. If it is [done] with outer seriousness, it must be with inner humor. If it is with outer humour, it must be with inner seriousness. Neither one alone without the other under it will do.... The utmost of ambition is to lodge a few [creations] where they will be hard to get rid of, to lodge a few irreducible bits.... In the process you will have "strengthened the impulses of life" (Frost 1964, p. iii).

Responsible practitioners should then be a long way beyond merely getting to know more and more about a challenge that the dismal figures about current scholarship suggest. Assembling and analyzing facts about the world's population "explosion" or communal violence or the flattening of management hierarchies amounts to responsible engagement only when harnessed and focused together with the actors for intervention. The concentration on "crises", which makes work dramatic but suspect even as science, diverts attention from the many promising social innovations and transformations that these same crises have set in motion in the last three decades and that are far more worth studying and highlighting. Some social scientists have participated in those directly, but more often as concerned citizens than as contributors of professional skills and experience; as if, like physicians till the advent of antibiotics, social science practitioners had nothing particular to contribute, not to strengthening the social fabric and governance, not to stepping up prevention and damage control any more than to curing the diseases decimating the public ill. Any scaling up now goes ahead with little or no input of what we profess to know and to be good at, and indeed advise clients about individually.

That social science practitioners train, counsel, and do organizational consulting, and that clients presumably find this useful (since they request and pay for this) does not brighten this picture. These are means and modes of practice, like Mallika's dancing and publishing or her (or anyone else's) administering and fundraising, whereas at issue here is directing that practice to coping with a "transcendent challenge that faces [humanity] within a thinkable timespan". That larger social direction we cannot leave clients to decide for us. On the contrary, we may have to leave clients aside who pursue other, private directions.

To engage any of the very large and complex challenges that face us all quite inescapably, calls in the first place for practitioners who are not merely highly competent in their craft but who also bring stout hearts and personal openness, and, in addition, also the readiness to enlarge and organize professionally so that many more colleagues sustain those qualities for social transformation. "Agreeable or not", Heilbronner concludes, "this is the direction in which humanity will have to travel...into a still unexplored world that must be safely attained and settled before it can be named" (Heilbronner 1990, p. 99).

For any practitioner personally, "it begins with a lump in the throat, a sense of wrong, a homesickness, a lovesickness...never a thought to begin with", Frost goes on. "It finds its thought or makes its thought. I suppose it finds it lying around with others not so much to its purpose in a more or less full mind" (quoted in Thompson and Winnick 1981, p. 225). So we return to images. What Frost calls "the sound of sense", the overall appreciation of what is the matter, no holds barred, will raise the lump in the throat that leads on to the needed thought much more surely than any additional columns of figures and reams of wordy analyses can. Frost hears people talking in the next room. He cannot make out the words, yet he is sure, from the sound in general, that it is *friends* talking, not strangers, and certainly not enemies. In the same way we *can* make out when a client or a public meeting is truly concerned with a vital matter and ready to move on it, just as as counselors and therapists we already listen beyond a client's words for tone and major themes and notice what body language "tells". In popular idiom, we hear and enjoy the music in a run of notes and see (or do not see) the forest for the trees. The "sound of sense", tantalisingly vague as it may be, points to an essential quality with which exploration and action on any transcendent challenge must go ahead. This and only thus will it reveal its essence and concrete opportunity. So I put it right next to transcendent challenge in the title to this chapter.

References

Balasubramaniam, D., 'Calibre's Yardstick of Measurement', *The Hindu*, Madras, January 21, 1991.

Boenhoffer, Dietrich, *Letters and Papers from Prison*, Macmillan, New York, 1972.

Day, Dorothy, *The Long Loneliness*, Dent, New York, 1952.

Delbecq, Andre L. and **Van de Venn, Andrew H.**, "A Group Process Model for Problem Identification and Program Planning", *Journal of Applied Behavioral Sciences*, Vol. 7, No. 4, pp 466–92, 1967.

Frost, Robert, *Complete Poems*, Holt, Rinehart and Winston, New York, 1964.

Gill, Eric,. *Autobiography*, Devin-Adair, New York, 1941.

Gutterman, Norbert, *The Anchor Book of French Quotations*, Doubleday, New York, 1989.

Heilbronner, Robert, in *The New Yorker*, September 17, 1990.

Henderson, L.J., "Hippocrates and the Practice of Medicine", in Curtis, Charles P., *The Practical Cogitator*, Houghton Mifflin Co., New York, 1945.

Lynton, Rolf P., *The Sound of Sense: What's So Hard About Being Practical*, Center for Applied Behavioural Science Studies and Action Research, Monograph Series No. 5, University of Delhi, Delhi, 1992.

Olesker, Michael, in *The New Yorker*, April 29, 1991.

Reik, Theodore, *Listening with the Third Ear*, Grove Press, New York, 1948.

Schoen, Donald, *The Reflective Practitioner*, Basic Books, New York, 1983.

Springstead, Eric O., *Simone Weil and the Suffering of Love*, Cowley, Cambridge, Mass., 1984.

Thompson, Lawrence and **Winnick, R.H.**, *Robert Frost: A Biography*, Holt, Rinehart and Winston, New York, 1981.

Van Woodward, C., *Thinking Back: The Perils of Writing History*, Louisiana State University Press, Baton Rouge, 1986.

Van der Post, Laurens, *The Lost World of the Kalahari*, Penguin Books, Harmondsworth, 1962.

Vergara, Camilo Jose, *The New American Ghetto*, Rudgers University Press, Brunswick, NJ, 1996.

Weil, Simone, *Waiting on God*, Routledge and Kegan Paul, London, 1951.

EPILOGUE

NET, CATCH, AND CREW

"Catches": What Gets Caught—And What Can
   Catch Practitioners
Several Runs, Same Course
The Inveterate Crew

... in this net it's not just the strings that count but the air that escapes through the meshes.

Pablo Neruda (quoted in Reid 1996, p. 68)

There are five contrasting schools of thought: the environmental pessimists; the business-as-usual optimists; the industrial world-to-the-rescue lobby; the new modernists; and those who advocate sustainable intensification.

Jules Pretty et al. 1996, p. 1

There is no end, and neatness is not to be had. What I *can* add, for now, are a few more anticipations I find useful. Two run side-by-side and pretty much determine what major work I now consider undertaking; they also tell me how to expect my part in it to end. Most of my time now I put on maintenance: keeping my professional networks alive and functioning well, and myself limber and connected.

Far from "settling down" in my advancing years, my penchant for thinking and creating afresh has even freer rein. I doubt that

Torschlussangst has much to do with it, that so-typical German nouns-strung-together for time running out and temptation escalating for taking shortcuts. I see no shortcuts worth taking and am more tolerant than ever of plausibly right people getting together, even if they then "mess about" for a while beyond my understanding—so long, that is, as they are about something that truly matters. No, if orthodoxies have brought us to where we are now and would hold us to the manifold social abuses and conflicts on an obscene scale which we see all around us and in endless prospect, that contrast is enough to lodge a lump in my throat with which any worthwhile work gets under way. If we elders, now that personal risks to livelihood and self-respect have become quite small, don't urge taking the long shots, who will?

The directions in which to put energies to work are not new. Most of the well-worn litanies open with several to which I can bring familiarity and experience. I go with those, not with calculating probabilities between the options in general—not for me and not for others. Nor do I look for niches, virgin space somewhere, in which to invent something brand new. I look in—test for would be the better term since choosing among opportunities offered is usually the issue these days—the actual concrete situations before me for two touchstones.

One is the kind of situation that "zero budgeting" is meant to produce: where a particular line of development and the resources for it have to make their case again from scratch, as if they were newly proposed (even if already under way)—virgin soil in *that* sense. If my involvement in that wide-open situation makes sense to the stakeholders in it, and they themselves and their commitments of time and other resources confirm they mean serious endeavor, then I will contribute what I can.

The second touchstone is high possibilities of access to actual experience when going about that challenge in the way proposed, at least to essential, large parts of it. That there is nothing new under the sun may be an exaggeration (state-of-the-art information technologies, for example, now make undreamed of connectedness possible), but it is also true that just about any combination of situation, people, means, and modes of facing any large challenge has been tried and is probably unfolding now, somewhere. This knowledge-of-acquaintance (anthropologist

Geertz calls it "local knowledge") can give a tremendously help-
ful leg-up to a new departure somewhere else. And the readiness
to respect local knowledge and to spend money and time to surface and use it is a telling test of stakeholder commitment to significant work.

"Catches": What Gets Caught—And What Can Catch Practitioners

Both kinds of catch have been much in evidence throughout this
book. If I now highlight the latter kind—the cautions—it is not
to calm down enthusiasms for what I hope have come through
as quite promising ways of working. On the contrary, I want to
free practitioners more by indicating some pitfalls and detours to
prepare for—the kind that buoys would mark for a sailing
course. Buoys do not mark or guard against the personal quirks
particular sailors bring; they mark places of risk for all who set
off on this particular course.

One catch is the temptation to expand the work at the first signs
that it "works", to "go with it", and "strike the iron while it is hot".
Euphoria is catching, especially when it deadens the initial anxieties that accompany fresh starts in vital directions. What needs
especially keen watching is, first, that enthusiasm has been
aroused not by a mere flash in the pan but by true, even if small,
signs that things are actually settling into proper working; and,
second, that stakeholders work through the implications of scaling up and do not just cheer. Powerful supporters are often
happy to encourage program leaders to "forge right ahead" without further ado when the sun is out and the winds fair. Later,
when the water gets choppy, as it will, they may complain they
were not warned; even that, with my gentle manner and general
friendliness, I had lulled them into going along with quick expansions which I had been set on from the beginning but kept
secret. Or, they were simply unprepared for further expansion;
did not, on reflection, really welcome it, at least right then. Early
and active intervention to prevent collusive enthusiasms or silences, patient waiting for confirmations of understanding and
collaboration, and also generally greater openness on my part
are learnings for negotiating this buoy.

With greater openness I also get more help now with making up for my increasing insensitivity, as it seems to me, to the personal distresses my colleagues and others experience from time to time as we work in new ways and often against the grain. I foresee likely points of stress well enough and include them in my maps and in discussions, but I tend to be blind to their actual onset and to the severity of distress others experience. Perhaps my own survival in good order of so many and such manifold crises has dulled me on that side, and also relaxed me too far into believing that without clear signaling for time out all others must be quite strong enough to work out any troubles by themselves and also become the stronger for it. Nor do I like to assume that I am the one to whom they should turn when the going gets too tough. My working more collaboratively distributes responsibilities and resources more widely too, and probably also itself lessens the stresses.

Whether it also helps with minding my time boundaries, I am less sure. Significant innovation and its amplification does make for open-ended tasks, so my portfolio must not get overcrowded—and that judgment is difficult. The more radical the innovation and the grander the amplification—and so also the more exciting to take part in—the more time it demands. The greatest amount of time, most unpredictably at that, goes into building and maintaining the many relationships involved. For building a community-based graduate school, I routinely managed and monitored 148 linkages with office holders and institutional units in the state and in the university, and many of those were sets: individual relationships were many more. And the relationships the school's program directors minded in the first place, but which still involved me indirectly, only partly overlapped mine. Under such pressures, working hours are never enough. With that, more subtly, I focus scarce time more narrowly on preplanned purpose. This then spreads the impression that I am really too busy to listen to the concerns others have with the next steps I propose, and that there is no point in burdening me as well with *their* agenda or asking me to take some part in it. Innovators tend to be too preoccupied to be available to others—or, at least, they appear so. Innovating is bound to touch off anxieties and radical changes the most; with this unavailability at the top, they fester. I know this, but I also know no alternative to letting innovative thrusts dictate their own pace. Even when all hands are on board and running with their parts, this always skirts the limits of available time. In every instance this is true in my experience.

The rapid unfolding brings all stakeholders into play (and not merely into view) and they jostle for all the time I have. Invariably there are more than I first expected. They are also more interconnected and involved with each other than I thought, so I propose meeting established clusters together. That I recognize their groupings by doing this may be even more important than saving time, which it may not do anyway: it may in fact take more time—for working out conflicts, for example.

Several Runs, Same Course

One way to put these many parts together is to approach each major work with the thought that it may well require several cuts to get properly started and several more for its run to get clearly established, and that my particular part will be making the first cut or two. Often I come for that—Aloka, SIET Institute, Population Center, School of Public Health, decentralizing the health services in Indonesia and in North India (to mention the big chunks in my career); always it is for major innovation or for recapturing an earlier one that lost its way.

The scenario then looks like this: I get the core innovation going quickly and use that to mobilize and confirm the supports that this actual practice shows it needs—quantities along with kinds, points of impact, timing (or at least sequencing), and also internal organization and external linkages.

With this, some months pass. The honeymoon period any new venture has ("the window" in current parlance), in which to unfold in sunny benevolence and show "what we have here" in actual fact, draws to a close. Doubts and insipient opposition surface from quarters where the innovation is already causing offence or threatens to at any moment. For a while longer they make no headway against the delights and/or hopes of beneficiaries. Who all the supporters are and who the opponents are and how they will eventually match up takes a while longer to clarify. This sorting out, before whatever hell to come actually opens, makes time to consolidate the venture and shore up outside support for it. Maintaining enthusiasm and quietly building further support without getting trapped in too early an expansion is what counts. The water is about to become choppy.

I, personally, tend to toughen under pressure, to hold fast to what the initial idea of the innovation specified and its early free unfolding showed: *that is* the development we all said we wanted, isn't it? I count on others to give way, or I will certainly resign rather than forego anything I see as essential to the integrity of the whole. I fear even temporary ("tactical") withdrawal lest that makes that piece seem less essential than I see it. I am not good at bargaining any of it away.

Instead I settle—battle—for prolonging the innovation as a whole just as long as I can. For my sake and also for others': I know that that first-hand, all-round experience with its working becomes the lasting legacy, the accomplishment to remember even when (indeed particularly when) the invention gets pared down later—as it usually is after I leave—or abandoned—as Aloka was. I am especially eager that institutional actors know from their own direct experiences that this innovation is indeed quite realistic: it *was* put in place, it *did* advance its purposes, and advancing them felt like *this*. My own experience includes two instances in which it took 20 years to re-establish components I had lost out on trying to preserve. If I caused some of the delay by my obstinate defence and the offence this caused, I did lodge "a few irreducible bits...where they [were] hard to get rid of" (Robert Frost quoted in Thompson 1981, p. 353).

The Inveterate Crew

From Nazi prison and still hopeful—wrongly—of release, political dissident Dietrich Boenhoeffer characterized to his best friend and fellow pastor the people who had influenced him most: They had "a kind of *hilaritas*,...confidence in their own work...a steadfast certainty that in their work they are showing the world something *good* (even if the world doesn't like it), and a high-spirited self-confidence.... It is a necessary attribute of greatness" (Boenhoeffer 1972, p. 229).

On like grounds, beyond immediate family and the other twin-like colleagues to whom I dedicate this book, this is my list:

Harold Bridger, Kamla Chowdhry, Bill Cousins, John Fitzsimons, Alexandra Kuebler-Merrill, Len Hirsch, Don Klein, George Lombard, Vijay Mahajan, Ravi Matthai, Loren and Polly Mead, George McRobie, Dorothy Nyswander, Mrinalini and Mallika Sarabhai, Charles and Edie Seashore, Elizabeth Sidney, Joe Stein, Suzanne Stier, Marjorie Sykes, Bob Tannenbaum, Joyce and John Weir, and Marvin Weisbord.

Of less acquaintance (with one exception), but important in my development, are also these great masters of "vital engagement" with their world (using Erikson's own phrase): Ken Benne, Erik Erikson, Vikram Sarabhai, Fritz Schumacher, Eric Trist, and, earlier still, Donald Tyerman. That they achieved prominence matters less here than the quality of engagement I am eager to convey. I like to think it is that quality by which they are remembered and by which far less prominent practitioners too are remembered. The masterful contact of the one I understand least may illustrate that total quality best: a boon for me pure and simple, unexplained.

This was with Donald Tyerman. We met over more than a decade, till I left for virtually continuous work and life overseas. I was 17 when we met: he an editor of *The Economist*; I, a German refugee just out of school and there for a menial job for the few weeks till I would be called up for work on war. Mentor, friend, one-person social service?

The settings were always public. I never visited his home, though he introduced me to others at theirs. I have no idea what it was that I offered or represented that warranted his attention. Yet he stayed in touch right through the war and for eight years after it, as long as I stayed in England in fact. After I left for Paris, then America, and then directly from there to stay in South Asia, the contact petered out. Perhaps I disappointed his hopes for me in England, but if so, I never knew what they were.

By then he had been top editor of *The Economist* and moved on to being editor of *The Times*, when it still was without dispute the most influential newspaper in England behind its quite unprepossessing front page of tiny personal advertisements. Every three or four months Donald Tyerman would send me a note asking me to lunch with him, just he and I, and I would call back and fix it for when I could be off from the factory. ("This staying in touch and mentoring young friends you also do", Ronnie says.

True, but I am not editor of *The Times* or of anything even nearly so august.)

Nor do I need two canes to walk, as Tyerman did, victim of polio. I can see him now as he lets himself down, expertly but with such labor, from the taxi, then climbs the steps to the Reform Club, and up more steps inside. Smiling, already asking. It is his so personal connection that stays with me, simply a gift.

In one brief note—his notes were always brief—he suggested I get in touch with Hermann Levy, a professor from the Frankfurt School, very senior in age and standing, and now settled in Richmond, on the outskirts. He is working on studies of social insurance and of workmen's compensation, and he and I have many things in common anyway, Tyerman suggests. Some years later Professor Levy dies, leaving an unfinished manuscript. I learn about it from Routledge, the publishers. Tyerman has proposed they ask me to complete it. I do, and earn my first fee: £100.

Still during the war T. asks whether I could help "a young friend" of his who is struck down with polio, is still bedridden but now recovered enough to catch up with his studies. Could I spend, say, two afternoons a week with helping him? Soon after VE-Day but with the war in the Pacific still to finish and the factory work continuing, he arranges for me to meet old Mr. Rowntree who is looking for a research assistant, full-time in York, for the next of his well-known social surveys. That position I failed to get. But a year after the war ended altogether and I was working with a small but quite well-known management consulting firm, T. contacts me with the suggestion I change and join instead the staff of a new periodical, *Future*, which is to be in Britain what *Fortune* is in the States. He has already introduced me. That position follows, and I research and write there for the next 18 months about a wide range of industrial and social developments and travel to many parts of the country. Till the quite common conflict between editorial and advertising policies (and the managing editor in her anxieties) "get me".

I leave not knowing what next. Immediately I get an inquiry from the brand new British Institute of Management. They have seen my letter in *The Times* that morning (about working hours in cotton mills). Would I consider a position with them? I do not know what, if anything, Donald Tyerman had to do with the letter or the offer. My book (about Incentives and Management) comes out soon after, and favorable reviews of it. At our next lunch, my august friend expresses his pleasure. "Good or not so good", says he, "most important is that your book *gets* reviewed." Engagement on and on. And always *hilaritas*, also when on crutches. "If it is done with outer seriousness, it must be with inner humor. If it is with outer humor, it must be with inner seriousness. Neither one alone without the other under it will do...."[1] Put together, they produce tunes on the blue guitar.

References

Boenhoeffer, Dietrich, *Letters and Papers from Prison*, Macmillan, New York, 1972.

Pretty, Jules N., Thompson, John and Hinchcliffe, Fiona, *Sustainable Agriculture: Impacts on Food Production and Challenges for Food Security*, Executive Summary, IIED Gatekeeper Series, International Institute for Ecological Development, London, 1996.

Reid, Alastair, "Naruda and Borges", *The New Yorker*, June 14–July 1, 1996.

Thompson, Lawrence and Winnick, R.H., *Robert Frost: A Biography*, Holt, Rinehart and Winston, New York, 1981.

1. Robert Frost, quoted in Thompson and Winnick 1981, p. 353.